Advance Praise for
Understanding Spanish-Speaking South Americans

"This is a must read for anyone interested in Spanish-speaking South America. The book is exceptionally well written and contains information of value to scholars, teachers, students, travelers and businesspeople. Even if you think you know the region well, you are certain to find new material.... If you don't know the region—and need to—this book is a very good, quick learner's guide that will pay dividends over and over as you travel the area. First rate in every way!"

—Stevan Trooboff, President and CEO
Council on International Educational Exchange

"Skye Stephenson's scholarly depth and keen, balanced insight are exhibited in this pragmatic but comprehensive analysis.... *Understanding Spanish-Speaking South Americans* offers a foundation of cultural understanding of one of the richest and most dynamic regions of the world."

—Kirk Simmons, Executive Director
International Affairs, University of Arizona

"A unique perspective on the culture in Spanish-speaking South America from a self-identified gringa living and interacting with Spanish-speaking South Americans for many years. Policy makers will benefit from absorbing the cultural understanding in these highly readable pages."

—Lori Bollinger, Senior Economist
Futures Group International

UNDERSTANDING

Spanish-Speaking South Americans

The InterAct Series

Other books in the series:

Au Contraire! Figuring out the French
Border Crossings: American Interactions with Israelis
Buenos vecinos: comunicandose con los mexicanos
A Common Core: Thais and Americans
Encountering the Chinese
Exploring the Greek Mosaic
A Fair Go for All: Australian and American Interactions
Finland, Cultural Lone Wolf
From *Da* to Yes: Understanding the East Europeans
From *Nyet* to *Da*: Understanding the Russians
Germany: Unraveling an Enigma
Good Neighbors: Communicating with the Mexicans
Into Africa: Intercultural Insights
Learning to Think Korean
Modern-Day Vikings: A Practical Guide to Interacting with the Swedes
Spain Is Different
Understanding Arabs
Vietnam Today
With Respect to the Japanese

UNDERSTANDING Spanish-Speaking South Americans

INTERCULTURAL PRESS
A Nicholas Brealey Publishing Company

YARMOUTH, ME • BOSTON • LONDON

First published by Intercultural Press, a Nicholas Brealey Publishing Company, in 2003. For information, contact:

Intercultural Press, a Nicholas Brealey Publishing Company
100 City Hall Plaza, Suite 501
Boston, MA 02108
Information: 617-523-3801
Fax: 617-523-3708
www.interculturalpress.com

Nicholas Brealey Publishing
3–5 Spafield Street
Clerkenwell
London, EC1R, 4QB, UK
Tel: +44-207-239-0360
Fax: +44-207-239-0370
www.nbrealey-books.com

Book design and production by Patty J. Topel

Printed in the United States of America

09 08 07 06 05 2 3 4 5 6

Library of Congress Cataloging-in-Publication Data

Stephenson, Skye.
Understanding Spanish-speaking South Americans: bridging hemispheres/ Skye Stephenson.
p. cm.—(InterAct series)
Includes bibliographical references and index.
ISBN: 1-877864-91-9
1. National characteristics, South American. 2. South America—Description and travel. I. title: Spanish-Speaking South Americans. II. title. III. Series.
F2210.S74 2003
305.8'0098—dc21

Dedication

This book is dedicated to my two children,
Kimberley and Nicholas,
who bridge the two Americas within themselves and who
have taught me so much more than I can ever teach them.

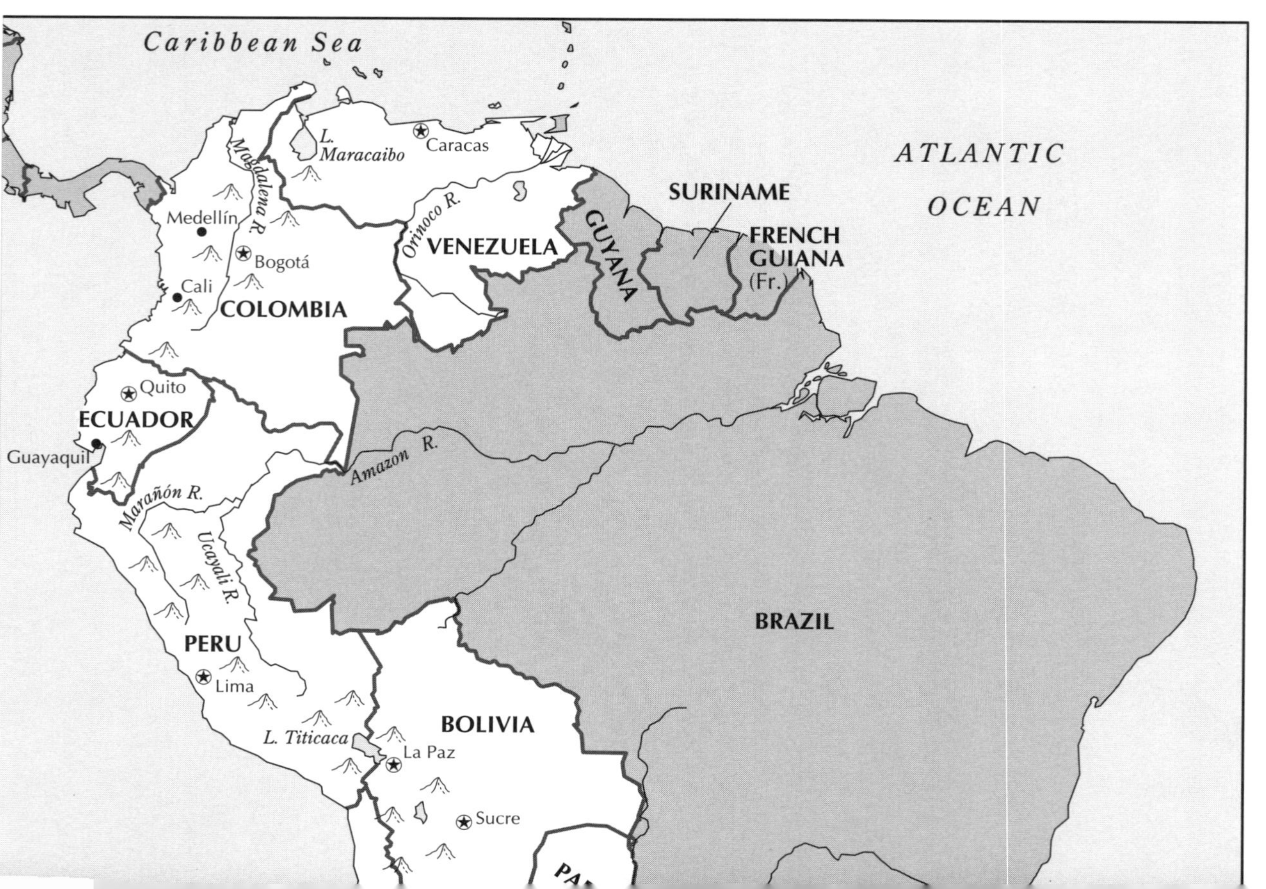
Caribbean Sea
ATLANTIC
OCEAN
L.
Maracaibo
Caracas
Magdalena R.
Medellín
Bogotá
Cali
COLOMBIA
Orinoco R.
VENEZUELA
GUYANA
SURINAME
FRENCH
GUIANA
(Fr.)
Quito
ECUADOR
Guayaquil
Amazon R.
Marañón R.
Ucayali R.
BRAZIL
PERU
Lima
BOLIVIA
L. Titicaca
La Paz
Sucre

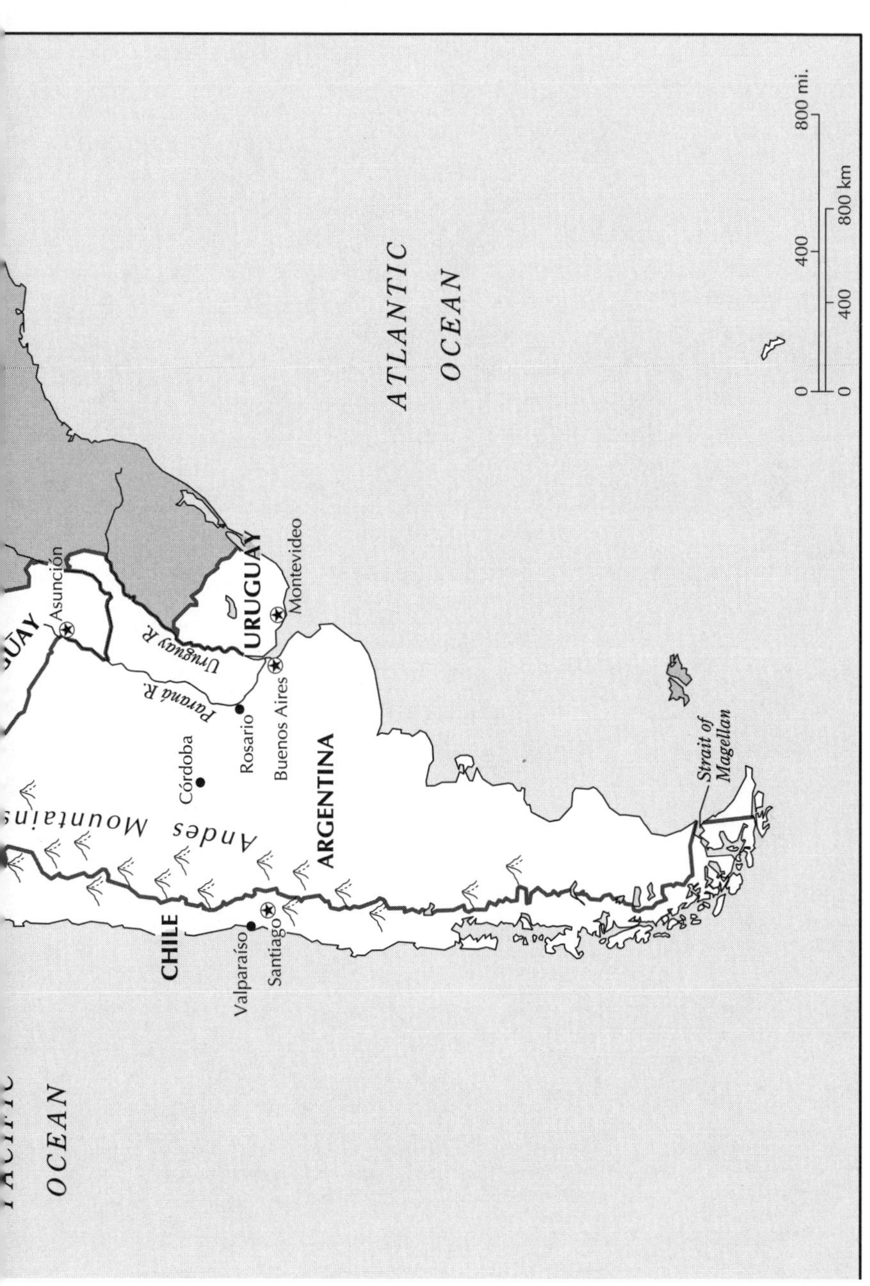
ATLANTIC
OCEAN
OCEAN
URUGUAY
Montevideo
Asunción
Uruguay R.
Paraná R.
Buenos Aires
Rosario
Córdoba
ARGENTINA
Andes Mountains
CHILE
Valparaíso
Santiago
Strait of Magellan
0
400
800 mi.
0
400
800 km

Table of Contents

Part II: Diversity and Divergence among the Spanish-Speaking South American Nations

Preface

To write about the cultural patterns of a particular group of people is to constantly walk a fine line between two equally dangerous outcomes. On one side lies the risk of cultural overspecification: emphasizing the differences between the cultural group being studied and others can create the false impression that all individuals from that particular culture are similar in their behaviors and beliefs and quite distinct from all others. Such oversimplification can obscure the common humanity of all peoples and can also exacerbate or even create new stereotypes about the cultural group in question, thus reducing the complexity of human beings and preventing true intercultural understanding.

On the other side lies the equally dangerous possibility of cultural denial. Ignoring the profound impact of culture on the individual and not acknowledging the significant differences that exist among the myriad cultures in the world prevent us from ever really knowing the "other" except through our own culturally based preconceptions. In fact, a long history of policy failures, many with detrimental consequences, has resulted from the lack of recognition that people from different cultures may indeed have quite different ways of perceiving and dealing with the same situation.

In writing about the cultural patterns of Spanish-speaking South Americans (SSSAs), I hope to walk the fine line between these two extremes and to avoid adding any more stereotypes to the already large number circulating in English-speaking North America (ESNA) concerning Latinos and Hispanics. Neither do I mean to imply that all SSSAs think and behave similarly. Significant differences among the many millions of SSSAs do exist and are to be expected. Some of these differences are attributable to community and national variations; these will be explored in Part II, "Diveristy and Divergence among the Spanish-Speaking South American Nations." Rather, my goal is that this book might help ESNAs achieve a more complete and realistic view of the SSSAs, a view that could lead to greater empathy among these hemispheric neighbors.

I approach the topic of SSSA culture not as an expert but as someone who is herself trying to understand this diverse, complex, and often misunderstood region. My own interest in SSSA spans more than a quarter century. I have lived in the region for nearly ten years and visited almost all of the countries on the continent. My academic work and scholarship have focused on this part of the world and my personal life is inextricably linked in numerous ways with SSSAs. In all of these endeavors and experiences, I have struggled, at times painfully, to better understand this part of the world that has become my second home.

Acknowledgments

Many individuals—more than can ever be mentioned here—have helped me better understand the Spanish-speaking South Americans (SSSAs) over the years. In some instances just a brief encounter, a chance remark, or a fleeting observation has given me additional insights into this group of people. Other times, a deeper understanding has resulted from relationships of a more profound nature. Many generous and kindhearted people have taken the time to share their thoughts and feelings, and I am truly grateful to each and every one of them.

In particular I want to thank two families—the Polakofs and the Glades—for welcoming me into their hearts and their homes and for their patient instruction of the gringa over the years. I would also like to thank the many study abroad students I have had the pleasure to interact with in my capacity as Director of the Council for International Education and Exchange program in Santiago, Chile. Their diverse experiences and insightful observations have served to propel me forward in my own efforts to understand SSSA culture. I want to thank my own family as well, for giving me the freedom to fly far away from them on wings crafted in large part by their own legacies and beliefs. Finally, a special word of gratitude to all the people at Intercultural Press, especially Toby Frank and Judy Carl-Hendrick, for believing in this project and guiding this fledgling writer through the process with great tact and patience.

To all I have met along the way I say *gracias*, and to all of you who are planning to live and/or work in SSSA, or who simply want to know more about the SSSAs, I wish you a *buen viaje*, or good travels.

—Skye Stephenson
2003

Part I

Patterns of Spanish-Speaking South American Culture

The Latin American search for something beyond the self, something above the world of the crass, everyday reality, deserves recognition in its own right and also in the interest of good international relations.

—John Gillin

1

The Spanish-Speaking South Americans and Their Lands

Yo espero siglos en que todos los hombre hablen español y hablen inglés sin que existen rivalidades entres estas dos formas de concebir y de soñar el mundo. El porvenir está hecho de nuestros sueños....

—Jorge Luis Borges

*I await centuries in which all people speak Spanish and English without there being any rivalry between these two ways of conceiving and dreaming of the world. The future is made of our dreams....**

These days, people in the United States and Spanish-speaking South America (SSSA)† are worried about the same thing...each other. In the U.S. we grapple with the implications of the increasing "Latinization" of the country. Today, more Spanish-speaking citizens reside in the U.S. than live in any one of the countries of SSSA. At the same time many SSSAs are confronting a cultural onslaught of U.S. businesses, products, and cultural exports. Neither group really knows what to think about this

* Unless otherwise specified, all translations of Spanish into English in the text are by the author.

† To avoid the awkwardness and repetitiveness of writing out Spanish-speaking South America (or Americans), I will refer to the region as SSSA and the people as SSSAs in most instances.

complex exchange, but both realize that their futures will be shaped significantly by it.

One reason that both groups have such difficulty figuring out how to address these increasingly large flows of people, products, and ideas is that we really don't know each other as well as we think we do. A few years ago, journalist Alan Riding made famous the term *distant neighbors* to describe the relationship between the United States and Mexico. If Mexico is distant according to the U.S. vision of the world, then the nations of SSSA must seem truly remote.

This book is designed to help bridge this perceptual gap by providing insights into the cultural patterns of the SSSAs. Currently, there is little material available in English on the subject; in fact, more published material can be found about other cultural or ethnic groups located much farther from the United States and with whom the U.S. has less exchange of both a human and a material nature.

Perhaps one reason little has been written about SSSA culture(s) in the English language is because of the often unstated assumption that the region is not "important" or "different" enough to warrant much attention. Such a belief is incorrect. Not only does this region have certain commonalities that mark it as distinct from other nations in the Spanish-speaking world as well as from the other countries located on the South American continent, but, more importantly, it is a place of great cultural interest and diversity.

Who Are the Spanish-Speaking South Americans?

The term *Spanish-speaking South Americans* (SSSAs) will be used to describe the approximately one hundred and sixty million people who reside in the nine nations in South America where Spanish is an official language: Argentina, Bolivia, Chile, Colombia, Ecuador, Paraguay, Peru, Uruguay, and Venezuela. Although it is not completely accurate to classify all these people as SSSAs (since a significant number either do not speak Spanish or speak it as a second language), this term seems to be the best choice to describe the inhabitants of this culturally distinct region. After all, Spanish is by far the most important language in the region's nine nations. More significantly, the cultural patterns shared by these nations are shaped in large part by the legacies of Spanish conquest and colonialism.

The SSSAs are a subgroup of the so-called Latin Americans—a category whose actual membership varies depending on which definition is employed. For some, Latin America includes all the countries in the Americas south of the Río Grande, thus incorporating all the Caribbean nations, whatever their cultural background and official language. Others include just the Spanish-speaking islands of the Caribbean (Cuba, Puerto Rico, and the Dominican Republic) in their definition. Yet others claim that only the continental nations from Mexico southward to Tierra del Fuego are truly Latin America. To make matters even more confusing, some critics reject the term *Latin America* altogether, preferring to call this distinct geographical and cultural zone *Hispanic America* or *Indo-America*, to name just two alternatives.‡

Whatever definition is used, the Spanish-speaking nations of South America are clearly included. However, notable distinctions still exist between the SSSAs and other South Americans. These differences are tied to numerous factors, including differing pre-Columbian, colonial, and postcolonial histories; varying ethnic and racial compositions; and distinctive economic and political realities.

‡ For our purposes, when the term *Latin America* is used, it will be defined as all those continental nations south of the Río Grande as well as the Spanish-speaking countries of the Caribbean. In general, this term will only be employed when there is the specific intention of incorporating more than the SSSAs into the discussion. Nonetheless, it is important to keep in mind that many of the cultural characteristics of the SSSAs may also be true of other nationalities and peoples in Latin America.

The Lands of Spanish-Speaking South America

The South American continent is the fourth largest in the world and covers about 17,611,000 square kilometers (6,798,000 square miles). South America's geographic diversity is notable. On this one continental landmass can be found dry deserts, snowy plains, soaring peaks, flat grasslands, and tropical rain forests. In many places the landscape in the Spanish-speaking countries of South America looks similar to parts of English-speaking North America (ESNA), and the two regions have much in common from a geological perspective.

Many erroneously attribute a tropical climate to South America when in fact much of the region is situated in temperate latitudes. For instance, the important cities of Buenos Aires, Santiago, and Montevideo are all located around the thirty-fifth parallel, which, if transposed to the northern hemisphere, would be about the same latitude as Washington, D.C. Even those South Americans who live close to the equator are often shielded from tropical temperatures by living in the mountains. Quito, located almost on the equator, nonetheless has a temperate climate year-round due to its altitude.

The Andes Mountains, nicknamed the *cordillera* (from *cordel*, which means "rope"), run north to south along the entire western coast of South America like a spiny backbone. This mountain range is younger than the North American Rockies; consequently, its peaks are higher and more jagged, since they have not been as worn by erosion. In fact, the highest peak in all the Americas is located in western Argentina; it is Mount Aconcagua and stands 6,960 meters (22,834 feet) high.

The Andes region of South America is located along the geologically active "ring of fire" that continues north through Central America and into California. This geological zone is very active seismologically because it is where two major tectonic plate systems meet. As a consequence, there are many active volcanos as well as bubbling hot springs in the Andes area, and numerous cases of volcanic eruptions as well.

This seismic activity also creates another geological phenomenon—earthquakes. For many of the countries in the region, earthquakes rank among the most memorable of national events. The strongest earthquake ever recorded on the Richter scale took place in the south of Chile in 1960. Measuring over 9.5, it caused massive destruction of roads, houses, and industries. Near the quake's epicenter, the sea level shifted permanently by several meters, and it was felt as far away as Japan.

Rivers are another important geographical feature of the South American continent. The Amazon is not the longest river in the world (the Nile beats it), but it is the largest and most extensive waterway. The Amazon River system, which includes the river and its myriad tributaries, spreads across about 40 percent of the South American continent. The contribution of this freshwater ecological system to the planet's well-being is incalculable in terms of oxygen production and the preservation of biodiversity.

There are other important rivers in South America as well. The Orinoco River begins in southeastern Colombia and southern Venezuela and flows into the Caribbean Sea. Further south, the commercially important Paraná-Paraguay River system drains an area of about 1.5 million square miles in northern Argentina, Paraguay, Uruguay, and southern Brazil. At the junction of the two rivers is the Itaipú Dam, one of the largest in the world and an important source of hydroelectric energy for the region. Further south, the merged river empties out into the 170-mile estuary of the Río de la Plata, which then meets with the Atlantic Ocean.

South America's largest lake is the unique Lake Titicaca, located on the border between Peru and Bolivia. This body of water is located 3,810 kilometers (12,507 feet) above sea level and is the highest navigable lake in the world; landlocked Bolivia operates navy maneuvers here. Some Native Americans make their home along its shore and on the islands in the lake's center. One group is particularly famous because their lives revolve almost entirely around the reeds that grow in the water. They weave these plants together to make floating structures several meters in diameter, and then build houses out of reeds on top of these human-made islands.

Though South America contains many important waterways, it also includes areas that are nearly bereft of water. The Atacama Desert in the northern third of Chile and much of coastal Peru is the driest desert in the world. There are places in this desert where it has not rained for over one hundred years. The landscape is even starker than the Sahara Desert, with areas that look like a moonscape.

From an economic standpoint, one of the most important regions in South America is the rich and fertile grasslands called the pampas, located in central Argentina and most of Uruguay. These temperate lands, which seem to extend toward an infinite horizon, contain some of the most fertile soil in the world. Cattle, horses, and sheep roam the pampas, eating the rich grasses and producing some of the most delicious meat and best leather products found anywhere. Grain, especially wheat, also proliferates here.

Below the pampas, the climate is much colder. Across the Andes, in southern Chile, the country breaks into numerous islands and inlets that look quite similar to the Norwegian fjords, some of which contain gigantic glaciers. Patagonia, one of the most remote places on earth, lies even further south, at the very tip of the continent. Wild animals roam these vast plains, where winds sometimes exceed one hundred miles per hour. The treacherous Strait of Magellan, located between Patagonia and Tierra del Fuego, became the graveyard for many clipper ships and other boats crossing between the Atlantic and the Pacific before the Panama Canal was built.

Some South Americans argue that their land does not end at Tierra del Fuego, where the South American landmass terminates, but includes Antarctica as well, since they are located closer to this frozen and uninhabited continent than any other people. Argentina and Chile are especially vociferous in their campaign to claim the territory, and national maps in both countries often include a large segment of this frozen continent. A few years ago the Argentines even sent a pregnant woman to Antarctica to give birth, and so were able to boast that Argentina is the first country to have had a native baby born there.

Continental Neighbors

The SSSAs share the South American continent with three other countries and one overseas territory. Along the northeastern shore lie the nations of Guyana (English-speaking), Suriname (Dutch-speaking), and the French overseas territory of French Guiana (French-speaking, obviously), where the infamous Devil's Island is located, as well as the launching site for French satellites.

The largest and by far the most significant neighbor is the Portuguese-speaking nation of Brazil. Of the nine SSSA nations, seven border Brazil. The country's formidable dimensions translate poorly on most standard maps, which tend to make the equatorial countries look smaller than they actually are. Suffice it to say that Brazil is the fifth largest nation in the world, bigger than the United States, excluding Alaska. It is also the country with the greatest number of Catholics in the world today. The reason that most of the South American continent is Spanish speaking but Brazil is Portuguese speaking is due to a papal agreement by the Vatican during the early era of colonization, which was designed to avoid conflict between the two most important Catholic nations at the time, Spain and Portugal. This document, the Treaty of Tordesillas (1494), divided the uncharted world between Spain and Portugal 370 leagues west of the Azores and the Cape Verde Islands, thus giving the Portuguese most of the eastern part of what is now Brazil and leaving the rest of the Americas to the Spanish. Originally, the Spanish thought they got the worst of the deal, believing that Africa (which fell to the Portuguese) was much richer and more important than the almost unknown American colonies. Such presuppositions soon proved incorrect as the Spanish encountered many more riches in their "half of the world." Consequently, the Portuguese and, later, Brazilians devoted much of their energies to expanding the Brazilian borders westward from the designated line of Tordesillas, through a combination of diplomacy, expeditions, and wars. By the end of the 1800s, Brazil had just about reached its current size, occupying about half of the South American continent.

Most SSSAs really like their Brazilian neighbors and enjoy many aspects of Brazilian life. They listen to samba music, watch Brazilian soccer, and ogle at the wearers of teeny-weeny Brazilian bathing suits. Nonetheless, they also recognize that they are culturally different from the Portuguese-speaking South Americans in significant ways. Many claim that the differences can even be heard in the two languages. Portuguese sounds gentler than Spanish, which includes more guttural tones and a more staccato beat. Some even nickname Portuguese "baby Spanish," because its pronunciation is similar to the way an infant might intone the harsher Spanish sounds.

The Brazilians seem to be gentler in other ways as well. Roberto Mangabeira Unger, a Brazilian, claims that his country's vocation is to "synthesize sweetness and greatness" (Page 1995, 496). A contrast between the two regions' struggles for independence illustrates this point. While the SSSAs' fight to wrest freedom from Spain was both protracted and violent, the Brazilians separated from the Portuguese without a drop of blood being shed. In a spontaneous and quite Brazilian fashion, the nation became independent from the "motherland" largely due to personal factors. The son of the Portuguese monarch himself—Pedro I—declared Brazil independent one night because he wanted to stay in Brazil rather than return to Portugal as his father, the king of Portugal, requested. This young and very Brazilian monarch led the fledgling nation in its early years of statehood.

Brazilians also tend to be more informal and relaxed than many SSSAs, due in part to different colonial settlement patterns in the two regions. For instance, Richard Hill's contrast between the Spanish and Portuguese can also be applied to some extent to the differences between the SSSAs and the Brazilians.

> The Portuguese personality reflects the mild, moist climate of the ocean littoral—a completely different world from the harsh, elemental environment of upland Spain.... Where the Spanish are at times sententious, even withdrawn, the Portuguese are outgoing and eager to please. (1997, 242–43)

In addition, the African element in Brazil is much stronger than in most of SSSA, with the possible exception of parts of Venezuela and Colombia. Many slaves were brought to Brazil, especially in the northeast, to work on the plantations. Due to varying definitions of race and ethnicity, it is extremely difficult to ascertain the actual percentage of Brazilians with African ancestry, but estimates suggest that anywhere from one-third to two-thirds of Brazilians are of African heritage, at least in part. This strong African presence can be noted in many aspects of Brazilian culture: in the look of the people, the beat of the music, the taste of the food, and even the form of the country's religion.

Other Spanish-Speaking Latin Americans

Although the SSSAs share the same language with Mexicans, Central Americans, and the natives of the Spanish-speaking Caribbean nations, significant cultural differences still separate them. In fact, many SSSAs, especially those from the Southern Cone[§] region, regard those nations located on the Central American isthmus and further north as more "exotic" and "different" in many ways than ESNA or parts of Europe are, and they often draw a sharp distinction between themselves and the "tropical" Spanish-speaking natives hailing from those nations located on the Central American isthmus and further north.

There are numerous reasons for such perceived differences. One is attributable to the nature of the indigenous imprint, which influences cultural patterns in these two areas even today. For

§ The Southern Cone nations include Argentina, Chile, Paraguay, and Uruguay.

instance, the Aztecs' fascination with death and human sacrifices did not occur to such a significant extent in the Andes region, where the Incan culture predominated. As a consequence, the folk views of death and the rituals involved with funerals vary significantly in the two cultural areas. The cuisine also reflects the different pre-Columbian lineages. For instance, a taco in Chile is a traffic jam, not a folded and filled corn tortilla, and peppery food is shunned by many SSSAs, particularly those from more southern latitudes.

In addition the Mexicans' approach to dealing with their indigenous roots has had a different dynamic. One consequence of the Mexican revolution in the early twentieth century was a more open incorporation of the Native American presence into mainstream Mexican culture and society. This acceptance and reverence for the Native Americans in Mexico, while at times more rhetorical than true, has not occurred to the same extent in most of SSSA, with the possible exceptions of Bolivia and Ecuador.

The patterns of foreign influence in the two regions are also quite distinct. From the start the Mexican, Central American, and Caribbean regions have been much more susceptible to foreign influences and interventions, especially from the United States. This susceptibility results largely from geographical factors, since these areas are much more "strategically" located in a global sense than are countries such as Chile or Paraguay. The SSSA nations, in contrast, have historically been less tightly linked with the U.S. from both a political and a strategic perspective.

Not only has U.S. government policies toward the two regions varied, but so too has the flow of people. Millions of Mexicans, Central Americans, and Caribbean Spanish speakers live in the United States, and more arrive every day. Fewer SSSAs have immigrated to the ESNA nations to live and work; in fact, many SSSAs from certain countries prefer Europe to the U.S. as a travel and residence destination.

As a consequence, the Mexicans/Central Americans, Caribbean Spanish speakers, and the SSSAs tend to have different self-conceptions and thus different perspectives concerning their relationships with the United States as well as with other countries. While the SSSAs usually bemoan what they perceive as excessive U.S. attention to (and in some cases intervention in) their affairs, they tend to be more ambivalent concerning their place in the international arena and can frequently worry more about being unknown than about being known too well. Many SSSAs begin conversations with noncitizens by plaintively asking, "Do you know where my country is located?"

Finally, SSSAs share important historical bonds that set them apart from their Central American, Mexican, and Caribbean neighbors. During the many centuries of Spanish colonial control in the Americas, the SSSA nations were administered separately from Mexico and much of Central America, a fact that instilled in the region a sense of shared experience and—for some—a shared destiny as well.

In fact many of the individuals involved in SSSA's independence struggles, the most famous one being the farsighted freedom fighter Simón Bolívar, dreamed of forming a "United States of South America." They wanted this new country to be set up much like the United States of North America, in which each part of the SSSA empire would form a separate state.

This dream has not yet come to fruition; the former Spanish South American colonies separated due to political and other divisions. Nonetheless, many continue to believe in the dream. Throughout the postindependence period, there have been various attempts to foment greater cooperation and even integration among the SSSA nations. These days, many SSSAs are trying to advance regional integration more though economic means than political ones.

2

Ethnicity and Identity

> *No somos ni indios, ni europeos, sino una mezcla...así nos hallemos en el caso más extraordinario y complicado.*
>
> —Simón Bolívar

> *We are not Europeans, we are not indigenes; we are a species midway between...thus our case is all the more extraordinary and complicated.*

The past seems to weigh more heavily on the Spanish-speaking South Americans (SSSAs) than on the English-speaking North Americans (ESNAs). This is quite understandable if one considers that the colonial period in the SSSA nations lasted more than a century and a half longer than it did in the United States. The Spanish arrived in the "New World" more than one hundred years before the English began establishing settlements in the Americas and did not leave their colonies until at least fifty years after the U.S. had become independent.

The colonization of the Spanish colonies of the Americas is one of the great adventure stories (and tragedies) of all times. It took just eighty years from the time of Columbus' first journey before most of the region was under Spanish dominion. Columbus' first incursion into the South American continent took place in 1498, on his third journey, when he and his crew explored the Venezuelan coast. Less than a century later, nearly the entire region that was to become SSSA was under Spanish control, except for some of the outlying areas.

The Spaniards' rapid and often violent expansion into South America had many repercussions. Perhaps the most important consequence of their colonization was that individuals from three continents—South America, Africa, and Europe—were forcibly brought into contact. In contrast to what happened in ESNA, where there was less contact among the different racial groups, in SSSA many types of relationships, including those of a sexual nature, occurred among peoples of great cultural and racial differences. Probably no other place in the modern world saw such diverse ethnicities come together so quickly as in the Latin American region during the past half millennium.

> Except in the dim past of Oriental history, mankind has perhaps never known a conflict between peoples of such opposite ways of life as the Hispanic Conquest of America. It was a clash of races, economic attitudes and contrasting modes of existence that still complicates the problems of social relationships in every country of Latin America. Anglo-Saxon civilization in North America was able to be far more flexible socially because it had only to confront the difficulty of populating vacant land after sweeping the unfortunate nomadic Indians from their vast plains and prairies.... From the empty wilderness, the Anglo-Saxon created his own community with a will like that of Robinson Crusoe and a resourcefulness that the Spaniard was unable to display in the relatively crowded world of strange inhabitants and highly developed rites and customs. (Picón-Salas 1962, 18–19)

The interface that occurred between the Europeans, Indians, and Africans during SSSA's colonial period has played a large role in shaping its contemporary cultural configuration, creating a people of great diversity. This ethnic and cultural diversity has proved, over the centuries, to be one of the major sources of both conflict and creativity throughout SSSA.

Principal Racial and Ethnic Groups

Native Americans

There were, and are today, many more indigenous peoples in SSSA than in ESNA. While estimates vary widely, it seems that at the time of the Europeans' arrival in the Americas there were about six times as many Native Americans residing in what was to become Argentina, Bolivia, Chile, Colombia, Ecuador, Paraguay, Peru, Uruguay, and Venezuela than in the region that became the United States and Canada.

That there should be so many more Native Americans clustered in the southern American continent seems odd; according to the most accepted hypothesis, the original inhabitants of the Americas were Asians who crossed over a land bridge into the very northern part of North America some time between 40,000 and 25,000 years ago. From there they are assumed to have gradually spread southward until they reached the southernmost tip of South America around 15,000 B.C.

It is now generally accepted that several waves of migration to the Americas, rather than just one, took place prior to the arrival of the Europeans in the fifteenth century. Thor Heyerdahl, one of the most famous exponents of this viewpoint, attempted to show that both Egyptians and Polynesians could have reached American soil on the sailing crafts they had at the time. Others promote different theories. Some scholars maintain that both the Chinese and Japanese visited the Americas during the pre-Columbian period. Still others have more "exotic" opinions, such as the idea that some Native Americans are descended from Atlantean people who fled to the American continent when their island sank into the ocean.

Whatever their origins, the indigenous people in SSSA are very diverse. Anywhere from one hundred to two hundred different groups exist in the region today, depending on the criteria used. Needless to say, there were many more prior to Columbus' arrival.*

Each of the Native American groups has its own cultural patterns and many also had their own language. The Incas are the most famous Native Americans in SSSA and are one of the three most important pre-Columbian civilizations, along with the Aztecs of Mexico and the Mayas of the Yucatan region in southern Mexico and Central America. At its height, from the mid-fifteenth to the mid-sixteenth centuries A.D., their empire extended for thousands of miles both north and south along the western flank of South America and was considered one of the most important of its time anywhere in the world.

Though the Inca empire fell to the Spanish conquistadores in 1532, many vestiges of it still remain. The Incan presence can be seen at many archeological sites such as forts, tombs, agricultural terraces, and roads that dot the Andean region. The most famous places of interest are the former Incan capital, Cuzco, and the ethereal Machu Picchu, a very well-preserved Incan city never found by the Spaniards due to its relatively inaccessible location. In fact, it was not until 1911, when Hiram Bingham stumbled upon it, that its existence was even known to the outside world. More significantly, the Incan heritage can be noted in the people of these lands. There are some places in Peru and Bolivia where over half the population are heirs of the Incas, and many still speak the Incan language, Quechua.

Other important Native American groups who resided in SSSA include the Mapuches of southern Chile and Argentina

---

* How a relatively small number of Europeans were able to subjugate the much more numerous and diverse Native Americans is one of the greatest riddles of modern history. Disease had a large part to play, and it is estimated that up to 90 percent of the Native American population died within the first one hundred years after contact. Disease not only killed individuals; it also served to disrupt entire communities, leaving them less able to defend themselves. Differences in technology as well as the Spaniards' serendipitous arrival at advantageous moments—such as during the civil war occurring in the Inca empire—also played important roles in the Spaniards' eventual victory.

and the Chibchas of Colombia. The latter numbered about 600,000 at the time of the Spanish conquest and resided in what is now highland Colombia. The Chibchas' stratified society included farmers, craftsmen, and nobles. Their elites not only demanded tribute but also decreed that the common people could not look into their faces and were required to scatter flowers in their paths when they passed. One interesting bit of trivia is that when a nobleman died, he was buried with his wives, who were sacrificed after being drugged!

The Mapuches of Chile and Argentina structured their society quite differently. Numbering about 1,500,000 at the time of the conquest, their society was relatively egalitarian. Although they had local chieftains, they did not make major social distinctions between their members. Partially because of this, the Mapuches proved hard for the Spanish to conquer because there was no elite with whom to negotiate and/or to subjugate. And since there was no dominant class, the Mapuches were not accustomed to submitting to orders and commands. In fact, it was not until the late nineteenth century that the Europeans could subdue the Mapuches.

There were, and still are, many other Native American groups with differing cultural patterns and lifestyles living in what became the SSSA region. Some hunter-gatherer societies were relatively small in size and relied for sustenance on foraging and hunting with simple tools. While most of these groups were decimated by the white man, some—particularly in the tropical forests of the Amazon basin area—have survived into the twenty-first century. A few groups still have had minimal contact with mainstream civilization. Two of the better known are the Yanomami, who reside along the Venezuelan and Brazilian border area, and the Waorani from Ecuador. Both ethnic groups have a reputation for being extremely fierce defenders of their lands and their way of life.

That so many Native Americans have survived into the twenty-first century, despite the difficulties that they have faced since their first encounters with the white people, attests to their cultural and physical resilience. The contemporary indigenous peoples of SSSA combine their own cultural patterns with those of the largely European mainstream groups in a variety of ways. Some of them maintain their traditional cultural patterns nearly intact. Many more incorporate aspects of both cultures into their lifestyles. Yet other SSSAs of Native American ancestry, especially in the urban areas, end up consciously or unconsciously adopting the ways of the dominant culture almost entirely.

Except for isolated tribal groups, it is very difficult to discern what is left of pre-Columbian culture. Today's indigenous cultures are the product of five hundred years of evolution in colonial and republican contexts. For instance, most of the so-called Indian garb actually derive from Spanish peasant costumes of the sixteenth century. Also, European foods such as *habas* (lima beans), wheat, and barley have become integral to most Indian diets.

Whether their lifestyles are traditional or modern, whether they are located in the countryside or in the cities, most Native Americans face a difficult existence, as statistics from nearly all the SSSA countries suggest. In many places, the life expectancy of the Native Americans is a full decade less than other citizens. In nearly all cases, their levels of literacy are lower and infant mortality rates are higher. It is said that Pope John Paul II, during his visit to the Paraguayan Chaco, cried upon hearing an account of the suffering of the South American Indians today.

Although the situation of the Native Americans in SSSA is certainly far from exemplary, many people from the English-speaking world harbor excessively negative opinions about how the Spanish treated these indigenous people. This critical view can be attributed in part to a propaganda campaign carried out by the Protestant British to discredit the Catholic Spanish in the sixteenth and seventeenth centuries when both countries were vying for leadership. This well-financed campaign has had repercussions lasting into the modern era, giving rise to what has come to be known as the Black Legend, which juxtaposes the cruelty of the Spaniards during their conquest of Latin America with a supposedly much more benevolent campaign of expansion carried out by the British colonists in North America.

Ironically, the seeds of the Black Legend actually began in the court of the Spanish monarchy itself in the early sixteenth century. There, a vociferous debate was carried out about whether the Indians actually had souls or not, and whether they should be used as slave labor. Bartolomé de Las Casas, a Dominican friar who had witnessed the early colonization, offered personal observations of the Spanish conquistadors' brutality toward the Native Americans and argued eloquently that "all peoples of the world are men" (Hanke 1974). His argument was so persuasive that the Spanish monarch at the time, Charles I, drafted specific guidelines intended to protect the Native Americans. Among these was a prohibition against using Indians as slaves.

Although the king's rulings were barely honored in the colonies, so distant were they from the European motherland, this discussion had two far-reaching consequences. The first was that Las Casas' arguments, presented in a tome titled *Brevisima Historia de la Conquista de las Indias (A Short History of the Conquest of the Indies)*, were seized upon by Spain's archenemy at the time, England. British publicists took excerpts from this moving treatise out of context and distributed them throughout the Protestant world. These writings served to "blacken" or denigrate the Spaniards' reputation internationally—hence the name Black Legend.

The second consequence was that Charles I's prohibition against the use of Indians as slaves in the colonies led the colonists to find another source of slaves—the Africans. Consequently, large numbers of Africans began forced journeys to the Americas in the bellies of ships. Inexplicably, there was never any discussion in Spain surrounding the nature of the Africans' souls or justifying their use as slaves.

The Africans

It is possible that a few black Africans may have accompanied Columbus on his journeys; this would not be surprising given the long history of African slavery in Spain resulting from centuries of Moorish control of these lands. In Spain, however, slaves had legal and social status as human beings, and it was often possible for a slave to improve his or her status; some were even able to purchase their freedom.

Whenever the first African stepped on South American soil, the real flow of black slaves began around 1510 after the prohibition of Native American slavery. Overall, SSSA did not receive as many African slaves as did Brazil, the Caribbean, or the southern part of the United States. Of the seven to ten million Africans who were brought as slaves to the Americas during the era of the slave trade, only about 500,000 to 750,000 ended up in SSSA.

Most Africans were settled along the warm coastal areas of the Caribbean Sea and the equatorial Pacific coast, where there were large plantations of different types. The rest of the Spanish colonies received fewer African slaves, although there were at least some slaves in all of the colonies during this period.

Today, the greatest percentage of blacks in SSSA are located in Venezuela, roughly 10 percent of the total population. About 5 percent of the population of Colombia, Ecuador, and Uruguay have African ancestry. The rest of the countries of the region have an even lower percentage.

The Europeans and Other Settlers

In contrast with the large Native American population in SSSA, the Caucasian presence was (and still is) significantly smaller than in ESNA. While over forty million immigrants, principally from Western Europe, settled in the United States alone, in the nine nations of SSSA altogether there were fewer than ten million European immigrants. These Caucasians came to SSSA in several waves—each of which had its own distinctive characteristics. The first wave, during the early colonial period, was made up primarily of Spaniards, although other nationalities were also represented. These immigrants congregated most heavily in areas where the Spanish colonial control was the strongest and the mineral deposits the richest—principally in what became Peru, Bolivia, Ecuador, and Colombia.

Later waves of European immigrants, especially in the postindependence era, were more diverse in origin and gravitated to other parts of SSSA. Particularly attractive were the southern cone region with its fertile lands and booming economies and Venezuela with its petroleum. Predominant among these immigrants were Italians, Spaniards, and—to a lesser extent—French and British.

Argentina attracted the most immigrants in the late nineteenth and early twentieth centuries. During that time there were more foreigners than native-born residents in its capital city of Buenos Aires. Italians were by far the predominant group. Between 1857 and 1950, more than 3.2 million Italians arrived in Argentina. Of this total, nearly 1.5 million eventually departed. Many were known as *golondrinas*, or swallows, because they would migrate annually between Argentina and Italy, taking advantage of the seasonal differences in the two hemispheres to do agricultural work.

Large numbers of Jews also arrived in Argentina as well as in other places throughout SSSA. While some of the early settlers were Sephardic Jews fleeing the Inquisition in the Iberian Peninsula, a significant number of Ashkenazic Jews, primarily from Eastern Europe, began immigrating to the region in the late nineteenth and early twentieth centuries. This phenomenon was partly created by Baron Maurice de Hirsch, a wealthy German Jew who believed that he could solve the "Jewish problem" in Europe by resettling Jews to agricultural colonies in Argentina and other places in the Americas; he spent over forty million dollars toward this goal. In 1909 more than 19,000 Jews lived in these colonies in Argentina alone. Although nearly all of them eventually experienced massive out-migration to urban areas, this social experiment helped to make Argentina's Jewish population the second largest in the Americas—following the United States. Later, many Jews escaping Hitler came to Latin America in the late 1930s and early 1940s. After the war, it was the Nazis who came to Latin America, fleeing legal prosecution in Europe.

While large numbers of Italians and Jews immigrated to Argentina, European colonists of other nationalities predominated in Chile. Many Germans settled in southern Chile in the late 1800s, due in part to a Chilean government campaign to bring hardworking and orderly people to this recently pacified region. Croatians congregated in other parts of Chile, especially in Punta Arenas and in the mining town of Antofogasta.

Immigrants of other origins have also made SSSA their home. For instance, there are relatively large Japanese and Chinese communities in Peru. While both of these Asian groups came primarily as coolie help under atrocious working conditions (some Chinese in Peru were given three days off per year!), those who survived managed to improve their lot, and some of their descendants have become quite successful in recent years. One of Peru's former presidents and most important contemporary political figures, Alberto Fujimori, is of Japanese descent. Another important immigrant group that settled throughout SSSA were people from the Middle East. Former Argentinian President Carlos Menem—of Muslim Syrian extraction—is one notable member of this contingent.

Cross-Cultural Interface: Conflicts and Commonalities

Each of these three groups—Native American, African, and Caucasian—confronted one another for the first time in SSSA during the colonial period. These encounters were often violent cross-cultural collisions, usually predicated upon inequality. Whether as colonizer and colonized, master and slave, boss and servant, or lover and mistress, the Caucasians generally dominated the encounter, sometimes quite aggressively. However, despite the asymmetry of their relationships, all three groups emerged from their initial contact changed in some way, forever transformed. The dynamics and consequences of this interface, in turn, laid the foundation for much of the region's cultural practices.

Contributing to the complexity of this intercultural exchange were the three racial groups' quite different cultural patterns and ways of envisioning reality. The Iberians, coming from the European peninsula where the Enlightenment was under way, valued individuality, achievement, accumulation of wealth, and the power of the written word. In contrast, the Native Americans of SSSA had never developed any written language, although the Incas did have quipu, a type of counting system that utilized ropes with knots for recording quantitative information. Their communication was primarily oral, and stories and myths were key elements in the transferal of knowledge; their history was based mostly upon myths and rites. The Native Americans viewed society as a collective and life as a sacred, ceremonial and—at times—sacrificial realm.

These contrasting cultural visions are well illustrated in how the two groups perceived their relationships to the land. For the Spaniards, terrains were something to be conquered, acquired, exploited, and used for personal enrichment. For the Native Americans, land was sacred and meant to be shared and used only to sustain life. The two groups used precious metals in strikingly different ways as well. For the Indians gold and silver were to be revered and used primarily for artistic and ceremonial purposes. For the Europeans, these natural resources were a means to obtain greater personal wealth.

Despite such contrasting and often conflicting mindsets, the fifteenth- and sixteenth-century Europeans, Native Americans, and Africans did share some cultural values. These areas of commonality became important in the emerging SSSA culture because they served as bridges of shared meaning, linking the three ethnic groups. It was through them that comprehensible cross-cultural communication could take place.

One area of cultural commonality was the importance all three groups gave to myths and lore. The world of the medieval Spaniard was full of magical creatures, a fact that is well illustrated by the ways that the first Iberians on the American continent interpreted what they observed. They told tales of giant Amazonian women beside the river that today bears this name, of big-footed humans in southern South America that gave rise to the name Patagonia, and of a legendary city with streets lined in gold called El Dorado, which was never to be found.

Myths were similarly central to all the Native American ethnic groups and to the African slaves as well. In fact, certain myths of the Andean Indians actually contributed to their conquest by the Spaniards. They thought that the early conquistadors were Viracocha, a bearded white-skinned god whom they believed created the other gods as well as all animals and men. They also believed in the notion of *pachacuti*, a catastrophe of cosmic proportions, whose purpose was to make the world new again. For them, the Spanish conquest was definitely a pachacuti.

The importance given to myths and stories carries over into the modern era. Some SSSAs claim that "we are all poets at heart, and you ESNAs are all engineers." There is some truth in this claim. Throughout SSSA, artists of all types abound. While in the United States many people tinker in their garages trying to invent a new or different machine or fix an existing one, in SSSA many "closet artists" leave their regular jobs and return home to pursue their true vocations as poets, painters, or craftspeople.

Artistic forms of all types are respected enormously. Known artists are considered prestigious members of society, often even awarded diplomatic posts and other governmental positions, and, in several cases, authors have reached quite high political office throughout the region. In Venezuela, one writer, Rómulo Gallegos, actually became president of the nation. Recently, in Peru, the well-known writer Mario Vargas Llosa ran for president but was defeated. Internationally, authors are some of the most famous SSSAs. Many of them, such as Gabriel García Márquez and Jorge Luis Borges, are noted for the mythic quality of their books.

Another important area of cultural commonality was the importance given by all three ethnic groups to ritual and ceremony. The Iberians were propelled by the ideas of the Counter-Reformation that stressed the sacraments, ceremony, and ritual as keys to salvation. For the Native Americans and Africans, ceremony and ritual were even more important, representing in many cases the manner in which their spirituality was manifested and bonds between members of the community created and maintained.

In the modern era, there are many manifestations of the centrality of ritual and ceremony in the culture of the SSSAs. Feasts and holidays abound throughout the region, and many have a religious dimension. In the secular realm, celebrations of all types are very important, and many workers are often paid, at least in part, through parties given by their bosses. For instance, when a building is completed there is often a "topping off" party for the construction workers featuring lots of wine and food. Nearly all SSSAs like a good party, whatever the occasion. It would be difficult to find anybody from this region who would not happily stay up nearly all night to "have a good time" with friends. Many see such activities as a very important part of enjoying life to its fullest.

Miscegenation and Mestizaje

Some of the most significant intercultural encounters that occurred in colonial SSSA were sexual in nature. That intimate encounters among the three racial groups were prolific should not be surprising. After all, there were many more Native Americans and many fewer Europeans in SSSA than there were in ESNA.

But additional factors beyond demographics account for the prevalence of these relationships. First, nearly all of the early Europeans in SSSA were males. In contrast to the settlement patterns during the later English colonization of North America, which included many female colonists and a large number of married couples, very few females came to the Iberian colonies, and even fewer spouses.

Because of the hierarchical nature of the relationships between the Europeans and the Native Americans and Africans, most of the sexual encounters reflected an asymmetry of power and different codes of conduct. European colonial males may have treated women of their own ethnicity in one way, but they usually treated indigenous and black females in quite another. Many of the sexual encounters that took place were forced; rape was widespread in some instances. Even if such interracial relationships were more than brief encounters, they rarely led to formal marriage, and the Caucasian men decided their course.

Second, the Spaniards' relatively open attitude about having sexual relationships with Native Americans and Africans can be attributed, at least in part, to the centuries of Moorish control of the Iberian Peninsula, during which time a multiracial and multicultural society existed. Again, this contrasts with most of the Anglo-Saxon colonists in North America, who tended toward greater racial separation.

Finally, the Catholic Church played a significant role in condoning, if not encouraging, these interracial relationships. From the Church's perspective, great benefits could be obtained from these intimate encounters between the Catholic men and their Indian or African consorts. Although Christian marriages between couples of different ethnicities were prohibited throughout most of the colonial period, the Church did recognize the large number of interracial couples as well as their offspring, who were usually baptized as Catholics.

The children born of these interracial unions proved to be one of the most important consequences of the entire colonial period, since these mixed offspring eventually came to form the largest segment of SSSA society. A new set of terms was needed to describe the different racial combinations born to the Spanish colonizers in a process that came to be known as *mestizaje*. Children of Caucasian and Indian ancestry was named mestizos; those of Caucasian and black descent, mulattos, and those of Native American and black parentage, *zambos*.

During the colonial era, these people of mixed ancestry were positioned in the middle tiers of the hierarchical social structure—between the Caucasians at the top and the Native Americans and Africans at the bottom. After independence, and even into the contemporary period, this social placement has generally continued.

The social, economic, and political importance of these mestizos and mulattos in SSSA cannot be overestimated, since they make up the majority of the citizenry in nearly all the region, with the exceptions of Argentina and Uruguay. These people of mixed ancestry straddle the gap—sometimes uncomfortably—between the predominantly white elite and the largely darker lower classes.

Questions of Identity

The prevalence of mestizaje among SSSAs has implications that transcend the purely racial. At its deepest level, the mixed ethnic ancestry of so many SSSAs raises perplexing questions of identity. Who are they and what do they represent culturally? Should they emphasize their Native American and/or African roots or their Caucasian lineage? Maybe they are truly different from either. But if that is the case, what is it about them that is unique? Do the sons and daughters of these sexual encounters represent only a cultural synthesis of the different racial and ethnic groups whose blood they blend, or are they, perhaps, something entirely new, a creation that transcends their own progenitors, a mixture leading to a never-before-seen human manifestation, both literally and figuratively?

Responses to these important questions of identity vary greatly according to both individual and group factors. Individually, some SSSAs of mixed ancestry proudly embrace their Native American and/or African roots, while others reject them even though their physiognomy clearly indicates their mixed parentage.

Nationally, some countries in the region, such as Ecuador and Bolivia, seem, at least on the surface, to venerate the mixed ancestry of their citizens. The actual implications, however, tell a different story. Those of mixed ancestry increasingly adopt the ways of the dominant Caucasian culture. In other countries, such as Chile, the mainstream "origin myth" emphasizes the Caucasian aspect of their lineage and minimizes the widespread miscegenation that occurred between the Europeans and Native Americans. The Chileans go so far, in fact, as to call themselves the "English of Latin America," even though the majority of the country's citizens are mestizos.

Whatever the individual and national views concerning this mixed ancestry, it is clear that "for many mestizo countries of America...few have achieved the tranquil acceptance of their own image" (Ribeiro 1972, 335–36). Many SSSAs are unsure of who they really are, and this identity crisis influences their perceptions both of themselves and of their place in the world. It is not surprising that the image most often used to describe the Latin Americans is the mask, a superficial disguise intended to hide one's true identity.

Blanqueamiento

One manifestation of the region's struggles with identity is the number of people of mixed ancestry who tend to prefer what is Caucasian over what is Indian or African, because the former is seen as the region's dominant culture and as having more status in the social hierarchy. In a process known as *blanquimiento* (whitening), many individuals try to appear "whiter" (both literally and figuratively) than they are. Blanquimiento can be noticed in many aspects of contemporary SSSA society. Although in many of the region's countries the majority of the population is of Native American descent, the media principally show people of Caucasian descent. Women frequently lighten their hair, and many job advertisements ask for somebody of *buena presencia* (good presence), which usually means not too Indian in appearance. Even within families, preference is often given to the child who looks "whiter"; the darker child is often called *negrito* and *feo* (ugly).

Such ethnic self-selection is made easier in SSSA than it would be in ESNA because of the different definitions of race in the two regions. While in the United States racial affiliation is based primarily on ancestry, in Latin America it is defined more from a cultural perspective. Thus, somebody who appears to have Indian features but who has few ties to the Native American culture might classify him- or herself as white.

Such attempts at blanquimiento go beyond the physical. At a deeper level, the concept implies a denigration of the racially Native and/or African aspects of many SSSAs. By elevating all that is Caucasian, those of mixed identity implicitly put themselves and their culture in a lower position. Blanqueamiento then has profound consequences for concepts of self-worth.

> One of the very last forms of European domination is the internalization by millions of mestizo Americans of ideals and other values based on white European characteristics as marks of superiority. This assumption of the self-image of "the other" is manifested in many ways.... For example, it is betrayed by the vanity of identification as white, made with the greatest naturalness, even with genuineness, by people who regard themselves as different and better and attribute their social precedence to their lighter skin...thus making even the aristocrats of the most clearly indigenous phenotype see themselves as white and explain their superior social status by this characteristic. (Ribeiro, 335–36)

This preference for what is "white" explains in part the SSSAs' attraction to many of the imports from Europe and ESNA, as it is often assumed that anything from "lighter" lands is superior and more advanced. This belief prevails not just in the realm of technology but also in fashion, art, ideas, and sometimes even people. Thus, many SSSAs often copy or imitate—even slavishly—what originates from beyond their region's borders and fail to appreciate what they have locally.

Persistent Cross-Cultural Divisions

Today, more than half a millennium after the first encounter between the Spaniards and the Native Americans and the Africans, many of the key issues of identity and position in society have yet to be comprehensively addressed, let alone resolved.

In many cities throughout SSSA, it is truly as though two different and mutually exclusive cultural realities coexist within the same geographic area. Areas inhabited by the elites, usually those of primarily Caucasian lineage, often appear quite similar to parts of the United States or Canada; with the effects of globalization, these areas seem even more similar to parts of ESNA, with fast-food restaurants, malls, and housing developments springing up constantly. In contrast, the poorer sectors of many urban centers are usually inhabited by individuals with darker skin and very different lifestyles. Many are just barely surviving. Here one finds a proliferation of folk religious figures and practices, shops that sell indigenous herbs and other medicinal objects, and a much more collectivistic lifestyle among family and neighbors.

Consequently, SSSA is not just multicultural, in many ways it is also culturally divided. Some even posit that the region at times demonstrates elements of cultural schizophrenia—with a split personality. These separate cultural divisions, based largely on ethnic affiliation, can be noted both externally in social structures and internally in values and perceptions.

3

The Cross and the Sword

El antiguo Conquistador se yergue todavía en su tumba, y dentro de nosotros, mira, muerto, a través de sus suenos frustrados, esa inmensidad promisoria aun, y se le humedecen de emoción nuestros ojos. Somos su tumba y a la vez la piedra de su honda.

—Ezequiel Martínez Estrada

The old conquistador yet rises from his tomb: he is dead, but within us he looks across his frustrated dreams at this immense and still promised land, and our eyes moisten with emotion. We are at the same time his tomb and [the] stone of his sling.

The Spaniards' legacy in their South American colonies extends far beyond the racial and ethnic composition of the region. The Iberians were able to accomplish an amazing feat, which was to control their vast and distant American colonies for nearly three hundred years during a time in which communication and technology were extremely slow and inefficient. They were able to maintain this control largely through the political, economic, and social structures that they implemented in the colonies. These social structures were initially shaped by the Spanish monarchs and their many advisers. The Catholic Church also played an important role in expanding the power of the Caucasian conquerors by disseminating spiritual concepts and values and through its more earthly impact on the realms of education, social services, and even politics.

In fact, the colonization of Spanish America has been dubbed the "Cross and the Sword" to indicate this intricate relationship between the Spanish political and military leaders and the priests and nuns of the Catholic Church. Together, the two entities directed and shaped the entire colonial interlude in Spanish-speaking South America (SSSA), contributing in significant ways to the development of many of the region's patterns and social structures. Even though the colonial period ended centuries ago, the influence of the cross and the sword was so profound and affected the diverse peoples of SSSA so deeply that it continues to shape much of the region's realities today.

The Cross

The Spaniards were motivated to conquer the New World not only by the promise of land and riches but also by missionary zeal. These medieval Iberians devoutly believed in the absolute and exclusive truth of their Catholicism. While it is easy to criticize this mentality from a modern perspective, one must recall what Europe was like at the end of the Middle Ages. As Mariano Picón-Salas reminds us,

> It is unfair to blame sixteenth-century Spaniards for a lack of anthropological insight or for a belief that only their own way of life had validity. It should be remembered, too, that every conquistador felt obliged by his religious convictions to further the spread of the Christian faith, which the Spaniard identified with his very being. (1962, 42)

The zealous bent of the early Spanish colonizers was strengthened by political events that occurred in the motherland during this period. It is more than mere coincidence that Columbus' first voyage to the Americas occurred the same year that the Spanish, under the united leadership of the monarchs Isabella of Castile and Ferdinand of Aragon, finally expelled the Moors from their last outpost on Spanish soil—Granada. The Catholics' reconquest of the Iberian Peninsula had been a long and protracted struggle, and the Christians' victory gave them the sense that God was truly on their side.

The Spaniards' hard-earned military victory ended a centuries-long, peaceful coexistence among the three religious communities then residing in Spain—Muslim, Jew, and Catholic. The Catholic monarchs, as Isabella and Ferdinand came to be called, demanded that all their subjects become Catholic. The many Muslims and Jews were faced with the difficult choice of converting to Christianity, leaving Spain, or maintaining their faith at the risk of being subjected to the infamous Inquisition.

The Catholic Spaniards' proselytizing fervor extended to their colonies in the New World. Ironically, it appears that some of the early Europeans who came to the American colonies were actually Spanish Jews who hid their religious affiliation, most likely thinking that they would be safer in distant America than in Spain. Most of the early Spanish who came to SSSA, however, were devout Catholics who firmly believed in the exclusive truth of their religion and who planned to promote these beliefs in the New World.

The Catholic Church's role in the colonies was not limited solely to the spiritual realm.

> No other institution has contributed as much as the Catholic Church to determining what Latin America has and has not become. The Spanish conquest was made in the name and the service of the Faith, and conquest and colonization were seen as one with Catholicism. Up to the nineteenth century—throughout the three hundred and fifty years during which the political and social structures of Latin America were decisively shaped—Catholicism formed both the brain and the backbone of Latin-American society. (Hanke 1974, 141)

The physical presence of the Catholic Church was an important element in the conquest and colonization of SSSA. In nearly every city, town, and village that the Spanish established, the first structures that they erected in the central plaza were the Church on one side and the government offices on the other.

In some places, such as Cuzco, they even built the church on top of sacred indigenous shrines.

This close juxtaposition of the Church and the political office in the main plaza reflects the interrelationship between the religious and political realms that existed in the Spanish colonies. It was assumed that the monarch, his or her colonial representatives, and the Catholic Church were allies working together for a common cause. After all, the viceroy in the colonies—the highest authority—was in charge of both political and religious affairs.

Some of the most dedicated Spaniards to arrive in South America during the long colonial period were the priests. Although they might be branded paternalistic from a modern perspective, numerous religious figures fought hard not only to convert but also to help the native people. During the early colonial period, several friars were among the most vociferous critics of the conquistadors' abuses of the Native Americans.

These religious critics were the minority among the colonial Catholic clergy, however. Most of the priests took a more conventional approach to their mission and concerned themselves primarily with two aspects of their priestly functions: (1) to meet the spiritual needs of those in the colonies who were already Catholics and to ensure continued adherence to their faith and (2) to convert the Native Americans and, later, the African "heathens" to Catholicism whenever possible. Especially in the early period of the Spanish conquest of the Americas, when the Spanish confronted and defeated large numbers of Indians, mass baptisms and forced conversions were common.

The Catholics imposed their religious ideas on the indigenous inhabitants of SSSA, often quite harshly. However, from the perspective of many of the Native American groups, most of whom believed in a pantheon of different gods, what they could understand of the Catholic faith (which often wasn't very much due to the language barrier) did not seem so incongruent with their own beliefs. Many Africans brought to the South American continent as slaves reached the same conclusion. Since neither group had an exclusive spirituality, many Indians and Africans converted to Catholicism while still remaining true to their own beliefs. This was done both overtly and covertly. While at first the figures and rituals of the Catholic Church were often utilized as a façade behind which the worship of their own deities could continue, albeit in a greatly modified form, over time the religions began to blend, especially at the popular level, until it often became difficult to distinguish the imposed Christian symbols and ceremonies from the indigenous and/or African ones.

Among the easiest aspects of the Catholic faith for the Indian and African to embrace were the numerous saints—each with its own personality. It was not so hard for the Native Americans and Africans to equate these Catholic saints with their own gods and goddesses. In a process known as syncretism, the two—Christian saints and indigenous spiritual figures—began to merge in the popular faith of the continent.

One of the most beloved figures was the Virgin Mary, whom many of the Native peoples could easily understand as a sacred maternal symbol. Most indigenous tribes had some type of goddess with whom they could equate the Christian Virgin Mary. Throughout the Spanish colonies, a cult to the Virgin Mary began to blossom even more than in European Catholicism, and the Virgin "appeared" to numerous people throughout the colonies. Each apparition was given a different name. Today, nearly every SSSA nation venerates at least one special virgin.

European Catholics and some Native Americans also shared a fatalistic view of life. The medieval Catholicism introduced to the Spanish colonies held that much of what occurred in a person's life was due to God's will and could not be altered—a perspective that was quite similar to the beliefs of many Native Americans.

A sense of fatalism continues to permeate SSSA culture. Many natives of the region—even the most secular—think that not everything in life can be explained, predicted, or controlled. Each person has a personal *destino*, or fate. One of the most frequent comments that SSSAs make in response to a tragic event of some type is "*Fue su destino*" ("It was his or her destiny").

Such a harsh fatalism, however, is not without some sort of remedy, and divine intervention sometimes does occur. Belief in miracles is still very strong in much of SSSA. In a study undertaken in urban (and seemingly very modern) Chile in 1998, over 80 percent of the people surveyed claimed to believe in miracles (FLACSO 1998). Plaques of thanks to saints and virgins for "favors bestowed" are present at many public and religious sites throughout the region.

Interrelated with attitudes concerning fate are those toward death, both one's own and others'. The theme of death is more overt in SSSA than is the norm in English-speaking North America (ESNA), and it is quite common for SSSAs to accompany any discussion about death or any tragedy, with a complacent sigh and the comment, "Fue su destino." The palpable sense of the possibility and reality of death can also be found in much of the art and literature from the region. In a comparative study of English and Latin American literature, the theme of death was raised at least twice as often in the latter works, according to the researchers.

Attitudes toward death are also reflected in the treatment of the dead in SSSA, which is strongly influenced by both Catholic and Native American traditions. Graveyards, for example, are a common place for outings, and it is not uncommon to see entire families visiting the tombs of their deceased kin. Many of the graves, which are typically mausoleums, are festooned with flowers, photographs, and other possessions of the loved ones who have passed on. This is particularly notable at the graves of infants and young children, which are sometimes decorated with favorite toys, pacifiers, and other such mementos. November 1, All Saints' Day, is a holiday throughout the region. According to the Catholic Church, it is the time when the spirits of the deceased are closest to the earthly realm. Consequently, people flock to graveyards to commune with dead loved ones, often bringing vibrantly colored flowers to lay on the graves.

Today, the nations of SSSA are among the most Catholic in the world. Despite recent inroads by some Protestant groups and the immigration of non-Catholics to these lands, the vast majority of the SSSAs are at least nominally Catholic. While some do no more than attend mass infrequently, and some not at all, many are quite devout. As one Latin American priest put it, "In Latin America, you are Catholic by breathing the air. The Catholic faith has so permeated the life of the people—the courtroom, the kitchen, the plaza, the architect's eye—it would take centuries for Latin America to sort all that out" (Rodriguez 1992, 176).

Although church and state are technically separate in all nine nations, the Catholic Church exerts enormous influence. At the same time, Latin America is also very important to the Catholic Church because it is the home of the largest Catholic population in the world. And the SSSAs have given Catholicism—at least at the popular level—a mystical and magical quality due to the influence of both the Native American and African religious beliefs upon the Catholic dogmas.

The Sword

When Columbus "discovered" the Americas, the Spanish nation was still in the Middle Ages in many ways. Neither the industrial revolution nor the beginnings of democratic rule had yet shaken the medieval structures of Iberia. Wealth was primarily equated with owning land and accumulating precious metals, especially gold.

The Spaniards who were involved in the early colonization of the Americas were motivated by these medieval concepts. Most were land-hungry younger sons, many from the poorest regions of Spain, who were compelled to look for their own land beyond Spanish borders because, under Spanish law, land went to the first sons only. The great majority of them were uneducated.

Most of the conquistadors dreamed of making their fortune in the New World and then returning to the motherland—Spain—to live the rest of their lives in comfort. Consequently, their time in the Americas was viewed principally as a means of achieving a prestigious lifestyle back in Spain. This outlook led to an exploitative approach to colonization that focused on how much could be "gotten out" of the American region for Spain and for the Spaniards.

The infamous story of the conquest of the Incas illustrates the Spaniards' rapacious attitudes. Francisco Pizarro, himself an illiterate and illegitimate son who had spent most of his childhood tending pigs, led the conquest of the rich Inca empire for the Spanish monarchy. Fortunately for him and his small entourage, they arrived in the Incan capital of Cuzco at a time when the Incas were beset by a civil war between two rivals for the Incan throne—the brothers Huáscar and Atahuallpa.

The Spanish managed to catch and imprison Atahuallpa. This royal personage, who had learned of the Spaniards' love of gold, offered to fill one room as high as his arm could reach with objects of pure gold and another room with silver if the Spaniards would release him. Pizarro agreed to this proposal.

It took two months to fill the room with gold, which came from throughout the extensive Incan domain. Ultimately 13,000 pounds of gold and twice that much silver were delivered to Pizarro. Most came in the form of beautiful objects of art, which the Spaniards melted down into bars for easier transport. The haul of gold and silver made not only Pizarro rich but all of his crew as well, even down to the lowliest foot soldier. According to the agreement, the Incan king should have been released, but Pizarro continued his imprisonment on the trumped-up charge of treason and executed Atahuallpa a short time later.

Not all confrontations between the Native peoples and the Spaniards were so clearly exploitative or treacherous. In fact Pizarro later encountered problems from the Spanish crown for breaking his word as a gentleman to the Incan king. Nonetheless, the nature of medieval warfare, with the spoils going to the winner, very much set the tone of the conquest.

Most of the early conquistadors were able to realize their dream of obtaining land, many ending up with more territory than they could ever have imagined. Their seizure of Native American territory was sanctioned by the Spanish crown, which awarded vast tracts of land as a prize for military success. To maintain Spanish control over this region, the Spanish monarchs devised a system known as the *encomienda* (from the Spanish verb *encomendar*, meaning "to entrust") or, later, latifundio. The encomienda was first introduced in the Spanish colonies as early as 1503.

Under the encomienda system, the Europeans were awarded control over both the conquered lands and the people residing there, on the condition that they take care of their subjects' well-being. The Native Americans, in turn, were obligated to provide labor and other services to their superiors and in compensation were to receive physical protection and religious instruction. In some of the encomiendas, African slaves were also employed; their status was often even lower than that of the Native Americans.

To the leaders back in Spain, this exchange seemed to be a fair one. The encomienda, in fact, was meant to moderate the early excesses of the conquistadors who initially seized many of the Indians and subjected them to slavery. In practice, however, the encomienda system ended up being very exploitative. Most of the encomenderos paid little attention to the health or interests of their Native American subjects and continued to seize lands and to enslave the indigenous people.

The Spanish crown tried unsuccessfully to end the encomienda system throughout the 1500s and 1600s, but because of the high stakes involved and its distant command, it was unable to do so until the late 1700s. Thus, the encomienda system remained the primary means of apportioning lands and structuring society in the Spanish colonies for nearly three hundred years.

The Spanish monarchs were less free in distributing political power to the South American colonists than they were in granting land rights. The colonies were divided into administrative units known as viceroyalties, the boundaries of which changed throughout the colonial period. In the Spanish-speaking region, there were eventually three viceroyalties. The first and most important was the Viceroyalty of Peru, with its capital in Lima. The second was the Viceroyalty of Neuva Granada, with its capital in Bogotá, created in 1717. The third, and the last to be formed (in 1776), was the Viceroyalty of Río de la Plata, with its capital in Buenos Aires. Colonial government remained almost entirely in the hands of Spaniards known as *peninsulares*, who were appointed by the monarch for limited terms. The top position in the colonies was that of viceroy. During his term in the colonies, the viceroy presided over all political and religious affairs.

As can be imagined, this created a very bureaucratized political and administrative structure during the long colonial period, a situation that carries over in many ways throughout the region even today. One of the most defining characteristics of daily life in much of SSSA is probably the bureaucratic red tape required to undertake many necessary activities of daily life. Sometimes it seems that nothing can be accomplished easily because of this bureaucratic proliferation that consumes so much personal time and energy. Isabel Allende wrote the following concerning this aspect of life in the region in a newspaper article in 1969:

> No *tramite* (procedure) requires less than three different papers with an equal number of copies, whose only finality seems to be to increase the public administration files...this paper trail not only employs several thousand otherwise useless people...it is also the sociological imperative of impeding any type of dynamic action within the national territory. To travel, marry, graduate, inherit, buy and die, you have to fill out so many papers, put together so much data, put on so many stamps and do so many lines that the victim gives up before beginning...the interminable spiral of papers can lead to very Kafka-like situations.

Most people, however, know how to maneuver the system to their advantage.

Despite the monarchs' attempts to exclude the locals (known as "Creoles") from participating in governing the colonies, there was one institution called the *cabildo*, similar to a city council, in which they did have some voice. Most of the major cities of the Spanish colonies had a cabildo, where issues of concern were raised and discussed. Influential citizens would be appointed to this council, or—in some cases—the position was "sold" to the highest bidder. During the struggle for independence, some of these cabildos played a decisive role in rallying the American-born colonists to fight against Spain.

The Spanish monarchs were not only concerned with exerting political control over their colonies but also with preserving the incredible riches of their American holdings. They demanded the "*quinto real*" (royal fifth) of all that was found in the New World. Galleon ships would sail annually from the American colonies, laden with gold and silver to satisfy the Spanish crown. The Spaniards became so focused on their mineral riches that they did not join the industrial revolution that was beginning to sweep the European continent. A century or so after the first colonization of the Americas, Spain was a nation in decline.

Spain's inability to shift successfully from a semifeudal to a capitalist society had important consequences for the colonies as well. The monarchs even went so far as to prohibit them from engaging in any sort of manufacturing whatsoever and also made it illegal for the colonies to have direct trade with any other foreign country or even among themselves. This meant, for example, that for the Viceroyalty of Rio de la Plata to legally trade with Peru, items had to be first shipped all the way to Spain and then routed back again across the Atlantic and through the Pacific passage to finally reach Peru.

Of course, the locals found ways to circumvent these restrictive trade policies, and smuggling was rampant during the entire colonial period. The colonists even coined what eventually became a well-known phrase to explain their manner of dealing with the many Spanish laws and edicts: "*Obedezco, pero no cumplo*" ("I obey but will not comply"). In fact, noncompliance with colonial edicts extended far beyond smuggling. Most Creoles knowingly violated Spanish edicts that were considered inimical to personal interests.

This lax attitude toward rules and regulations carries over into contemporary life. Many SSSAs pretend to follow orders, but in reality they do whatever they consider to be in their own best interest. Such noncompliance ranges from mild cases of bending the rules to more blatant illegalities. Tax evasion is rampant throughout the region, as are cases of corruption and bribery. Although many of the contemporary SSSA leaders are attempting to create a more orderly and rule-abiding environment, in part as a way to attract foreign investment, it is extremely difficult to change centuries-old patterns of behavior.

The monarchs' long-ago prohibition against industrialization and their encouragement of the export of raw materials have also proved hard to modify. Despite many efforts to promote industrialization, all of the SSSA nations today—even the more economically successful ones—are mainly exporters of primary goods.

Although the encomienda system officially ended centuries ago, its influence on social patterns in contemporary SSSA lingers. For example, the very unequal roles accorded to the Caucasian overlords on the one hand and to the Native American, black, and somewhat later, mestizo workers on the other have contributed in large part to the hierarchical and paternalistic nature of many labor relationships in the region. Typically, the boss is known and often addressed as the "patrón," is accorded much higher status than his employees, and expects obedience and respect from them. In turn, the patrón is ostensibly responsible for the personal well-being of employees, a duty that extends beyond the work arena in many cases.

The encomienda system has also led to an unequal apportionment of land and economic resources. In fact Latin America has the most inequitable distribution of resources of any region in the world. While some people (many descendants of early settlers) have enormous landholdings and great inherited wealth, many more (often of Native American descent) barely make a living either by farming minuscule plots of land or by laboring in the urban areas. This still holds true in many parts of the region, despite diverse efforts, particularly in the last fifty years, to redress such glaring inequalities. Such attempts have ranged from limited redistribution of lands and resources to outright revolution in a few instances. In fact, this issue of inequality is perhaps the single most volatile arena in SSSA.

4

Relationships and Personalismo

Soy otro cuando soy, los actos míos, son más míos si son también de todos, para que pueda ser he de ser otro, salir de mí, buscarme entre los otros, los otros que no son si yo no existo, los otros que me dan plena existencia, no soy, no hay yo, siempre somos nosotros.

—Octavio Paz

I am another when I am, my actions are more mine if they are also everyone's. So that I can exist I must be the other, I must leave myself to look for myself among the others, those who would not exist if I did not, those who give me my own existence. I am not, there is no I, always it is we.

The cultural patterns of the contemporary Spanish-speaking South Americans (SSSAs) have been shaped by numerous factors, including historical influences, ethnic composition, social structures, and contemporary realities of the region's inhabitants. As with all distinct cultural groups, the SSSAs have certain practices and beliefs that are particularly emphasized. These distinguishing cultural orientations serve several important functions. First, they help establish the parameters for perceiving and interpreting the social milieu. They also provide guidelines for framing culturally acceptable values and behaviors. Finally, they encourage a sense of group affiliation and provide a means of distinguishing one's own cultural group from "outsiders."

One of the most notable distinguishing cultural orientations of the SSSAs is a preferred means of relating to others known as *personalismo*. Personalismo is a way of structuring human interactions in which—as the term implies—the personal element is emphasized. Illustrations of this personal element include creating ties of emotional warmth, preferring face-to-face communication whenever possible, having at least some knowledge about another's personal life (i.e., family, children, health, partner, etc.), and enjoying a sense of interconnectedness.*

Such feelings of interconnectedness are crucial and explain why SSSAs do not typically draw boundaries between themselves and others as sharply as do many English-speaking North Americans (ESNAs). Neither do they view themselves as entirely autonomous and independent. Instead, SSSAs are more communal in orientation, usually defining their own individuality largely by how they relate to other people, especially those with whom they have established ties of personalismo. Richard Rodriguez succinctly sums up these cultural differences as follows: "The point in the United States is distinguishing yourself from the crowd, the point of Mexico [and SSSA] is the crowd" (1992, 165).

These cross-cultural differences can even be noted linguistically. There are fewer Spanish words based on "self" than in English and many more words to describe interpersonal relations. For instance, the language includes numerous terms to express the nature of affection, and the nuances between them can be quite subtle. Just a few examples of such words are *querer* (to like or love), *amar* (to love), *adorar* (to adore), *estar enamorado* (to be in love), *sentir afección* (to have affection for), and *apreciar*

---

* Personalismo is characteristic of Latin American culture in general and not limited to the SSSAs. It is most likely an important component of many other cultural groupings around the world as well. However, the manner in which personalismo is actually weighted, interpreted, and actualized in different societies can vary considerably depending on myriad other characteristics of the particular cultural group under consideration.

(to appreciate).† Some of these words cannot even be adequately translated into English. One of the most important of these affection terms is *cariño*, which means "warm affection," but it is actually more encompassing than its best English equivalent. For most SSSAs, relationships that exhibit a marked element of cariño are highly valued. To describe someone as *cariñoso/a* is considered among the highest of compliments, and many SSSAs actualize such behavior when possible, as manifested in close physical contact, the expression of concern and attention for the needs of the other, a gracious hospitality, and a sense of being emotionally present during personal encounters.

This cultural emphasis on giving and receiving cariño and reaching out emotionally to others is motivated in part, if often unconsciously, by the desire to connect with what SSSAs consider to be the most important aspect of humans—their *alma* (spirit or soul). Most people from this region, even the secular, believe that everybody has such an alma imbued in them by forces larger and more powerful than mere human efforts and capabilities.

Connecting to others' almas is a primary means by which to nurture one's own, and such personal connections are thought to be important for both emotional sustenance and individual realization. Actually, feeling and perceiving another person's alma serves a double purpose. It is both a means of knowing another person's most intrinsic qualities and a way of accessing—through the relationship—the most significant aspects of life, those immeasurable and nonmaterial elements that some may call spiritual. Because of this, SSSAs believe that they achieve fullest selfhood by relating to others; it cannot be done alone.

---

† Not only are there more words in Spanish that describe the many different types of affection than in English, but also SSSAs tend to be more circumscribed in their employment of such words and are often surprised at how freely many English speakers use the word *love* to describe their opinion regarding a food, a movie, and so on. This would never be done in Spanish!

Given this cultural perspective, it should not be surprising that many SSSAs find it difficult to understand why ESNAs often strive to be as autonomous as possible and, in many instances, even prefer to live alone. They actually feel sorry for ESNAs, whom they consider to be rich materially but frequently poor in what is most important in life—human warmth and affection.

Illustrations of personalismo abound in contemporary SSSA culture and can be seen clearly in how people in the region greet and take leave of each other. Typically, great care is taken to make physical contact with each and every person present in an overt demonstration of emotional warmth. This cultural practice can make both greetings and farewells quite time-consuming; however, these rituals are considered central to maintaining bonds between people.

In practice, it works as follows—when SSSAs enter or leave almost any type of gathering, including most business meetings, they will circle the group and either kiss, hug, or, less frequently, shake hands with everyone present. The appropriate form of salutation depends on gender, level of familiarity, degree of formality of the event, and other factors. Typically, males will either shake hands with other men or, in the case of close friends or family members, give a firm hug or even a kiss (depending on the context). Females usually give one or two kisses (depending on the country) on the cheek to everyone. Between men and women, a salutatory kiss given lightly on the cheek is the norm. When departing, the same procedure is followed.

Personalismo also manifests itself in other daily routines. Many errands and activities that would usually be accomplished by a phone call or by mail in ESNA must often be done in person in SSSA. Fewer places offer self-service; there are nearly always people to "help out" in restaurants, in stores, at gas stations, and when parking, even if such assistance is not solicited. In fact, it is hard to be left alone when carrying out such activities. Such personalized connections extend even into the inanimate realm. In some places, buses and trucks are given names and sometimes even baptized by their owners.

Personalismo is even expressed in the way that many SSSAs perceive their relationship with the "higher forces." Religion, especially its popular manifestations, stresses a sense of intimacy with the myriad saints and virgins of the Catholic pantheon. These religious figures provide the primary means of communicating with God; typically, individuals will have a favorite entity with whom they feel a special connection, and when in need, they will petition this saint or virgin for assistance in much the same way one would ask a friend for help.

Personalismo and Intimate Relationships

Of all the different realms in SSSA culture where personalismo is manifested, its presence is strongest in intimate relationships—typically family members and close friends. This should not be surprising, because it is among such familiar people that the strongest cariño can be exchanged and where the greatest possibility for accessing the alma of the other exists. Due to the great value accorded these intimate relationships, most SSSAs devote the greatest time and personal attention to them, frequently giving preference to family and friends over broader-based and less personalized human groupings such as clubs and organizations, both secular and religious. Empirical studies have corroborated these cross-cultural differences. In one such project, carried out in Chile, the following results were obtained:

> [Chile] demonstrates a high incidence of people gravitating to relationships with people who are known to them, which contrasts with the English-speaking North American tendency to relate with strangers, that is to say friends and neighbors.... The proportion of people who live under the same roof with their mother, father and/or siblings is 3 to 1 between Chile and the United States.... In Chile, only about half of the population belongs to some kind of association, while in the United States this figure rises to 70 percent. This difference is made even more significant if the intensity of participation is taken into consideration: the United States has an average of 1.7 associations per person, while

> in Chile the average is only .7. The most significant contrasts are in the areas of religious association..., education and work, that is to say in those areas where they organize collective interests.... Only in the realm of sports does Chilean participation come anywhere near that of the United States. (Valenzuela and Cousiño 2000, 326–27 and 333–34)

The Family

The most significant relationship for nearly all SSSAs is their family. While some ESNAs may retort that family is also important to them, the differences can be noted both in (1) the degree of the intensity of familial ties and (2) the perceived purpose accorded to the family unit in these two cultural regions. Many people from the United States and Canada consider a primary purpose of the family unit to be the formation of a home base for the individual members so that they can become capable of achieving their goals individually in the larger (and often, implicitly, more important) world that exists beyond the family confines. SSSAs, however, usually view the role of family in just the opposite way, as a refuge from the vagaries of the world and as the group with whom they can achieve their own greatest personal realization through common affiliation. Thus SSSAs, as a general rule, do not itch to leave their family but, rather, long to return to it whenever they are away.

Most children live at home for practical as well as cultural reasons until they get married. Whereas most ESNAs somehow consider a person to be a "failure" or "not to have made it" if he or she is still residing in the parents' home as adults, many SSSAs think just the opposite. An SSSA host mother for an exchange program described her own impression of the differences between SSSA and ESNA conceptions of family as follows:

> I see that in the United States the people are more liberal and independent. There are advantages and disadvantages of this but I believe that humans, all humans, need "cariño." There would not be drugs if there were more love in the family. We have these close-knit families and we have the idea that in the United States there are more independent families.

When SSSAs speak about their family, they envision it expansively—both numerically and generationally. Family does not include just the nuclear family—mother, father, and children—but the extended one as well. It is quite common for diverse members of an extended family to live under the same roof or, at the least, near each other. Relations with uncles, aunts, cousins, grandparents, and so on are usually accorded great importance, and much time is dedicated among family members to keeping up with the news and knowing what is happening with one another. Many SSSAs feel sorry for people who have few relatives, believing that they are missing certain opportunities for social activity and the exchange of cariño.

If having relatives is considered positive, children are accorded even greater importance and are often showered with unconditional affection by family members, since their mere presence ensures generational continuance. As a rule, children in SSSA are viewed not so much as individuals to be raised and taught until they are ready to strike out on their own but rather as cement between members of the family and a reaffirmation of the bonds of relationships. As one essayist explained it, "The [Latin American] child does not represent distance from the past, but reflux. She is not expected to fly away, to find herself. He is not expected to live his own life" (Rodriguez, 56).

It is rare for an SSSA couple to consciously decide not to have children, and they generally start their family not long after getting married. Although birthrates have decreased in recent decades, they are still higher than in ESNA.

One of the most delightful aspects of living in SSSA as a foreigner with children is the fact that nearly everyone in the region, whatever his or her age or station of life, really seems to like children and usually relates extremely well to them. It is a rare SSSA who will not happily interact with a child when given the opportunity.

Having a child in SSSA can be less personally demanding than is often the case in ESNA, for several reasons. First, because most SSSAs live close to family members, there is almost always a relative willing to help. In addition many people from the middle class upward have access to domestic help; many even have live-in maids, who provide assistance to the parents in countless ways. Finally, public policies also underwrite the importance of motherhood through liberal maternity-leave laws and other rules and regulations that support the parent-child relationship.

Interconnected with the importance accorded to children is that given to parenthood, and particularly the parent-child relationship, which at times seems almost reverential in its manifestations. Most SSSAs remain very tied to their parents, especially their mothers, throughout their lifetime, and even as adults interact with them frequently, in many cases every day. In turn, most parents (especially mothers) consider it their responsibility to take care of their brood by attending assiduously to concrete personal needs, often claiming to enjoy "spoiling" them, and by missing them deeply when they are not nearby. Even during the turbulent adolescent years, SSSA teenagers somehow seem less rebellious than do many of their counterparts in the northern latitudes of the hemisphere. These youth often fail to understand why so many university students in ESNA try to study as far away from their homes as possible.

The way that the parent-child interaction is actualized, with its characteristics of unconditionality, devotion, and service, is evident not only in the nature of familial relationships themselves but also in many other types of social exchange. Among friends and working colleagues, between employer and employee, and in other relationships, there is often the underlying assumption (and expectation) of dependence, rather than independence, among the individuals involved. Thus, it is not considered a positive attribute, as is often the case in ESNA, to be a "loner" and to prove that you can "do it on your own." Rather, relationships are often cemented by the exchange of favors or service of one type or another. As the sociologists Eduardo Valenzuela and Carlos Cousiño explain it,

> In the case of our society (SSSA), where the dimension of parent-child predominates over that of the spouse as the defining element of the family structure,...the parent-child relationship thus offers the model of all significant social relationships. People are worth something when they become real, which means, literally, "when we receive something from them." No relationship can be founded on the promise of a future benefit, but rather on the certainty of something received here and now, which is the certainty that a child has with respect to its parents. In conformity to this model, our relationships always aspire to closeness, the proximity of the familiar, which means that they open to those who are or could be present and now have or can give us something. (325)

The emphasis on meeting concrete needs as one of the defining characteristics of family interaction brings up another reason why the family unit is so important. In many instances, the family serves as a crucial source of assistance. In a region where few people have insurance of any type and social provisions are often woefully weak, people typically turn to family members for help when needed. Such help can take the form of material support and/or assistance of other types. Conversely, if times are good and/or if a family member is successful, at business or whatever, the entire family will reap the rewards.

The importance accorded to family in SSSA culture is reflected in numerous ways linguistically. In contrast to most ESNAs, SSSAs employ both parents' surnames as their official last name. When women marry, they continue to use their maiden name, adding their husband's last name to their own. At the workplace, many women use only their maiden name. Many employees, both men and women, find it hard to understand how the apparently "liberal" ESNA women so willingly "give up" their own family name when they marry.

Conversational topics also reflect the significance of the family. Most verbal interchange, whether in a social or business setting, begins with inquiries about family, and only after this information has been exchanged will other topics be introduced. This practice carries over into the written media. Many of the region's newspapers and magazines commonly indicate next to peoples' names their marital status, number of children (and grandchildren in some cases), and so forth. In interviews, questions often revolve around the individual's personal life and views of family.

The family theme carries over even when talking with foreigners. Probably the most frequently asked question is "Don't you miss your family?" to which the expected response is "Yes, I do." If the affirmation is not emphatic or sincere enough—or particularly if a negative is proffered—the SSSA interrogator may be quite surprised and perhaps even suspicious of the individual.

Once the discussion proceeds beyond the initial interchange, it is rare for SSSAs (except with intimates) to openly discuss anything that might be interpreted as casting their family or some member of their family in a negative light. This stands in sharp contrast to the often very open and sometimes quite critical comments that many ESNAs make to people they might not even know very well concerning members of their own family and/or family relationships.

Given the almost sacred nature of the family unit, it should not be surprising that the most offensive slurs in Spanish are negative comments about family members, particularly mothers. In fact, many Spanish speakers cannot understand why certain words regarding sexual acts may be considered "worse" in English than derogatory words about loved ones.

While much of the importance accorded to family and familial relations is indeed authentic, there is also an element of ingroup behavior that serves, in many cases, to mask a very different reality than that put forward by the mainstream rhetoric. In truth, the SSSA family unit was not based on a two-parent household (as was the case among most of the settlers in ESNA) but rather on a very present mother and an often absent father, who in many cases may have been from a different social class and/or ethnicity from the woman he impregnated. Furthermore, he may never have assumed any responsibility for the offspring.

While social dynamics have changed very much since colonial times, nonetheless there is still some carryover from those early years. Throughout the region, there are quite high levels of illegitimate births. The employment of both maternal and paternal last names serves an ancillary purpose, which is to distinguish legitimate from illegitimate children: the latter must employ their mothers' last name twice, because they have no legitimate paternal last name. This can sometimes be quite a heavy social burden to carry.

Despite the beliefs of the Catholic Church, consensual unions are also quite common throughout the region. In Venezuela, the country with the highest percentage of such relationships, recently close to 30 percent of all households were headed by a couple in such a union (Valdés and Gomariz 1995, 62). An even more recent phenomenon is a marked rise in divorce rates (except for Chile, where divorce is not permitted), which range from between 10 to 23 percent, depending on the country (59). Today about 20 percent of households are headed by women. These statistics all serve to reveal the actual gap that exists in many cases between the mainstream cultural rhetoric (also known as the cultural ideal) in regard to family and the actual reality of many SSSAs' familial situations.

The Compadre *System*

The centrality of family in SSSA culture can be noted in other aspects of the region's cultural patterns, such as how favored outsiders are "brought into the family circle." One practice that illustrates this inclusive behavior is that of designating godparents, known as *compadres* in Spanish, to be "second parents" for one's children. Compadres are chosen when an infant is just born, and it is an honor to be asked. Usually, compadres are either family members or close friends. In other cases, especially in the rural sector, a compadre may be selected from a higher social class in the hope that this designated individual will be in a better position to help out the child. A male compadre is called a *padrino* (godfather) and a female, *madrina* (godmother).

Although one of the primary functions of a compadre is to participate in the infant's baptism ceremony, his or her duties extend far beyond this rite. Compadres are expected to assist children both emotionally and materially until they reach adulthood. In some cases, the compadre's obligations even entail adopting the child should the natural parents pass away.

This godparent system was brought to SSSA by the conquistadors and was a common practice throughout medieval Europe. In the Spanish colonies, this practice played an important role in spreading the rite of baptism during the era of mass conversions by incorporating more people into the ceremony. Today, the compadre system has all but disappeared in most of Europe, but it remains quite common in many parts of SSSA, especially in rural areas.

Over the centuries, the nature of compadre relations has broadened to encompass not only the one between the compadre and his or her *ahijado* (male godchild) or *ahijada* (female godchild) but also that developed between the adults involved (the infant's parents and compadre). Individuals so linked call each other "compadre," and the relationship is predicated upon expectations of both affection and sometimes assistance, if requested. Thus, a compadre can be an additional source of support in times of need.

Sometimes, *compadrazgo* relationships can develop more informally, and many SSSAs address friends or people who can help them as "compadre," even if they are not officially linked through any formal baptism ceremony. Such relationships usually do not impose extensive obligations on either party. Rather, the term is used to indicate affection, and sometimes even as a familiar greeting. Typically, one person might say to a friend, "*¿Como estás, compadre?*" to which the other would reply, "*Bien, compadre.*"

Friends

The importance accorded to familial relationships in SSSA culture has several implications for the nature of friendship among

SSSAs, which tends to play out somewhat differently from that of ESNAs. Not surprisingly, friendships are envisioned similarly to relationships with one's family and thus tend to be inclusive and intense rather than broadly based and diffuse, as is often the case among ESNAs. Most SSSAs stress quality rather than quantity in friendship. Friendship is not entered into lightly because it usually involves a significant investment of personal energy and commitment. Rather than having many scattered friends who might not even know each other, as is often the case in the United States, SSSAs usually prefer to have a tight-knit group of intimate peers.

A recent empirical study corroborates these cross-cultural differences in friendship patterns. People in both the United States and Chile were asked how many close friends they had, and while the average among people from the U.S. was over 6, among Chileans it was about half that figure, around 3. In fact, 30 percent of the Chilean respondents stated that they had no friends at all, compared with only 5 percent of the U.S. respondents. Conversely, while 40 percent of Americans in the survey said they had 6 or more friends, only 17 percent of the Chileans fit into this category (Valenzuela and Cousiño, 325).

Because of the family-oriented nature of most SSSAs, becoming friends usually involves some degree of inclusion within the family unit of both individuals. In many cases, getting to know the family is an integral aspect of developing and maintaining friendship between two individuals of whatever age and gender. In fact, much of the legendary hospitality of the region can be attributed to the SSSAs' sense that potential friends must be presented to their households in order to become actual friends. Eduardo Valenzuela and Carlos Cousiño explain this perception as follows:

> Among us, the relationship of friendship needs to be purged of all elements of distance through the procedures of incorporating the friend rapidly into the home space. True friends are, by this definition, those that can be considered "part of the house"....

> Our culture is hospitable, but not friendly, because as a stranger goes to the house and sits down at the table, he/she becomes part of the known people. This consolidates the relationship through the elaboration of a permanent tie with the family. (325)

The structure of many social institutions in SSSA encourages the consolidation of intimate and tight-knit friendship groups. For example, in most elementary schools each class maintains the same members throughout the entire elementary period, often keeping the same teacher for several years as well. Thus, from an early age, SSSAs become accustomed to constancy in their friendships and relationships.

Even most university programs have a rigid and prescribed curriculum that places entering students in the same group, which they will remain in throughout their university studies. Because of the limited number of individuals with university degrees in many of the SSSA nations, university companions often become professional colleagues as well.

The example of university education points to another way that SSSA culture tends to encourage the creation of close support groups among friends. Just as with one's own family, friends serve not only each other's emotional needs but can also serve a more practical purpose. Because completing one's degree can often be quite an accomplishment, given the frequent difficulties in obtaining course materials and in fitting in the large number of core curriculum courses, having a close group of friends can be extremely helpful in getting through the university. Typically, friends help each other by sharing notes, splitting up projects, participating in study groups, and in many other ways.

The importance accorded to mutual help among friends in the academic setting can even extend to helping each other during examinations, quite a common and accepted practice among SSSAs and one that is viewed quite differently in ESNA, where the practice is considered cheating and is vigorously condemned. In contrast, many SSSA professors turn a blind eye when students copy from each other during tests, because they realize that the students usually put friendship before the abstract concept of breaking the rules. An Argentine professor who taught in the United States describes his realization of the divergent attitudes toward cheating between his home and host cultures as follows:

> In the universities in the United States, it is very rare that somebody cheats. They could risk their whole career in this one gesture. When there is an examination, the professors leave the room. I mean, the students stay alone! They told me that that was how things were done when I gave an examination for the first time to seniors in Maryland. Since I could not believe it, I entered a few times by surprise, pretending to have forgotten papers or a book. Nothing irregular happened…[they explained to me that] the students take care of themselves in the examinations, because if somebody copies, the person on the side or behind will denounce him or her. Nobody seems to think that a person who does this is a tattler; rather, they are defending themselves and maintaining the principle of social honesty. For us, accustomed to a more savage culture,…telling on a companion that is cheating will always have an air of infamy, be looked down upon…. Here [In Argentina], anyway, the kids are still going to keep on cheating...even the [former] President Menem said that he cheated when he was a student and nothing happened to him. (Tomas Eloy Martínez 1999, 179–80)

Vergüenza *and Dignity*

Because human relationships are accorded such importance, most SSSAs are quite concerned with what other people think of them. "Fitting in" and "being accepted" by others—especially those with whom one has close personal ties—are highly valued. So too is social approbation, at least from one's own circle of intimates or social equals. Thus, the opinions of others are often given significant weight in evaluating personal behavior and deciding upon appropriate actions.

This focus on others' opinions, especially for self-evaluation, is encouraged in most SSSAs from a very young age. Parents commonly chide their offspring when they behave inappropriately or do not fit into the group to "be careful" or they will experience shame (*vergüenza*), because others will think or speak badly of them. This approach to discipline is more common than that used by many ESNA parents, who often try to shape their children's behaviors and beliefs by referring to personal conscience, an internalized sense of "right and wrong."

Many adult SSSAs maintain this concern with group approbation throughout their entire life and function in such a way as to avoid being shamed whenever possible. Consequently, exhibiting "good manners" is accorded great importance: knowing the social niceties, exhibiting correct table manners and decorum, and dressing appropriately, for example, are deemed very significant. So too is being generous and sharing, at least with one's circle of intimates.

Closely linked with the attention accorded to vergüenza is that given to maintaining the feelings of interconnection and cariño between individuals. Thus, any action or comment that might be perceived as disrupting this sense of group harmony and affection can be judged as shameful. Contrary to the widespread belief of many ESNAs, most SSSAs are neither hot-tempered nor prone to frequent yelling. Rather, as a general rule, efforts are usually made to keep human relationships smooth by creating and maintaining an emotionally warm ambience.

One of the ways that harmony can be disrupted is by saying or doing anything that might offend another person's dignity. In SSSA culture, one's dignity, as well as that of one's family, is imbued with great value because of the belief that dignity is inextricably linked with the unique alma of a person and so must be protected at all cost. Dignity can be damaged even by verbal comments that are interpreted as personally disparaging or derogatory in some way. Consequently, the English saying "Sticks and stones may break my bones, but words will never hurt me" does not ring true in SSSA, where words can hurt a lot if they are perceived to damage one's inner integrity or worth. This supposition is elucidated in the following quote by Latin Americanist John Gillin:

> Every person is supposed to defend his inner integrity to the utmost of his ability, and a person who submits abjectly and without emotion to slurs upon it is usually regarded as much "lower" than one who merely breaks the laws established by society. Thus, words or actions that are interpreted as insults to the individual's soul are highly explosive; they evoke emotional reactions which to the average North American seem to be sometimes exaggerated and "unrealistic." (1965, 18)

In order to preserve this sense of harmony, SSSAs are usually quite careful in their conversations not to bring up anything that might be construed by another as personally offensive or hurtful in order to avoid a potentially explosive situation, even if such avoidance leads to greater complications later. When potentially controversial topics must be brought up at all, they are usually touched on indirectly and often even metaphorically. This more circuitous communication style is often hard for ESNAs, with their preference for clarity and directness, to decipher and properly interpret.

A corollary of this phenomenon is that SSSAs usually attempt to present both themselves and their families in positive ways so as not to damage their own dignity. Thus, they typically stress the positive in their lives and do not bring up anything that might make them not "look so good" to other people. This is particularly the case when interacting with people they do not know well. Consequently, modesty is not a highly valued virtue, and many people from this region can seem boastful when speaking about themselves. Ironic humor, especially at one's own expense, is also not typical; people prefer instead to employ verbal agility and plays on words for levity.

Implications for the Workplace

The importance accorded to personalismo, relationships with intimates, and the avoidance of vergüenza has numerous repercussions for the conduct of business affairs in SSSA. Given the proclivity for interacting with people one knows well rather than with outsiders, it should come as no surprise that there are many more family-run businesses in this region than in ESNA. Whereas many people in the United States and Canada think it best to separate business from personal affairs, many SSSAs have the opposite opinion. They consider family members the most trustworthy and best people to work with.

Not only do many SSSAs prefer to work with family members when possible, they also frequently rely on family and friendship ties for both obtaining and maintaining their jobs to a far greater extent than ESNAs do. As a general rule, networks for recruiting and advertising for employment, especially at the higher echelons, are far rarer than is the case in many urban locations in ESNA, and many employment decisions are made through "who you know" or "what others know about you." In ESNA most people believe that one should get ahead on one's own merits, and many "men feel that they cannot call themselves successful unless they can say that they have gained their success by their own efforts" (Whyte and Holmberg 1956, 6). SSSAs, in contrast, openly acknowledge their debt to their family and friends in the work arena and usually try to cultivate personal ties with as many people as possible in order to help promote and consolidate their professional careers.

Once hired, such personalized connections can be extremely useful in several ways for successful job execution. First of all, they can help one obtain useful knowledge through the network of contacts. This can be even more useful than is often the case in ESNA because information is not always available and accessible in SSSA. In addition family and friends who are well connected can often prove immeasurably useful in carrying out transactions of many types, reducing or even eliminating the often ubiquitous bureaucratic red tape. Finally, such personalized connections can be a great source of support, both practically and emotionally, in the often unpredictable business environment of SSSA.

This cultural penchant for personalized relationships, often elevated above objective criteria in making decisions, can sometimes prove to be a barrier for foreign businesspeople, who do not typically have close or long-term connections with members of the local business community. This problem, however, can be remedied in some situations through pairing up with a local person who has such connections and whom one can use as an associate to facilitate business dealings. Also helpful is trying to establish personal connections with key locals, which can sometimes be accomplished through a common university affiliation and/or mutual friends. In fact it is not uncommon in certain business circles in SSSA to find that many of one's local counterparts have studied and received advanced degrees from important institutions of higher learning in ESNA.

Another arena that can sometimes prove to be challenging for ESNA businesspeople working in SSSA involves issues related to shame and personal dignity. Due to the manner in which these concepts are actualized in SSSA culture, people are highly sensitive about criticism of their work performance. Not infrequently, comments made by ESNAs with the intention of being open and honest in order to contribute to improved performance can have unintended consequences. Instead of being perceived as open dialogues, the ESNAs' comments may be construed as an affront to personal dignity. Thus, the foreign manager must be careful in the phrasing of feedback, evaluations, and other comments. It is preferable in many cases to err on the side of subtlety rather than directness when framing critiques of any type.

5

Differences and Corporatism

Dime con quien andas, y te diré quien eres.
—popular Latin American saying

Tell me who you hang out with, and I will tell you who you are.

A second distinguishing cultural orientation of the Spanish-speaking South Americans (SSSAs) is their way of envisioning and structuring their societies based more on differences than on similarities among members. These differences are considered a natural and integral aspect of being a member of society, and SSSAs of whatever subgroup recognize both their own place in society as well as those of other subgroups. Thus, hierarchy (and segmentation) rather than equality are the norms in SSSA culture, although more heavily manifested by some SSSAs and in some locales than in others.

This method of organizing society according to status differences among members can be traced back to the influence of the region's Native American civilizations and of the Spanish conquistadors. Many of the indigenous groups that hailed from what is now SSSA, with the Incas being perhaps the most well-known example, structured their societies very hierarchically. Typically, clearly marked distinctions were made between groups of different social status (i.e., farmer, artisan, noble, etc.), and society was organized along these distinctions.

The colonizing Iberians also brought with them a vision of human society that was based on functional differences among community members. This belief system was heavily influenced by certain medieval Catholic scholars, the most well known being Thomas Aquinas (1225–1274).

These scholars posited a view of human society that has come to be known as corporatism, so named because they thought that society should be organized in much the same way as a human body (corpus) is. Just as each part of a body carries out its unique and necessary purpose, so too each sector of society needs to carry out its particular role effectively in order for the entire community to run properly. Implicitly, this theory of corporatism dissuades individuals or groups from attempting to assume functions different from their designated ones, for such role aggrandizement could weaken the entire system. In the ensuing centuries since the Spanish colonial enterprise, many other more modern currents of political and social thought have swept throughout SSSA and been adopted to varying degrees; nevertheless, all have been grafted onto a societal structure that is still strongly shaped by colonial and precolonial concepts of organizing society according to differences in status, position, and function.

Such emphasis on differences among members of society may appear to conflict with the effusive warmth and human compassion embodied in personalismo, but in fact they both spring from the same source: the strong conviction that much of a person's life is shaped by forces beyond human control. While such forces endow everybody with a unique alma, they also work in such a way as to place people in their own particular life circumstance, as rich or poor, light or dark. Thus, while most SSSAs consider everyone to be equally human due to their unique internal qualities, they do not expect all people to have the same external realities.

This way of envisioning human society influences the current social structure of all the countries in the region as well as the nature of interpersonal relationships among SSSAs. It also shapes public and private organizational structures and the policy initiatives undertaken by them and serves as an underlying explanation for many of the marked dichotomies and polarities that exist in SSSA today.

Class

Almost all the SSSA countries have social structures that are pyramidal, with a large segment of the population belonging to the lower or working classes and a much smaller elite positioned at the top. While this hierarchical structuring has been modified significantly in the past century and while there are several SSSA countries today that have quite a large middle-class sector,* marked class distinctions still persist in nearly all the countries of the region.

Statistics corroborate the marked economic and social divides in SSSA. While other parts of the world are decidedly poorer in macroeconomic terms, it is Latin America (including SSSA) that exhibits the most unequal income distribution. This pattern of economic inequality nearly always persists even in periods of positive economic growth and is perhaps the most defining economic characteristic of the region as a whole.

Class in SSSA, however, is more complex and multifaceted than is reflected purely in such statistics. Class issues spill over and influence nearly all aspects of life. For most SSSAs, class affiliation is a crucial aspect of identity, and knowledge of one's place in the hierarchy as well as that of others influences the dynamics of social interactions and self-perception. This holds true for people from all echelons of society.

SSSAs are typically quite open about their classist orientation. In a survey of nearly one thousand individuals conducted in a large urban city in the region, over 75 percent identified themselves as classist. Of this 75 percent, over 50 percent said they

* This phenomenon is particularly notable in the nations of Argentina, Chile, and Uruguay as well as in Venezuela.

were very classist. In this same survey, only 4 percent identified themselves as socially egalitarian (FLACSO 1998, 10).

Despite this openly recognized classism, many SSSAs can be a bit ambiguous about what exactly constitutes a specific social class and how many actual classes might be present in society. John Gillin makes this point well in the following story:

> Although the class situation is universally recognized, it seems that precision regarding the structure is not...I made a small inquiry in three Latin American countries regarding the extent of social classes.... The question in essence was, "Which social classes are there here?" The answer varied from two to as many as seventeen. (1965, 10)

Three aspects of class in the SSSA context need to be considered in order to better comprehend how class is constructed in the region. First, class is not measured by material wealth alone but is a more complex social construct that includes family connections, personal history, and educational level. Having attended certain exclusive private schools, living in certain neighborhoods, vacationing in elite resorts, and other criteria are characteristics of many elites from the region who may hail from a long line of family dating back generations as prominent in national life.

Care must be taken, however, not to overemphasize the closed nature of class in SSSA. It is not as rigidly structured as a caste system. Possibility for social mobility does exist in the region, although it tends to be more difficult to achieve than in English-speaking North America (ESNA). Although SSSA has no Horatio Alger myth, every nation lays claim to at least several historically important figures who emerged from the lower classes to "make good." For instance, Evita Perón's greatest appeal to many Argentines was her humble beginnings.

Finally, the concept of class is often inextricably entwined with the issues of race and ethnicity. The long colonial and postcolonial legacy of relegating people of Native American and African ancestry to the lower rungs of the social hierarchy means that today the vast majority of poor SSSAs are decidedly "darker" in complexion than the elites.

Despite this often blatant link between class position and racial affiliation, this phenomenon is not always openly acknowledged by many SSSAs themselves, who often criticize—justifiably in many cases—the racism of ESNA society. In fact, a favorite phrase that many from this region flippantly use to describe their own attitude is "We are not racist, but we are classist."

Interactions between Social Unequals

Status differentiation takes many forms and is manifested both verbally and nonverbally. Despite individual variations, nearly all SSSAs, in some form and to some degree, relate distinctly to people who are from a different social class than their own. In fact, there are certain culturally encoded rules of conduct that govern interactions between social unequals that nearly all SSSAs implicitly know and act upon. When social unequals interact, the person of higher status often behaves in a dominant fashion, expecting respect from an individual of lower status who, in turn, is supposed to act deferentially. Often, the person of lower status will be addressed using the informal you (*tú*) and the individual's first name. The person of lower status, in turn, will usually maintain a subservient or at least relatively passive demeanor during the interaction and will nearly always use the formal you (*usted*) when addressing a social superior. If the first name is used at all, a prefix such as *señor* or *señora, don* or *doña* is usually added, particularly in situations where a request is being made. In some cases, people in a subservient position still call their boss "patrón" or "patrona" as a sign of respect.

This deferential communication style extends far beyond forms of address and colors the entire exchange between individuals of different social status. Especially in work situations, orders and commands given by those of higher position in the hierarchy are usually treated as sacrosanct by those of lower position. As a consequence, sometimes workers will appear to accept orders, even if they do not fully understand them or if they do not want to carry them out. The great care that such workers take not to contradict or question a social superior can prevent them from honestly raising issues in the work setting, even when such avoidance leads to greater difficulties in the future.

The fact that communication patterns between social unequals are predicated on status and power differences can often, not surprisingly, lead to an undercurrent of resentment exhibited by both parties. Much of the overt communication is really just a form of superficial posturing, and deeper down there is often an underlying sense of distrust and suspicion.

This tension often plays out in subtle and not-so-subtle ways in exchanges that take place between individuals of different social position. Commonly, individuals of lower status will only appear to be submissive and respectful but will actually be calculating the possibility of not complying with orders and getting away with doing so. In some cases, taking advantage of a social superior can involve trickery and cunning. Some employees even steal items from their boss or workplace, and many bosses have elaborate ways to foil such attempts. One of the most famous involves the founder of the Concha y Toro winery. He discovered that many of his workers were stealing his best wines, kept in a special cellar. To stop this, he donned a devil's outfit and scared his employees so much that he had almost no more wine losses. This event also gave rise to the name of a line of the firm's more popular wines, "Casillero del Diablo," which means "Devil's Cellar"!

This story illustrates how many SSSAs of higher status are very concerned and, in some cases, even obsessed with being taken advantage of by their lower-status workers. It is common to hear them expressing these worries, bandying about such statements as "My employees are so lazy" or "I can't leave the house when my maid is there because she will steal my things," to name but two. This preoccupation is often coupled with the belief that the best way to discourage such behavior from social inferiors is to exercise a "heavy hand" and to be "firmly in control" when dealing with them.

Thus, individuals on both sides of the societal divide are deeply aware of the possibility of being taken advantage of by the other and are often figuring out how they can get the most personal gain from any particular situation. One woman from the region explained this cultural proclivity as follows: "We are always trying to get the greatest personal advantage out of situations without thinking of the damage it might cause to others" (Delpanio 1999, 13).

Picardía

This approach has even been given a specific name, *picardía*, which loosely translated means obtaining what one wants through a combination of charm and deviousness, with an extralegal element sometimes involved. Despite its possible negative connotations, picardía is embraced by many SSSAs as one of their most defining cultural characteristics, and sometimes people who exhibit marked picardía are lauded for their skills. There are numerous popular figures in the political, economic, and sports fields whose fame is due in large part to their ability to unabashedly carry out clever deeds with cunning. Some of the most beloved characters in the widely popular and locally made soap operas typically personify elements of picardía, as do other fictitious figures in SSSA popular culture.

This attitude of picardía, in turn, tends to create an overall lack of confidence in people who are either not well known or who hail from a different social group. Usually, interactions with such individuals are entered into with a healthy dose of skepticism and often a ritualized jesting to try to figure out what, if anything, the other person is trying to get away with. This approach contrasts quite sharply with the attitude typically taken by ESNAs, who usually begin an encounter by assuming the best about another person. In a recent worldwide survey on trustworthiness, the SSSAs ranked among the least trusting people in the world, with only 4 percent of those polled agreeing that they could trust the majority of people (*El Mercurio*, 7 October 1997, A1).

Different explanations have been offered as to why SSSAs have such little confidence in people they don't know well or who seem somehow different from them. Some suggest that this attitude is tied, at least in part, to SSSAs' preference for intimate familial-type relationships, and personalized relations are not possible with people one does not know well. Others claim that the Catholic religion might play a role in creating this dynamic of distrust toward the unknown person. As Eduardo Valenzuela and Carlos Cousiño explain,

> It is possible that the differential aptitude to establish ties with strangers is religiously based.... The Protestant faith refers to a God that is invisible and distant, that does not manifest itself in the world and which can only be reached by faith (which is exactly the ability to believe in what one does not see and the capacity to confide in what is only a promise). [In contrast] the Catholic faith is directed to a close God that is constantly actualizing its presence in the world. The distance of the Protestant God seems to favor relations of confidence between unknown people, while the closeness of familiarity of the Catholic God seems to inhibit the unfolding of these relations in the corresponding countries. (2000, 323)

Whatever the explanation, SSSAs' tendency to mistrust outsiders and, in some cases, to even carry out personal picardía, helps to explain certain aspects of life in the region, such as why people who are usually excruciatingly polite with people they know well can be incredibly rude in public spaces, where the law-of-the-jungle approach more often applies. At a deeper level, these attitudes may account in part for the tendency toward corruption and even authoritarianism, which has been a marked historical characteristic of many parts of the region over the centuries. After all, the consolidation of a diverse national society can be challenging if most citizens with power elevate their personal interests and those of their intimates to such a degree as to exclude or ignore the interests of other segments of the national population.

Appearance

Another quite different way that social differences are manifested in SSSA cultural practices is in the importance accorded to appearance, since it can often be a concrete indicator of status. Most SSSAs are experts at interpreting others' appearance and thus discerning their position in the social hierarchy. This explains, at least in part, the almost cultlike importance given to "how people look," an attitude that contrasts sharply with that of many ESNAs, who often think "Looks are deceiving" and "It is not what you look like on the outside, but rather what you are like inside that really counts."

Appearance for SSSAs involves physiognomy in many cases. Due to the often close linkage between race and class in SSSA, it is often quite easy to discern an individual's social status based on skin tone, hair and eye color, height, and other such features. This explains to some degree the fact that many advertised jobs, especially at the clerical level, ask for a photograph to be sent with the resumé. In some cases they even clearly state that they want someone with "*buena presencia*," which, indirectly, means someone who is not too dark and/or too indigenous-looking in features.

In general, people from this region are quite open about bringing up such physical attributes, a characteristic that can often shock ESNAs when they first encounter it. Just as SSSAs will freely discuss social class and position, so too will they talk about a person's skin color, hair, and other such characteristics to an extent that many supposedly politically correct ESNAs find hard to deal with. For instance, they will commonly call someone *negro* (dark) or *pelado* (bald) or any of a number of other such terms. Depending upon the circumstances, such terms are often used affectionately and indicate both closeness and affection toward the party so designated.

Attire is another way that SSSAs classify people, figuring out "where they fit in" both socially and ideologically by what they wear. As a general rule, clothing is chosen not so much as a way to express individuality and uniqueness but rather as a demonstration of both status and group affiliation. Many SSSAs, especially those with the means to do so, often devote a significant amount of attention and resources to having the proper clothing, jewelry, and so on, and fashion norms are often quite closely followed. Also, uniforms are more widely used in the region than in ESNA; for example, most schoolchildren in SSSA wear uniforms, which usually have a clear designation on them showing what school the child attends.

As a general rule, SSSAs of all walks of life and social classes are well dressed and take great care to appear clean and neat, especially in public. This is often one of the first characteristics that visitors to the region note, along with the fact that there tends to be less variety in clothing styles and colors than is seen on many streets in ESNA. Visitors may also begin to recognize that sometimes they are being judged by their own attire, and the treatment they receive from some SSSAs can be significantly influenced by what they wear and how they present themselves.

Implications for the Workplace

The dynamics of the work environment in many SSSA businesses are strongly shaped by the class distinctions and their repercussions. As a general rule, most SSSA businesses are structured somewhat like their national societies, with a marked hierarchical configuration. Usually, relationships between individuals of different position are clearly established, and the nature of communication between people of different status is quite formal.

Typically, those in the lower echelons are accustomed to working under a rather authoritarian and paternalistic type of management and usually await specific orders rather than demonstrating initiative. Some businesspeople who have worked in SSSA note that there are fewer opportunities for advancement and training given to those in lower positions than might be the case in the United States or Canada. One such expatriate businessman describes his perceptions of the differences in the command structures of businesses in the U.S. and SSSA as follows:

> SSSA uses a more rigid hierarchy than is common in the United States. Who reports to whom is more important here. Also, in the United States there is more flexibility about doing things and then getting them approved. Here, following the formula to the letter is the key. The way I see it is [either] you value where you are in the hierarchy or...you value getting the work done.

While it is not expected that ESNAs should adopt the management style of the SSSA workplace, and while many workers actually enjoy the ESNAs' more egalitarian approach, some accommodation to local cultural patterns is likely to enhance work performance in the region. In fact, sometimes maintaining at least a degree of distance and formality with workers as a demonstration of status can serve to make many of them feel more comfortable.

As noted earlier, the sense of distrust and, in some cases, even picardía, which is common in SSSA are often most fully demonstrated in the workplace. As a consequence, many employers closely supervise their staff and express concern about potential thievery. On the one hand, it is important not to exaggerate this phenomenon, since many South Americans themselves tend to overemphasize this aspect of life in their society. On the other hand, neither should one be naïve when conducting business in the region.

Finally, due to the importance accorded to attire in SSSA, clothing in the business world is a very important indicator of class and power, and businesspeople are frequently judged on how well (or badly) they dress. This holds true for both local and foreign businesspeople and is a reality that should be taken into consideration by people trying to conduct business in the region.

6

Male and Female

El hombre, un pájaro apenas.
Y la mujer, un vilano.
(Apenas casi un vilano.)

—Rafael Alberti

The man, barely a bird.
And the woman, a thistledown.
(Just barely a thistledown.)

Stressing gender differences is another characteristic cultural orientation of Spanish-speaking South Americans (SSSAs). Obviously, this criterion differs both in nature and implication from class considerations. Because the biological distinctions between males and females are both immutable in character and crucial for species survival, they are encoded into role differences by all cultural groups, but the degree to which gender differences are emphasized varies significantly from culture to culture.

SSSA cultural patterns tend to highlight the apparently unique and distinct aspects of both sexes. While there is considerable variance among the many millions of SSSAs, as a general rule most people from this cultural group firmly believe that males and females are not only biologically distinct but that these biological differences serve to indelibly shape the way that both genders perceive the world and act in it.

Gender differences, then, are perceived as not only natural but also pleasurable, one of the gifts of life. Rather than trying to downplay gender distinctions, SSSAs usually seek to acknowledge and appreciate them. Both men and women play the part of their gender; women tend to be quite concerned with projecting their femininity and men with acting according to accepted norms of masculinity.

Both, in turn, want acknowledgment of their gender identity from members of the opposite sex. Generally, SSSA women enjoy having men notice and respond to their physical attributes and often act quite coquettish with them, especially in social situations. SSSA men, for their part, try to appear invincible and infallible. This way of construing gender identity has underlying implications for intergender relations.

Although SSSAs typically celebrate the distinctions between men and women, mutual companionship and open communication between the genders is not emphasized. Rather, both genders participate in a shifting combination of admiration and manipulation of the other.

Men seem to almost venerate the whole concept of femaleness. They particularly treasure the supposed nurturing ability of women, a quality which encompasses their reproductive capability as well as their maternal senses and perceptions. This reverence for the abstract concept of femininity is most clearly represented in the Catholic Church itself, which, especially in Latin America, stresses the role of women through the concrete representation of the Virgin Mary and countless other virgins who are considered sacred and even miraculous in many cases. There are also several important female saints who are very popular figures of worship in SSSA.

The proclivity to venerate maternal figures applies not only to the religious realm but also to the more secular one. In SSSA, the figure of the mother is accorded great importance both rhetorically and in practice. While the family unit is so central to SSSA culture, within the family it is the mother who reigns supreme in many ways. Often it may appear that the father is the patriarch who wields the power, but in actuality it is the mother who has far greater influence, albeit more indirectly and more subtly manifested in many cases. In fact, some have even gone so far as to describe the region's cultural patterns as a hidden matriarchy.

It is rare for SSSA children of any age to speak ill of their mothers, and even teenagers will rarely criticize their mothers to the extent that is common in English-speaking North America (ESNA). In fact, many grown SSSA males are still "mama's boys" in many ways and often communicate with and visit their mothers whenever possible. SSSA mothers, for their part, typically consider their role to be one of providing both physical and emotional support to their brood and usually like to "take care" of their children to an extent that many ESNA mothers, often focused on instilling autonomy and independence in their offspring, do not.

Even public policies throughout the region underwrite the importance of motherhood through liberal maternity-leave laws and other rules and regulations. In most of the countries, working women who are pregnant are awarded a minimum of several weeks of leave prior to delivery and several months afterward at full pay. Their jobs are guaranteed, and they are even given time off during the first months back at work in order to breastfeed their infant. It is not uncommon to see special parking spaces designated for pregnant women and special lines at the supermarket as well.

Sometimes it can be difficult for actual, real-life women to live up to the near perfection represented in the numerous female figures of Catholic liturgy; it can be equally difficult for many SSSA men, with their patriarchal tendencies, to directly acknowledge the symbolic and real implications of such a strong female presence in popular religion and culture. Consequently, men may overcompensate by either denigrating women or by emphasizing their inherent weakness—focusing on those same qualities for which women are venerated: a supposed emotionality and lack of rationality.

This view can lead to a sense on the part of men that women are special and that they need to be protected and sheltered: that is, women should be taken care of, because they can't really take care of themselves very well. Women are also often perceived as not understanding or feeling entirely comfortable with the supposedly "masculine" realms of power and aggression.

However, such a view is not consistently held for all women in society. Due to the strong classist orientation in the region, most men treat women of their same or of a higher class differently from those of lower social status. While the former are usually placed on a pedestal, with all the positive and negative associations this implies, the latter are often regarded as inexpensive labor or, in some cases, as a means of satiating sexual desire. Lower-class women who fulfill neither of these roles are most likely ignored, considered beyond the circle of interest.

This view is a carryover from the way that many male-female relationships developed during the colonial era. While much has changed in the ensuing centuries, nonetheless there is still a tendency to divide women into "good women" (the type that one would consider marrying and who are nearly always from the same social class) and "bad women" (those who might be acceptable sexual partners but would never be part of one's intimate family circle). This distinction holds true even if, as sometimes happens, the female involved becomes pregnant. In such cases, marriage is usually out of the question, and the woman typically ends up raising the child on her own. Sometimes the child is recognized by the father, who might provide some financial support. In other instances, even this recognition is denied.

While not nearly so predominant as it once was, there is still the sense among many SSSAs that males and females have different levels of sexual desire. Men, it is thought, have a much stronger sex drive than do women, one that is sometimes considered even beyond the control of the male himself. Women, in contrast, especially "good women," are thought to have more of a psychological need than a sexual one and consequently will only enter into a sexual relationship if they believe that there is emotional involvement as well. Thus men must "conquer" and "win over" women they are sexually interested in, primarily by convincing them, whether truthfully or not, that they (the men) are very attracted to them (the women), both physically and emotionally.

Most SSSA women, in turn, consider men to be a complex combination of the highly capable and the incredibly child-like. Men are looked up to for their physical prowess, financial capabilities, emotional support, and the power they typically exercise, at least in the public domain. Women, especially in public, usually abdicate leadership and decision making to men, often appearing almost passive in their attitudes.

However, in private and among themselves, women often poke fun at the apparent invincibility of their male cohorts. Although they are quite indirect about it, SSSA women are experts in subtly manipulating their men in order to achieve what they want. In keeping with the importance of appearance in SSSA cultures, women let it appear that the men are in charge, even though they are often the ones who exert far greater control in a relationship.

This leads to an interesting and somewhat paradoxical phenomenon: SSSA women tend to consider men to be as weak as many SSSA men consider women to be. And both sexes, in turn, relate across gender lines based at least in part on this unstated premise of weakness concerning the other and the concomitant need of one for the other.

These culturally based attitudes and beliefs about gender roles influence affairs in the public arena, where women are often treated differently and where some laws perpetuate gender differences in subtle and not-so-subtle ways. All the nations of the region do have a Ministry of Women's Affairs and active government organizations to help women in various ways. However, in many of the nations of the region, women achieved the right to vote quite late into the twentieth century. There are some places where even in the twenty-first century, males and females vote at different locales, in large part to prevent husbands from influencing their wives to vote for certain candidates.

Socially, these gender perspectives serve as a backdrop to how men and women communicate with one another. Typically, in social gatherings, the two end up separating for conversations according to gender. Women usually discuss what are considered women's issues (such as family, food, friends, and fashion) in one group, while the men talk about sports, cars, and trips in another.

In general, the concept of men and women just "being friends" is rare, especially if both parties are unattached. Although this is not always true, men and women who have enough in common to be potential partners usually view each other primarily through the lens of courtship rather than companionship. More than one ESNA woman has had a rude awakening when relating to SSSA males, finally realizing that despite her directly expressed desire to "only be friends," the man never intended a friendship and was always looking for something more.

Machismo

When discussing gender differences and how they are played out in SSSA culture, care must be taken not to oversimplify or exaggerate such differences. The reality of male identity in SSSA is more complex than is recognized by many outsiders who, lacking firsthand knowledge, sometimes harbor incorrect stereotypes about males from this region.

In fact, the now widely popularized concept of machismo has done a real disservice to intercultural understanding between Anglos and Latinos by presenting a narrow and oversimplified view of Latin men. According to this stereotype, Latin men (including those in SSSA) consider females primarily as objects for sexual conquest and are only concerned with projecting an image of physical prowess.

Recent scholarship has illuminated how this concept of machismo has a decidedly racist origin, and how it first arose partly as prejudice directed against Mexican immigrants in the United States. In fact, *machismo* is a relatively new term in Spanish, and its first use has been traced to the time of the Mexican revolution in the early twentieth century when Mexican and Latin American nationalist leaders encouraged the growth of this concept to promote an image of masculinity with attributes similar to those highly prized among fighters—bravery, courage, and strength.

Actually, male identity in SSSA culture involves much more than sexual conquest and heterosexuality (although these are considered crucial elements of masculinity). Being a "true man" means shouldering responsibility and being strong at all costs. A man should not cry or appear weak, especially in public. Even more importantly, he should be a person of honor, one in whom people can confide and someone who is willing and able to provide for those weaker than he is, most particularly children, women, and elders. To be such a man can be difficult and painful at times, and it implies compliance with duty no matter what the personal cost.

Given the importance accorded to family, it seems logical that much of how men perceive their role revolves around their ability to create and support a family. Working in order to provide for one's family is considered by many men to be a central aspect of their role in society and perhaps the most defining one in terms of maturity and prestige.

Juan Pablo, a thirty-eight-year-old middle-class male, explains how he feels about assuming the responsibility for being his family's provider as follows:

> It is something that makes me feel anxious sometimes, a necessity, a burden. I can't get sick, I can't give myself this luxury, and I can't do anything stupid. I am not complaining, however, because I truly do it with the best feeling, I do it for my children. I believe it also helps me project myself as a person. (Valdés and Olavarria 1998, 32)

Contemporary Changes in Gender Roles

As in many other places around the world these days, many SSSA men and women are reevaluating the traditional male and female roles in very significant ways. Many more women than in previous generations are viewing their lives as made up of much more than just the bearing and raising of children. These changes are attributable, at least in part, to demographic realities. Since 1950 the average life expectancy for women in SSSA has increased by twenty years, from 55.7 to 75.6 years. At the same time, the average number of children per family has decreased from six to three.

Partially due to the decrease in time dedicated to family concerns that stems from the changing realities of the region, large numbers of SSSA women are entering the workforce out of both necessity and interest. From 1960 to 1990 the number of economically active women in Latin America increased more than three times, from 18 to 57 million, while the number of economically active men did not even double during this same period (80 million to 147 million) (Valdés and Gomariz 1995, 36). That so many women are now contributing to the economic support of their households has gone far in changing the nature of the power distribution within the family unit. It has also changed how females perceive their role in society.

Like women in many other cultures, working women in SSSA often have to do "double duty" and carry a much greater domestic burden than their spouses. While it is common for middle- and upper-class women to have domestic help, many women from the working sectors must put in long hours at work and then do most of the chores in their own household as well. In fact, about one-third of all women employees in the region actually work as domestic servants for other families.

However, patterns of gender relations are changing dramatically among many SSSAs—particularly for the younger generations and for people in the urban middle to upper classes. The traditional division between the private domain as the realm of the female and the public as that of the male is weakening. More women are entering the workforce, and increasing numbers of men are participating in the home environment.

The once sharp distinction between the "good" girl and the "bad" girl is breaking down as well. Nowadays, a large number of young SSSA women have sexual relations before marriage, and the assumption that females should enter into sexual relationships only with their husband no longer prevails. In fact, it is increasingly common, especially in urban areas, for couples to live together. Also, many females of the younger generation feel comfortable taking a more active role in initiating dates as well.

In fact, the whole concept of machismo and male supremacy is considered outdated by many SSSAs. This is especially true for people with more education and in areas that have been more exposed to globalization, with all the information and images that brings. Many women make an effort not to be in relationships with men who are too macho, while some males are trying to figure out their new role in relationships and in society generally.

Homosexuality

The way that gender identity is construed in SSSA has strong implications for how homosexuality is dealt with. The emphasis upon heterosexual relationships as an important aspect of masculinity means that any breach of this norm is considered deviant behavior. The Catholic Church, which clearly considers homosexual behavior to be aberrant and sodomy unnatural, also plays a very important role in shaping attitudes toward homosexuality in the region, where government policies in many countries are based on this religious perspective and make sexual relations between people of the same gender illegal, even in the twenty-first century.

As a consequence, the whole issue of homosexuality generally remains "in the closet" throughout much of the region, except in a few urban and progressive sectors of society. There is little public discourse on the topic in most places, and consequently many SSSAs have little knowledge about homosexuality. They often feel uncomfortable discussing it, and if it is addressed, it is often with stereotypes predicated on incomplete information and ignorance.

Many adult SSSA males go to great lengths to show their heterosexual tendencies in order to make it clear that they are not gay. In a 1997 survey carried out in the region, 43 percent of adult males exhibited some degree of support for the following quote: "Homosexuality should be prohibited, because it goes against human nature" (Fundacion Ideas 1997, 47). In fact, there are many fewer individuals in SSSA who openly declare themselves gay than is the world average. In several recent surveys carried out on this theme in the region, less than 1 percent of the respondents identified themselves as homosexual or bisexual. Those who do admit to this sexual orientation experience social ostracism in some cases, although this varies widely depending on the locale and group within which the individual involved functions.

Due to views of female sexuality and perceptions of womanhood, lesbians are even less understood than are male homosexuals and bisexuals, and there are even fewer women in the region than men who declare themselves gay. As one lesbian explained it, "The life of lesbians in Chile is almost anonymous: very few admit that they are; some hide behind a conventional family, and others avoid telling their children, and all complain of the lack of space for them in society" (*Qué Pasa* 2001, 57).

However, just as gender relations are changing rapidly among SSSAs, so too are many people's views regarding homosexuality, bisexuality, and lesbianism. In recent years there has been a burgeoning of organizations in some of the larger cities in the region designed to advance the cause of gay rights and some increased acceptance by mainstream society for gay rights.

The SSSAs' tendency to avoid discussing controversial issues also facilitates the treatment accorded to many homosexuals, bisexuals, and lesbians, especially among family members and friends. In many cases, such individuals will be warmly treated and well received. Although some may suspect that an individual has a "different" sexual orientation, the topic will rarely be directly discussed or confronted.

Women in the Workplace

The differences attributed to males and females by SSSAs tend to be replicated, at least to some degree, in the workplace. Despite the great strides made in recent decades toward greater female participation in the workplace, sharp salary and position differences still exist between men and women, which are more marked than in some other parts of the world. Some sectoral differences influence this phenomenon, and it is indeed more common to see women in relatively high positions in nonprofit and educational sectors than in the business realm. Although there are some prominent women executives in banking and the private sector in the region, they are more the exception than the rule.

Although this overall pattern is important to recognize, what is probably more striking for foreign women working in SSSA is the daily reality of functioning in an environment that has a decidedly different attitude toward gender roles than is the norm in ESNA. These differences are felt most directly in the social ambience of the workplace.

In SSSA, the concept of political correctness has yet to arrive, and comments regarding decidedly nonprofessional aspects of female employees are frequent. Such comments can range from the topics of attire and physical appearance to inquiries regarding family, male companions, and even a woman's views regarding having children. Most of these remarks are made quite innocently and are not considered derogatory or hostile to a pleasant work relationship. Nonetheless, sometimes foreign women perceive these behaviors as condescending and disrespectful. A female foreign business executive described her experience working in SSSA as follows:

> The atmosphere for women is different here. Women are uncommon in the corporate world and comments are made that highlight the differences, i.e., people will talk more about your appearance, the fact that you are a woman. It is obvious that you are different and it is commented on. In the United States, such topics are taboo.

In some cases, the attention foreign female workers receive may seem excessive or inappropriate. While this attention can usually be attributed to cross-cultural miscommunication, in instances where there is actual harassment, a woman has little formal recourse. In fact, the concept of sexual harassment does not exist either legislatively or in terms of policy standards throughout most of the region, and there are very few, if any, SSSA women who would bring a suit on these grounds.

Actually, though, being a foreign woman working in SSSA can sometimes be used to one's advantage if handled correctly. In some situations, women are considered to be less threatening than men in a comparable position and thus can sometimes acquire information or accomplish certain tasks more easily. Unfortunately, more often women, no matter how well qualified, are not taken as seriously as a male counterpart would be. Sometimes, it can take quite a while for foreign women to prove themselves equally capable.

7

Unpredictability and Life

Todos los días pienso que, en Latinoamerica, vivimos por milagro. No es una reflexión derrotista, ni siquiera pesimista. Es un pensamiento a t'onito. Las cosas que ocurren en nuestros países son tan inesperadas, que siempre nos toman por sorpresa. Como si no hubieramos podido poner en orden nuestra memoria, ni nuestra experiencia, los hechos nos atacan por la espalda y muchas veces nos hieren mortalmente, sin que sepa, los ni por qué, ni cuando, ni quien ha sido.

—Marta Traba

Every day I think that in Latin America, it is a miracle that we survive. This is not a defeatist or even a pessimistic reflection. Rather, it is an intuitive thought. The things that occur in our countries are so unexpected that they always seem to take us by surprise. It is as if we have not been able to put into order our memories and experiences, and, consequently, events seem to attack us from behind, and many times they mortally wound us, without us ever knowing why or when or even who did it.

The Spanish-speaking South Americans' (SSSAs') most important cultural characteristics—personalismo and social differentiation—not only profoundly influence identity and social interactions, they also provide important sources of stability amidst the perceived unpredictability of life. Indeed, at the core of the region's belief system is the assumption that many of the events that transpire are ultimately beyond human control, shaped and directed by forces much more powerful than those of mere mortals. Acknowledging the significance of this belief in life's unpredictability and understanding its implications can help illuminate many aspects of SSSA culture.

Perspectives on Life

SSSAs believe that life is like a torrential river that is powerful, magnificent, and beguiling. An all-encompassing, vital force that runs along a self-directed course, its intentions are often unfathomable to and unalterable by humans. Life can exhibit all the changing temperaments of a river system—it can be gentle, it can nourish, it can heal, but it can also be capricious and unpredictable. At times life seems to flow according to a clear plan and set order; in other instances, it changes direction unexpectedly, flooding into new channels and leaving others to dry up.

This vision of life powerfully affects how SSSAs conduct their own lives. Since they tend to attribute much of what occurs to forces beyond their control, they often adopt the strategy of adjusting themselves to the currents, rather than trying to modify the flow of events—an alternative that they consider to be a vain expenditure of personal energy. In contrast, adjusting to circumstances permits them to survive the vicissitudes and to bask in the pleasures that the larger life force brings. Actually, perceived in this way, individual life and universal life cannot be separated but are inextricably linked.

This does not mean that SSSAs view their lives in an entirely passive or fatalistic way. Quite the contrary! Much of the region's history attests to the concerted efforts made by many brave individuals to change, oftentimes radically, aspects of life and society. Rather, this perspective serves as an ultimate point of reference, a final marker against which human efforts are appraised. Thus, the actual outcome of intended actions and goals—whether success or failure—is not attributed solely to individual enterprise and initiative. Rather, individual and even group efforts are considered to be but one component of a larger constellation of forces, events, and energies that interact to influence the final result.

This perspective has numerous implications for how personal energies and efforts are directed in SSSA. While it lessens personal accountability in many cases, it also promotes the drive to decipher in some way what the "larger powers" might have in store for us mortals. Not surprisingly, there is much focus in SSSA on revelatory experiences or divination of various types, especially at the popular level. In fact millions of SSSAs from all walks of life and educational backgrounds consult religious figures, fortune-tellers, tarot readers, astrologers, and other such diviners regularly. In many communities throughout the region, people who have the "gift" to read the future are held in high esteem.

A second quite different implication of this vision of life is that it creates a focus on the present and, though to a lesser extent, on the past rather than the future. Since tomorrow is considered to be so unpredictable and uncontrollable, the best one can do is to savor the moment, taking pleasure from what is currently going on and living life to its fullest. The focus is on the tangible "now" rather than on a more nebulous and often indecipherable future.

This focus on the present can be noted in the relish with which many people approach life, especially enjoying social activities, parties, and fun. There often seems to be a savoring of the moment, with a relaxed attitude (or sometimes even a reckless nonchalance) concerning tomorrow. For example, conspicuous consumption is high and savings are low throughout the region; purchasing on credit is widespread. Few people earmark much of their earnings toward insurance, even when they have the means to do so. Instead, they often "hope for the best," and if events transpire that dash such hopes, they typically shrug and suffer the consequences, often turning to family and close friends for help and support. Related to this somewhat carefree approach to life is a lack of opportunity to redress grievances through the legal systems. Consumer rights are weak, if not nonexistent, in many places in SSSA, and medical malpractice suits are nearly unknown.

In fact, the whole approach to planning tends to be envisioned differently by SSSAs than by English-speaking North Americans (ESNAs), an often overlooked fact that can sometimes lead to uncomfortable consequences, especially in the business realm. For many SSSAs, plans are considered to be general guidelines for intended direction and hoped-for results. Typically, no one assumes that plans will be rigorously followed because, after all, the future can be so unpredictable. Often, even the concept of how plans are constructed in SSSA is different from in ESNA, tending toward eloquence and generality rather than specificity and feasibility.

For foreigners visiting and/or living in the region, such realities can often be disconcerting, disheartening, and in some cases, even frightening. The best adage with which to address these circumstances is "Expect the unexpected," which can be interpreted both positively and negatively. Sometimes, what one plans for and anticipates just does not occur, for a variety of possible reasons. At other times, inexplicably, events transpire quite differently, unfolding so naturally and rapidly that one is astounded by their effortlessness.

Whether this at times frustrating yet often very alluring aspect of life is conditioned by the perspective of the inhabitants who live there, or whether the inhabitants who live there have somehow adjusted their way of perceiving life to the manner in which events seem to occur in the region is impossible to discern. However, it should come as no surprise that the genre of magic realism first emerged from the pens of SSSA authors.

Time

If life is the greater force, then time is its handmaiden, propelling individuals from birth toward death, inevitably and, at times, mercilessly. Consequently, time in SSSA is envisioned like life itself—often beyond human control and direction. Rather than attempting to control, direct, or dominate time, people prefer to flexibly adjust to it, finding pleasure in whatever way circumstances transpire as time moves us all toward our ultimate and most predictable destiny—death.

In contrast to the predictability of death, time can often be most unpredictable indeed. Even in the realm of daily transactions, it can often be impossible to know how to schedule one's activities and how much time to allot to performing certain errands and tasks. Well-intentioned promises can be impossible to fulfill for a variety of reasons. As Richard Hillman explains,

> Venezuelans [and other SSSAs]...tend to promise everything with good intentions at the moment. However, constraints such as traffic, power outages, availability of materials, or other difficulties often intervene, causing inability to control events or follow through on promises. Often frustration and misunderstanding ensue, especially for North Americans whose sense of rationally ordered efficiency is offended.*

Even appointments and other scheduled gatherings are not always convened at the agreed-upon time, or even, in some instances, at all. This more relaxed attitude concerning punctuality holds true in both the work and social realms, although it tends to be more pronounced in social situations. The underlying assumption is that "Time is an unlimited good, there is always more of it, later, tomorrow, in the indefinite future" (Hirschkind†).

Foreigners attempting to conduct business and other work-related activities in SSSA should not assume, however, that the people they will be dealing with will necessarily be tardy. Many professionals and others from the region are punctual in their work habits, and timeliness varies widely due to factors such as individual inclination, national affiliation, and social status.

---

* Richard Hillman is author of chapter 18, "Venezuela: the Tropical Beat," in Part II of this book.

† Lynn Hirschkind is author of chapter 14, "Ecuador: In the Middle of the World," in Part II of this book.

As a general rule of thumb, assume timely behavior and wait if the appointment is delayed, rather than show up late and risk making an unfavorable impression.

Once an appointment or meeting begins, it will probably last longer than is the norm in ESNA, typically moving along at a leisurely pace. Usually, the event will commence with general conversation, often accompanied by tea and/or coffee. Such small talk is very important because it serves to create the right atmosphere for the more substantive discussion that will follow by developing bonds of emotional warmth. It is especially important in instances where the parties involved do not know each other very well.

SSSAs and ESNAs have diametrically opposite ways of viewing time as it relates to status. Whereas in ESNA "Time is money," and an important person is one who is very busy, in SSSA the opposite holds true. High-ranking people are often those who act as though they have significant time at their disposal to graciously entertain those they deem worthy and potentially useful. They can function in such a way precisely because they have subordinates working for them to carry out the mundane tasks. In fact, it is a sign of high rank to not be rushed.

This sense of a leisurely pace applies even more to the social realm than to the work setting. Typically, social encounters of all types in the region last much longer than is common in ESNA, and events just seem to "flow along," the hours passing imperceptibly. It is rare to see SSSAs frequently glancing at their watches. Acting rushed is considered detrimental to enjoying human interactions and relishing the moment, and even very busy people do not typically present themselves as being in a hurry.

If ESNAs firmly believe that "Early to bed and early to rise makes a man healthy, wealthy, and wise," SSSAs generally take the opposite approach when scheduling their daily activities. Later hours are often preferable, due perhaps, in part, to the assumption that much of what is considered most pleasurable typically transpires when the lights are low. Activities both begin and end later in SSSA. For instance, most people do not even eat dinner until eight or later in the evening, and many nocturnal activities, such as nightclubs, discos, and so on, do not even open until midnight, and many movie theaters offer midnight or 1:00 A.M. showings.

Even children stay up late, especially during the summer, when it is not uncommon to see them playing at ten or eleven o'clock at night. Some parents consider the schedules imposed during the school year so onerous that during holidays children are allotted large amounts of free time and permitted to go to sleep whenever they desire. The adults themselves tend to take this same approach during the weekends and holidays, and on Sundays in many households no one gets up before noon. Then they visit with family for lunch, and then take a long afternoon nap, often recuperating from a late Saturday night.

Not only are activities typically scheduled differently in SSSA, but the way in which these activities are conducted is different as well. Edward T. Hall, a well-known cultural anthropologist, distinguished between cultures that are monochronic and those that are polychronic in their ways of meeting the numerous demands placed on individuals in the course of their daily activities. According to this categorization, "monochronic time emphasizes schedules, segmentation and promptness. Polychronic systems are characterized by several things happening at once. They stress involvement with people and completion of transactions rather than adherence to present schedules" (1989, 17).

SSSAs clearly fall into the polychronic category, and most people from this region are usually quite comfortable, and in fact prefer, engaging in several different activities simultaneously. Often, meetings or appointments are interrupted by phone calls, staff entering and leaving, and other myriad activities, between which events the people involved in the meeting seem to shift their attention with ease.

Dealing with such multiple activities can sometimes prove quite stressful for ESNAs, who are usually more monochronic in their handling of tasks. They sometimes find it difficult to follow events that are transpiring around them while they are trying to have a meeting with someone. ESNAs can lose focus and/or concentration and often become annoyed with what seems to them rude behavior. Hall comments on this potential for a cross-cultural "clash" as follows:

> Americans overseas are psychologically stressed in many ways when confronted with polychronic time systems such as those in Latin America and the Middle East. In the markets and stores of Mediterranean countries, one is surrounded by other customers vying for the attention of a clerk. There is no order as to who is served next, and to the northern European or American, confusion and clamor abound.... Things are constantly shifted around. Nothing seems solid or firm. (17–18)

Communication

SSSA communication patterns are construed in such a way as to accommodate unpredictability and even in some cases a personal lack of accountability. The Spanish language itself leaves more open to interpretation than does English, which is usually so direct and specific. For example, if a glass falls and breaks, a Spanish speaker will typically say "*Se cayó*," or "It dropped," leaving undefined how this occurrence actually transpired and who, if anybody, might be responsible. The widespread use of the conditional verb form also lends a connotation of ambiguity to many statements, encouraging speakers to focus on what "might" or "could" or "should" happen, rather than on what actually "did" or "will" take place.

Sometimes SSSAs utilize this linguistic lack of precision as a method for dealing with potentially contentious issues, especially when human relationships and feelings might be at stake. Rather than be direct and say the truth, even if it hurts, as many ESNAs are culturally conditioned to do, SSSAs tend to prefer indirectness as the way to convey unpleasant or potentially disturbing information. In some situations, individuals will even avoid the word *no*, preferring instead to substitute a broader *maybe* or even, in some cases, an insincere *yes*. As an SSSA explains,

> To say yes [sometimes] only means "I wanted to say yes." It is an educated yes, a yes without conflict because the truth brings conflict.... Rather, what they have said is an inexact truth, or a weak promise. (Otano 1998, 9)

This proclivity for emphasizing human interactions in the present, even at the cost of veracity, can in some cases cause misunderstandings with the more literal ESNAs. For instance, many foreigners visiting the region have learned after several exasperating experiences that many locals, when asked for directions, will proffer incorrect instructions rather than admit that they do not know.

> In the United States, if you are stopped and asked for directions to a place you are unfamiliar with, you are expected to be honest and say you don't know. In most Latin American countries, that would be considered disrespectful toward the person who has asked you, since you appear to be simply dismissing him or her without even making an effort to help. It is considered more appropriate to at least try to provide an answer, even if your response is inaccurate and sends the person in the wrong direction. (9)

This approach of emphasizing the positive at the expense of accuracy often holds true in the business realm as well, as the following incident written by an ESNA businessman illustrates.

> I tried to write a letter to some Chilean government officials expressing my annoyance and frustration about the proceedings concerning the mine. I wrote the letter in English, and a Chilean geologist translated it. The geologist came to me several times and said, "I don't think we should say this exactly because it will offend or give the wrong impression to the official. It is better to say things in a restrained manner and assume the official will read into them their true meaning." I can go to a meeting and think everything went all right, but after the meeting the Chil-

> ean will tell me, yes, that is what they said, but what they really meant was.... It seems that people intentionally hide behind the formality so that they won't insult anyone. Chileans hate giving negative information. Even if the whole place is falling down, they'll tell you that one side is still standing. (Mizon 1998)

This communication style is a concrete manifestation of deep-seated views concerning the power and purpose of words. For SSSAs, words are not so much tools used to convey concrete reality and to promote specific results—a perspective typical of many ESNAs, with their no-nonsense, direct, and honest communication style—as they are timely works of art used to create a mood, present an intended or desired image, or paint a verbal picture. It is not assumed that words will necessarily convey realistic or completely accurate information; their purpose is, in part, to create a different reality, one that might be more enticing, more beautiful, and more interesting than the actual one.

Thus, words are given great importance in SSSA culture, not for what they actually express but rather for what they have the potential to create. Verbal dexterity, confident discourse, originality in expression, and even in some cases clever lies are all lauded.

> Latin Americans are enamored with the word. Everyone who is anyone has written something. To be a man of letters carries immeasurable prestige and certainly some of the greatest writers of this century are Latin Americans. For the Latin American, there is something noble, sublime and transcendental in the eloquent expression of the word. (Spencer 1991, 7)

This fervent appreciation of verbal language can be noted in SSSAs' rhetorical style, which often takes uninitiated ESNAs by surprise with its verbosity, ornateness, and, sometimes, apparent lack of grounding in reality. Compared with the North American style of discussion, in the Latin American pattern,

> Great value [is] given to words and their manipulation, as in

> argument, compared to the comparatively low rating accorded to the empirical investigation of premises and data. Every visitor to Latin America, who goes with a working knowledge of the language, has been astounded by the enormous verbal facility of his hosts. Even in published scientific works in the social sciences...the North American reader is often treated to a virtuosity of argumentation, phraseology, and theory to which he can only weakly and perhaps discourteously reply by asking, "Where are the facts?" (Gillin 1965, 13)

The importance of the word even spills over into attitudes concerning how words themselves are actually written. Most SSSA adults artfully create their own personal signatures, which are often so stylized as to make the actual reading of the name virtually impossible. In some situations, particularly those involving financial and/or bureaucratic transactions, great ceremony surrounds the whole process of signing documents. The use of notaries to legalize and formalize signatures to important documents is widespread throughout SSSA.

8

Work and Leisure

Nosotros trabajamos para vivir, pero ustedes viven para trabajar.
—Popular Latin American saying

We (SSSAs) work to live, but you (ESNAs) live to work.

Attitudes toward Work

Cultural perceptions of life and time powerfully shape how Spanish-speaking South Americans (SSSAs) view work and its place in the overall scheme of life. It should come as no surprise that, as a general rule, work is not considered to be as central to personal identity and societal recognition as it is in English-speaking North America (ESNA). In fact, in SSSA work is often considered to be a necessary evil, the most important function of which is to provide needed resources to support oneself and one's intimates.

This different emphasis on work is even present in conversation openers. Whereas ESNAs who are getting to know someone frequently ask, "What do you do [for a living]?" or inquire about a person's position, it is much more common for SSSAs to begin an exchange by asking about family or other types of relationships.

The roots of this perspective toward work can be traced back to the colonial era. In marked contrast to the Puritans and other early settlers of ESNA who believed that work was a virtue and a primary means of achieving salvation, the conquistadores and other foreigners who settled in SSSA were of the opinion that work, especially manual labor or anything that dirtied the hands, was a chore to be relegated to those of the lowest ranks (Indians and Africans), while the elites employed their energies in such a way as to have as much leisure time as possible.

Even today, almost two centuries after achieving independence and despite the tremendous economic transformations that have occurred since then, work productivity in SSSA can be quite sluggish, as has been cited in empirical studies designed to measure workplace efficiency cross-nationally. In all such investigations, SSSAs were ranked quite low compared with people from other regions of the world.

Such low ratings in workplace productivity are not, however, usually attributable to short working days. In fact, in most of the region, workdays are actually longer than in ESNA, extending in many cases until seven or even eight in the evening. In recent decades, rapid urbanization and economic problems have mired many of the SSSA nations, and many people have had to invest tremendous amounts of time and effort in making a living. While the region typically recognizes a greater number of official holidays and allows more vacation time than is the norm in ESNA, the total number of vacation days annually is about equal to those in many European nations.

There are numerous reasons for low workplace performance in SSSA, including (in some cases) infrastructural problems, economic instability, and/or the sense of unpredictability that can make long-term planning problematic. One of the most significant explanations, however, is the amount of time that is often dedicated to cultivating and maintaining relationships—activities that are sometimes given a higher priority than completion of the task at hand. In many cases, this is a very rational response to employment and business realities in the region, since these personal connections often prove vital in assuring personal survival and, in some cases, organizational success. For instance, personal connections can be crucial for navigating through the often extensive bureaucratic procedures endemic in much of SSSA. Such connections are highly prized and often vigorously solicited by SSSAs from all walks of life. So prevalent is the practice of calling on one's connections that all the countries in the region have a specific term to describe it, such as *pituto* in Chile or *palanca* in Colombia, to name but two. One Colombian researcher, Kristine Fitch, explains the importance of a palanca in the following way: "Palanca constitutes a cultural myth that underscores the importance of interpersonal connections, revolving around the notion that almost any goal may be accomplished by way of strong relationships with appropriately powerful others" (1998, 11).

Sometimes, in situations where one lacks such a facilitator or the transaction is considered too mundane to "use up" one's contacts, it is possible, for a nominal fee, to hire people to do the actual paperwork or stand in line in one's place. Such individuals, known as *juniors*, *tramitadores*, or other words depending on the country, actually make their living in this way and can serve a very useful function indeed.

Individuals in high-status positions of authority typically invest considerable time in solidifying and expanding their circle of contacts through such means as phone calls, social lunches, and so forth. For many, these efforts are an excellent expenditure of time and energy. In this way, as in so many others, personalismo comes to the fore.

The importance accorded to personal relationships in the workplace also affects the way SSSAs evaluate foreigners. Especially in the initial stages of contact, more energy is devoted to getting to know the people involved in a project than to actually conducting business. This approach is considered only natural because one needs to discern whether the individuals under consideration exhibit those qualities that will make them good working colleagues. Such qualities might include, but are in no way limited to, the following: a pleasing physical presence and presentation, courteous behavior, emotional warmth, and a sense of humor. As a Peruvian businessman explained in an interview with the author,

> The North American should have in mind that the business will not necessarily finish in one morning. It takes time for us to meditate and think about what is being presented. We need to understand the people we are involved with and, above all else, have a sense of the person. If somebody is very dry or dull, then it will be hard for us to have dealings with him or her.

Entertaining and Leisure

Given the importance of family in SSSA, it is understandable that much of the social life throughout the region takes place in personal residences. For an outsider, an invitation to a local's home is a sign of acceptance and can denote a greater degree of intimacy than a similar invitation from an ESNA would.

Typically, there is a clearly marked division between private and public spaces that can be noted both literally and psychologically. Nearly all residences in the region are bordered by walls and must be entered by passing through a gate. Many have guards or other forms of surveillance as well. Although much of family life in the United States and Canada is carried on publicly, in full view of neighbors or those passing by, in SSSA such events take place behind closed doors, in the interior of the dwelling and beyond the eyes of strangers.

Passing into a native's private realm means that you are entering the family's domain and that they are now in charge. What this usually implies is a clear distinction between host and guest and the desire to be the most gracious hosts possible. In fact, the hospitality of many SSSAs is legendary, as is illustrated by a favorite saying that many people from this region use when entertaining—"*Mi casa es tu casa*" ("My house is your house").

Although most hosts will patiently put up with faux pas from foreigners, knowledge of certain expectations can help make social encounters proceed more smoothly and promote a greater personal connection. Although it is not always expected, a small gift of flowers, chocolates, or wine will be warmly received. Even more important for making a positive first impression is to properly greet people, making sure to individually kiss, hug, or shake hands with everyone present at the event.

As a general rule, a greater degree of formality governs such visits than many ESNAs may be accustomed to. Visitors are usually expected to stay in the living room or dining room area. Going to the kitchen to "help out" is not usually appropriate, expected, or appreciated unless the household is decidedly informal. In fact, in many families the kitchen is considered to be the domain of the female head of house and the maid, if there is one, and household members will feel quite uncomfortable having outsiders intrude here.

Because meals typically include several courses, they are often quite long. Not infrequently, after dessert members of the dinner party retire to the living room or patio to drink coffee and/or liquors and continue talking. Leave-taking can also be an extended affair, and departing guests are typically implored to stay longer. It usually takes a while to gracefully depart without undue protestations from the hosts. When leaving, everyone present should be individually told good-bye. Thanks should, of course, be proffered, but effusive gratitude is not expected and can even be considered a bit odd.

The warmth of SSSA hospitality, however, does not suggest that intimate ties can be quickly established. Given the importance accorded to one's circle of intimates in SSSA culture, it can be hard for foreigners—especially those with weak language skills—to break into such closely knit groups.

Since many South Americans devote much of their leisure time to being with family and close friends, there are fewer organized events to promote business relationships outside the workplace setting, as is often the case in the United States and Canada. For instance, while some SSSAs might play golf, the game is not as popular as it is in ESNA and Asia. Soccer is by far the most popular sport throughout the region, but it is not usually engaged in to promote business purposes. In some circles, attending cultural activities of various types can be an important way of making and consolidating work-related contacts.

9

Bridging Hemispheres: Views on English-Speaking North Americans

Si el norte fuera el sur, serían los Siouxs los marginados
Ser moreno y chaparrito sería el look más cotizado…
Los yanquis de mojado a Tijuana
Y las balsas de Miami a la Habana, si el norte fuera el sur—
Seríamos igual o tal vez un poco peor.

—Ricardo Arjona

If the North was the South,
the Sioux would be the marginalized ones.
To be dark and short would be the most sought after look…
The Yankees would be wetbacks to Tijuana
And the Balseros would go from Miami to Havana,
If the North was the South—
We would be the same, or perhaps a little worse.

One of the frustrations that Spanish-speaking South Americans (SSSAs) feel when dealing with people from the United States is that they really do not know what to call them. They almost unanimously discard the designation *American* because they maintain (correctly) that they are also Americans. Sometimes they use *estadounidiense* (United Statesian), but it sounds awkward and also is not popular. More frequently, especially in informal settings, more colloquial terms are used instead.

The most common is the word *gringo*, its etymology traceable to the Mexican War. During this conflict, the U.S. soldiers donned green uniforms, and Mexican nationalists would say in English "Green go home" as a rallying cry for their struggle against the northern intruders. The phrase eventually evolved into the abbreviated term *gringo*, which is not nowadays usually meant to imply anti-United States sentiments when used to classify English-speaking North Americans (ESNAs).

In fact, the exact attributes and nationality of a gringo can be a bit ambiguous at times. Some SSSAs find it less appropriate to use the term when describing Canadians or people from the United States who are of African or Asian lineage, feeling somehow that these people are not quite "gringos." However, some SSSAs are more expansive in their designation of gringos and include Nordic and Germanic Europeans as well,

In contrast with most of the rest of the region, Argentineans and Uruguayans tend to dub people from the United States *yanquis* (yankees), pronouncing the word with the typical Río Platense *sh* sound for the *y*.

Whatever term they use, both myths and realities shape what many SSSAs think about their northern neighbors. Because of the extensive and growing influence of ESNA popular culture throughout much of SSSA, many people from this region have absorbed large amounts of information regarding ESNAs (from television, movies, newspapers, etc.)—some of which is fairly accurate and some of which is decidedly distorted or simplistic.

In some ways, SSSAs find much to appreciate about the United States and Canada, including their material progress, modern focus, and political and economic stability. Although they may wonder how this has been achieved and why ESNAs seem to drive life rather than let life drive them, they sense that somehow things are more predictable, less random, and less sudden in the northern realms of the Americas than in their own domains. Perhaps some SSSAs even feel a bit of inferiority vis-à-vis their northern neighbors.

Nonetheless, many SSSAs still harbor the conviction that many of the great achievements of their northern neighbors have been brought about at great personal cost. They see the alleged pragmatism and individualism of ESNAs, which propels them so decisively toward material progress and concrete achievements, as excessive. The ESNAs' drive to succeed is seen as excluding them from the most significant aspects of life and living, in particular human relationships, creativity, and personal relaxation and enjoyment.

This viewpoint is most succinctly characterized in a work by the Uruguayan author José Enrique Rodó entitled *Ariel and Caliban*. Written almost a century ago, this book is still very influential throughout the region; Rodó associates the United States with Caliban—heavy, plodding, and grounded only in this world. Latin Americans, in contrast, are considered to be like Ariel—ethereal and able to fly to realms that Caliban could never reach. This symbolic juxtaposition is often echoed by SSSAs today, even those who are unaware of Rodó's work. For instance, one Ecuadorian, according to Lynn Hirschkind, had the following impression of ESNAs:

> My image of North Americans isn't very positive. I think the average North American citizen is a good person, but confused. They have an extraordinarily pragmatic sense of life, are uncultured, lacking totally in a background of humanistic aspiration that we Latin Americans have. While the North Americans know perfectly well how to tighten a screw and nothing more, the Latin Americans can speak of Dante and el Quixote and many other things, but when we have to tighten a screw it probably wouldn't be done right.

Related to this opinion about ESNAs is a corollary assumption that they are cold and emotionally distant because of the excessive energy they dedicate to personal achievement. Hirschkind also elaborates on this perspective.

> In general, North Americans are thought to be "cold and dry," meaning not emotional or sentimental, without affect. They are indifferent to their families, and thus leave home as soon as possible and move as far away as possible. They are naïve and thus easily fooled.

Whatever views SSSAs may hold regarding ESNAs, their emphasis on personalismo, warm human relationships, and formal social niceties typically makes them welcoming hosts to any visitors to their lands. Even in the very contentious areas of politics and economics, so divisive over the years in governmental relations between the two regions, SSSAs quite consciously separate their personal feelings for individuals from their opinions about the English-speaking north in general.

One of the best ways for ESNAs to create a positive image of both themselves and their own culture is to make a real effort to learn as much as possible about the SSSAs. One of the most frequently voiced complaints of many in the region is that they typically have much greater knowledge about their English-speaking northern neighbors than the latter have about them. Learning more about the history, politics, and economics of SSSA, as well as reading representative works by some of the region's many renowned authors, can go far in promoting goodwill among hemispheric neighbors.

References and Selected Bibliography Part I

Adler, Larissa. 1994. *Redes Sociales: Cultura y Poder*. México City: Angel Porrua.

Alabarces, Pablo. 2000. *Peligro de Gol: Estudio sobre el Deporte y Sociedad en América Latina*. Buenos Aires, Argentina: CLACSO.

Alvarez, Julia. 1997. *Yo*. New York: Penguin Books.

Alvarez, Sonia E., Evelina Dagnino, and Arturo Escobar, eds. 1998. *Cultures of Politics/Politics of Cultures: Revisioning Latin American Social Movements*. Boulder, CO: Westview Press.

Anderson, Charles W. 1967. *Politics and Economic Change in Latin America: The Governing of Restless Nations*. New York: Van Nostrand Reinhold Company.

Arbena, Joseph L. 1988. *Sport and Society in Latin America: Diffusion, Dependency and the Rise of Mass Culture*. New York: Greenwood Press.

Atkins, G. Pope. 1989. *Latin America in the International Political System*. Boulder, CO: Westview Press.

Baddeley, Oriana. 1989. *Drawing the Line: Art and Cultural Identity in Contemporary Latin America*. London and New York: Verso Books.

Beezley, William H. 2000. *Latin American Popular Culture*. Wilmington, DE: SR Books.

Benavente, M. Cristina, Jacqueline Gysling, and Teresa Valdés. 1999. *El Poder de la Pareja, la Sexualidad y la Reproducción*. Santiago, Chile: FLACSO.

Berger, Peter, Norbert Lechner, Manuel Mora y Araujo, and Pedro Morandé. 1999. "Cultura y Desarrollo Económico." In *Estudios Públicos* (Chile), 40.

Bethell, Leslie. 1995. *The Cambridge History of Latin America: Latin America since 1930: Ideas, Culture and Society*. Cambridge, England: Cambridge University Press.

Bosrock, Mary Murray. 1997. *Put Your Best Foot Forward: South America*. St. Paul, MN: International Education Systems.

Brunner, José Joaquín. 1995. *Cinco Estudios sobre Cultura y Sociedad*. Santiago: FLACSO.

———. 1994. *Bienvenidos a la Modernidad*. Santiago: Ediciones Planeta.

———. 1990. *Tradicionalismo y Modernidad en la Cultura Latinoamericana*. Santiago: FLACSO.

———. 1988. *Un Espejo Trizado. Ensayos sobre Cultura y Políticas Culturales*. Santiago: FLACSO.

———. 1983. *La Cultura Política del Autoritarismo*. Santiago: FLACSO.

Brunner, José Joaquín, and Angel Flisfisch. 1984. *Los Intelectuales y la Organización de la Cultura*. Santiago: FLACSO.

Brysk, Alison. 1996. "Turning Weakness into Strength: The Internationalization of Indian Rights." *Latin American Perspectives* 23, no. 2 (Spring): 38–57.

Bueno, Eva P., and Terry Caesar, eds. 1998. *Imagination beyond Nation: Latin American Popular Culture*. Pittsburgh: University of Pittsburgh Press.

Canclini, Néstor García. 1995. *Hybrid Cultures: Strategies for Entering and Leaving Modernity*. Translated by Christopher L. Chiappari and Silvia L. Lopez. Minneapolis: University of Minnesota Press.

———. 1991. "Los Estudios Culturales de los 80 a 90. Perspectivas Antropológicas en América Latina." In *Punto de Vista* (Argentina), no. 40.

———. 1987. *Políticas Culturales en América Latina*. Mexico City: Grijalbo.

Caponnetto, Antonio. 1991. *The Black Legends and Catholic Hispanic Culture: Liberation Theology and the History of the New World.* Translated by Jose R. Lopéz-Gaston and Rosa M. Lopéz-Gaston. St. Louis: Central Bureau of the Catholic Central Verein of America.

Casanova, Pablo González, ed. 1993. *Latin America Today*. New York: United Nations University Press.

Casella, Ronnie. 1999. "Pedagogy as View Sequence: Popular Culture, Education and Travel." *Anthropology and Education Quarterly* 30, no. 2.

Chilcote, Ron, and Frederick Stirton Weaver. 2000. *Latin America in the World Economy: Mercantile Colonialism to Global Capitalism*. Boulder, CO: Westview Press.

Conference on Latin American Culture. 1942. "Cultural Bases of Hemispheric Understanding." Sponsored by the Institute of Latin American Studies, University of Texas, Austin, April 14–15.

Crahan, Margaret E. 1991. "Church and State in Latin America: Assassinating Some Old and New Stereotypes." *Daedalus* (Summer), 131–58.

Dahl, Victor, ed. 1987. *Culture and Nationalism in Latin America.* San Diego: San Diego State University Press.

D'Allemand, Patricia. 2000. *Latin American Cultural Criticism: Re-interpreting a Continent*. Lewiston, NY: E. Mellon Press.

De la Cadena, Marisol. 2000. *Indigenous Mestizos: The Politics of Race and Culture in Cuzco, Peru. 1919–1991*. Raleigh, NC: Duke University Press.

Delpanio, Maria Olga. 1999. *El Mercurio* (21 August).

De Soto, Hernando. 1989. *The Other Path: The Invisible Revolution in the Third World*. Translated by June Abbott. New York: Harper and Row.

Echegollen, Alfredo. 1998. "Cultura e Imaginarios Políticos en América Latina." *Metapolítica*, no. 7.

Edmonson, Munro S., Claudia Madsen, and Jane Fishburne Collier. 1968. *Contemporary Latin American Culture*. New Orleans: Middle American Research Institute, Tulane University.

Falcoff, Mark. 1998. *A Culture of Its Own: Taking Latin America Seriously*. Transaction Publishers.

Fitch, Kristine L. 1998. *Speaking Relationally: Culture, Communication and Interpersonal Connection*. New York: Guildford Press.

FLACSO. 1998. Informe de Encuesta: Representaciones de la *Sociedad Chilena*, Vols. 1 and 2. Santiago: FLACSO.

Foster, George McClelland. 1965. *Contemporary Latin American Culture: An Anthropological Sourcebook*. New York: Selected Academic Readings.

Foxley, Ana Maria, and Pablo Halpern, eds. 1988. *América en la Encrucijada Cultural*, no. 21. Santiago: Ministerio Secretaria General de Gobierno.

Franco, Jean. 1967. *The Modern Culture of Latin America: Society and the Artist*. London: Pall Mall.

Fuentes, Carlos. 1992. *The Buried Mirror: Reflections on Spain and the New World*. Boston: Houghton Mifflin.

———. 1992. *El Espejo Enterrado*. Mexico City, Mexico: Fondo de Cultura Económica.

Fundacion Ideas. 1997. *Primera Encuesta Intolerancia y Discriminacion: Informe y analisis*. Santiago: Fundacion Ideas.

Galeano, Eduardo H. 1991. *El Descubrimiento de América que todavía no fue y Nuevos Ensayos*. Caracas. Alfadil Editores.

———. 1989. *América Viva: 1492–1992—Quinientos Anos Después*. Madrid: Editorial Revolución.

———. 1985. *Memory of Fire*. Translated by Cedric Belfrage. New York: Pantheon Books.

———. 1980. *Las Venas Abiertas de América Latina*. México City: Siglo Veintiuno Editores.

———. 1973. *Open Veins of Latin America: Five Centuries of the Pillage of a Continent*. Translated by Cedric Belfrage. New York: Monthly Review Press.

Garretón, Manuel Antonio. 1992. "América Latina: Cultura y Sociedad en el Fin de Siglo." In *Transformación Cultural: Cuatro Documentos de Reflexión Preliminar*. Santiago: FLASCO.

———, ed. 1999. *América Latina: un Espacio Cultural en el Mundo Globalizado*. Bogotá: Convenio Andrés Bello.

Gassett, José Ortega y. 1983. "El Hombre a la defensiva." In *Obras Completas*, vol. 2. Madrid: Alinza Editorial. Article originally published in 1929.

Gillin, John. 1965. "The Ethos Components in Modern Latin American Culture." In *Contemporary Cultures and Societies of Latin America*, edited by Dwight B. Heath and Richard N. Adams. New York: Random House.

Gissi, Jorge. 1982. "Identidad, 'Carácter social' y Cultura Latinoamericana." *Estudios Sociales CPU* (Chile), no. 33: 141–72.

Godsland, Shelley, and Anne M. White, eds. 2002. *Cultura Popular: Studies in Spanish and Latin American Popular Culture*. New York: Peter Lang.

González, Luis. 1982. *Filosofía de la Cultura Latinoamericana*. Bogotá, Colombia: El Buho.

Gordon, Raymond L. 1995. *Living in Latin America: A Case Study in Cross-Cultural Communication*. Chicago: National Textbook Company.

Guntermann, Gail, and the Center for Latin American Studies, Arizona State University. 1984. *Contemporary Latin American Culture: Unity and Diversity*. Tempe, AZ: Center for Latin American Studies.

Gwynne, Robert N., and Cristobal Kay, eds. 1999. *Latin America Transformed: Globalization and Modernity*. Cambridge, England: Cambridge University Press.

Hall, Edward T. 1989. *Beyond Culture*. New York: Anchor Books.

Hanke, Lewis. 1974. *Latin America: A Historical Reader*. Boston: Little, Brown.

———. 1949. *The Spanish Struggle for Justice in the Conquest of America*. Philadelphia: University of Pennsylvania Press.

Harrison, Lawrence E. 1985. *Underdevelopment Is a State of Mind: The Latin American Case*. Lanham, MD: Center for International Affairs, Harvard University, and University Press of America.

Henríquez Urena, Pedro. 1966. *A Concise History of Latin American Culture*. Translated by Gilbert Chase. New York: Praeger.

Herring, Hubert. 1968. *A History of Latin America*. 3d ed. New York: Alfred A. Knopf.

Hill, Richard. 1997. *WeEuropeans*. Brussels: Europublications.

Hopenhayn, Martín. 1994. *Ni Apocalípticos ni Integrados: Aventuras de la Modernidad en América Latina*. Santiago: Fondo de Cultura Económica.

———. 1988. "El debate post-moderno y la Dimensión Cultural del Desarrollo." In *Imágenes Desconocidas: La Modernidad en la Encrucijada Postmoderna*. Buenos Aires: CLACSO.

Hunt, Lynn, ed. 1989. *The New Cultural History*. Berkeley, CA: University of California Press.

Inman, Samuel Guy, ed. 1959. *South America*. New York: Van Nostrand Press.

Inter-American Development Bank. 1990. "Economic and Social Progress in Latin America 1990." Report, Washington, DC. Distributed by Johns Hopkins University Press.

Jaguaribe, Helio. 1973. *Political Development: A General Theory and a Latin American Case Study*. New York: Harper and Row.

Jaquette, Jane S., ed. 1991. *The Women's Movement in Latin America: Feminism and the Transition to Democracy*. Boulder, CO: Westview Press.

Jerman, William. 1975. *Repression in Latin America*. Nottingham, England: Spokesman Books.

Keen, Benjamin, ed. 2000. *Latin American Civilization: History and Society, 1942 to the Present*. 7th ed. Boulder, CO: Westview Press.

Kliksberg, Bernardo. 1996. "Como enfrentar los déficit sociales de América Latina? Acerca de Mitos, Ideas Renovadoras y el Papel de la Cultura." *Revista Venezolana de Gerencia* (Venezuela), no. 2: 163–82.

Koschutzke, Alberto. 1989. *Y Hasta Cuando Esperaremos Mandam-dirun-dirun-dan: Mujer y Poder en América Latina*. Caracas: Nueva Visión.

Lande, Carl H. 1977. "The Dyadic Basis of Clientelism." In *Friends, Followers and Factions*, edited by Steffan Schmidt. Berkeley, CA: University of California Press.

Landi, Oscar. 1988. *Reconstrucciones: Las Nuevas Formas de la Cultura Política*. Buenos Aires: Punto Sur Editores.

Larraín, Jorge. 1996. *Modernidad: Razón e Identidad en América Latina*. Santiago: Editorial Andres Bello.

Larsen, Neil. 1995. *Reading North by South: On Latin American Literature, Culture and Politics*. Minneapolis: University of Minnesota Press.

Lechner, Norbert, comp. 1987. *Cultura Política y Democratización*. Santiago: FLACSO/CLASCO/ICI.

Mander, John. 1969. *The Static Society: The Paradox of Latin America*. London, England: Victor Gollancz.

Marcuse, Herbert. 1968. *Cultura y Sociedad*. Buenos Aires: Editorial Sur.

Martínez, Tomas Eloy. 1999. *El Sueño Argentino*. Buenos Aires: Edición Planeta.

Masiello, Francine. 2001. *The Art of Transition: Latin American Culture and the Neoliberal Crisis*. Raleigh, NC: Duke University Press.

Mason, Tony. 1996. *Passions of the People? Football in South America*. London, England: Verso Books.

Mato, Daniel, ed. 2001. *Estudios Latinoamericanos sobre Cultura y Transformaciones Sociales en Tiempos de Globalización*. Buenos Aires: CLASCO.

Matus, Teresa. 1993. "Legitimaciones Culturales de Violencia." In *Revista de Trabajo Social* (Chile), no. 63: 25–38.

McGuirk, Bernard, and Mark I. Millington. 1995. *Inequality and Difference in Hispanic and Latin American Cultures*. Lewiston, NY: E. Mellon Press.

Mintz, Sidney W., and Eric R. Wolf. 1977. "An Analysis of Ritual Co-Parenthood (Compadrazgo)." In *Friends, Followers and Factions*, edited by Steffan Schmidt. Berkeley: University of California Press.

Mizon, Maria Isabel. 1998. Interview with author regarding a questionnaire she wrote and distributed. Santiago.

Montecino, Sonia. 1996. *Madres y Huachos: Alegorías del Mestizaje Chileno*. 3d ed. Santiago: Editorial Sudamericana.

Montes, Luis. 1998. "Modernización y Cultura Política en América Latina." In *Revista de Trabajo Social* (Venezuela), no. 6.

Morandé, Pedro. 1995. "Identidad Cultural." *El Mercurio* (Santiago), 8 October.

Morrison, Terri, and Wayne A. Conway. 1997. *The International Traveler's Guide to Doing Business in Latin America*. New York: Macmillan Spectrum.

Neruda, Pablo. 1991. *Canto General*. Translated by Jack Schmitt. Berkeley, CA: University of California Press.

Olavarria, José, and Rodrigo Parrini, eds. 2000. *Masculinidad/es. Identidad, Sexualidad y Familia*. Santiago: FLACSO.

Ortiz, Renato. 2000. "América Latina: de la Modernidad a la Modernidad-Mundo." *Nueva Sociedad* (Venezuela), no. 166: 44–61.

Otano, Rafael. 1998. "No somos mentiroso, solo inexactos." *Ya*, 3 March.

Oxhorn, Philip D., and Graciela Ducatenzeiler, eds. 1998. *What Kind of Democracy? What Kind of Market?: Latin America in the Age of Neoliberalism*. University Park: Pennsylvania State University Press.

Page, Joseph A. 1995. *The Brazilians*. Reading, MA: Addison-Wesley.

Paz, Octavio. 1994. *El Laberinto de la Soledad*. Santiago: Fondo de Cultura Económica.

Perez de Mendiola, Marina, ed. 1996. *Bridging the Atlantic: Toward a Reassessment of Iberian and Latin American Cultural Ties*. Albany: State University of New York Press.

Pescatello, A., ed. 1977. *Female and Male in Latin America*. Pittsburgh, PA: University of Pittsburgh Press.

Picón-Salas, Mariano. 1972. "The Initial Encounter." In *Man, State and Society in Latin American History*, edited by Sheldon B. Liss and Peggy K. Liss. London: Pall Mall.

———. 1962. *History of Spanish America: From Conquest to Independence*. Berkeley, CA: University of California Press.

Rajevic, Pia. 2000. *El Libro Abierto del Amor y el Sexo en Chile*. Santiago: Editorial Planeta.

Rangel, Carlos. 1976. *Del Buen Salvaje al Buen Revolucionario: Mitos y Realidades de América Latina*. Caracas: Monte Ávila Editores.

Ribeiro, Darcy. 1972. *The Americas and Civilization*. New York: E. P. Dutton and Company.

Rodríguez, Ernesto, and Bernardo Dalezies. 1989. "Primer informe sobre la Juventud en América Latina." Proceedings from the III Conferencia Intergubernamental sobre Políticas de Juventud en Iberoamerica, San José, Costa Rica, 5–8 June.

Rodriguez, Richard. 1992. *Days of Obligation: An Argument with My Mexican Father*. New York: Penguin Books.

Rosenberg, Tina. 1991. *Children of Cain: Violence and the Violent in Latin America*. New York: William Morrow.

Rowe, William, and Vivian Schelling. 1991. *Memory and Modernity: Popular Culture in Latin America*. London: Verso Books.

Ryan-Ranson, Helen, ed. 1993. *Imagination, Emblems and Expressions: Essays on Latin American, Caribbean and Continental Culture and Identity*. Bowling Green, OH: Bowling Green Popular Press.

Santa Cruz, Eduardo. 1996. *Origen y Futuro de una Pasión: Fútbol, Cultura y Modernidad*. Santiago: Universidad Arcis.

Santiago, Silviano. 2002. *The Space In-Between: Essay on Latin American Culture*. Raleigh, NC: Duke University Press.

Schechter, John Mendell. 1999. *Music in Latin American Culture: Regional Traditions*. New York: Schirmer Books.

Silva, Osvaldo. 1985. *Civilizaciones Prehispánicas de América Latina*. Santiago: Editorial Universitaria.

Silverman, Susana Chavez. 2000. *Reading and Writing the Ambiente: Queer Sexualities in Latino, Latin American and Spanish Culture*. Madison: University of Wisconsin Press.

Skidmore, Thomas E., and Peter H. Smith. 2000. *Modern Latin America*. 5th ed. Oxford, England: Oxford University Press.

Sowell, Thomas. 1996. *Migrations and Cultures: A World View*. New York: Basic Books.

Spencer, Berkley A. 1991. "Understanding Latin American Underdevelopment and Tensions with the United States: A question of applying the right paradigm." Brigham Young University.

Stewart, Edward C., and Milton J. Bennett. 1991. *American Cultural Patterns: A Cross-Cultural Perspective*. Rev. ed. Yarmouth, ME: Intercultural Press.

Sunkel, Guillermo. 1994. "El Péndulo de la Cultura." In *Diálogos de la Comunicación*, no. 40.

Trompenaars, Fons, and Charles Hampden-Turner. 1998. *Riding the Waves of Culture: Understanding Diversity in Global Business*. 2d ed. New York: McGraw Hill.

Valdés, Teresa, and Enrique Gomariz, coords. 1995. *Latin American Women: Comparative Figures*. Santiago: FLACSO.

Valdés, Teresa, and José Olavarria, eds. 1998. *Masculinidades y Equidad de Género en América Latina*. Santiago: FLACSO.

Valenzuela, Eduardo, and Carlos Cousiño. 2000. "Sociabilidad y Asociatividad: Un Ensayo de Sociología Comparada." *Estudios Públicos* (Santiago), no. 77 (Summer): 323–34.

Varas, Augusto. 1981. "Cultura y Poder en el Marco Geopolitico de Latinoamericano." Santiago: FLACSO, Documento de Trabajo, no. 111.

Varese, Stefano. 1996. "The Ethnopolitics of Indian Resistance in Latin America." *Latin American Perspectives* 23, no. 2 (Spring): 58–71.

Wagley, Charles. 1968. *The Latin American Tradition: Essay on the Unity and Diversity of Latin American Culture*. New York: Columbia University Press.

Waldmann, Peter, and Ulrich Zelinsky. 1984. *América Latina: Síntesis Histórica, Política, Económica y Cultural*. Barcelona: Herder.

Whyte, William F., and Allan R. Holmberg. 1956. "The Contrast of Cultures: United States and Latin American." *Human Organization* (Fall).

Willems, Emilio. 1975. *Latin American Culture: An Anthropological Synthesis*. New York: Harper and Row.

Winn, Peter. 1999. *Americas: The Changing Face of Latin America and the Caribbean*. Updated ed. Berkeley, CA: University of California Press.

Yudice, George, Juan Flores, and Jean Franco. 1992. *On the Edge: The Crisis of Contemporary Latin American Culture*. Minneapolis: University of Minnesota Press.

Zea, Leopoldo, coord. 1993. *América Latina en sus Ideas*. México City: Siglo Veintiuno Editores.

Zemelman, Hugo. 1996. "Pensamiento, Política y Cultura en Latinoamérica." In *Revista Latinoamericana de Estudios Avanzados* (Venezuela), no. 1: 115–34.

Part II

Diversity and Divergence among the Spanish-Speaking South American Nations

Introduction

If any single word could sum up the Spanish-speaking South Americans (SSSAs), it would be *contrast:* contrasts of race, class, gender considerations, linguistic patterns, historical privileges, and current realities, to name but a few. To this already complex mélange will now be added yet another type of contrast: national differences. An examination of national differences serves our purposes for several reasons. Because citizenship is the primary criterion that most people use to distinguish among the SSSAs, it is important to have a relatively accurate picture of what these national traits include, both for the holders themselves as well as for others.

For visitors to the region, awareness of national differences in the SSSA context can be very helpful in understanding many aspects of SSSA cultural patterns and behaviors as well as some of the intraregional dynamics. The study of national differences also serves as a portal through which other very important aspects of the nine SSSA societies can be approached, aspects such as levels of development, economic dynamics, social structures, and communication styles.

What follows is a brief look at each of the SSSA countries, with special attention given to what makes each of them different from the others in the region, particularly in cultural and social aspects. The intended purpose of the country chapters in this part is not to provide extensive background information on the history, economics, and/or politics of the countries, themes that would involve many more pages than are possible here and that have already been written about in English, for the most part. Neither is it to be a type of "guidebook" to the countries of the region, a genre within which there is no lack of material available. Rather, the aim is to provide in a few brush strokes, in straightforward language, a feel for each of the countries, a sense of what it means to be, for example, an Argentine or a Colombian or a Bolivian.

The country chapters will be presented in alphabetical order, although such an ordering is not the most valid from either a geographical or a cultural standpoint. Although numerous different subdivisions of the SSSA countries can be made, the most common is to divide the nine nations into three distinct groups. The first is made up of Venezuela and Colombia, the two SSSA nations that have coastlines along the Caribbean Sea; these countries are notable for having the largest black populations of the region, as well as for their many citizens who exhibit a rather "tropical" approach to life, especially those who reside in the coastal areas. Moving along the Pacific flanks of the continent is the second subgroup, the Andean nations of Peru, Ecuador, and Bolivia. These three countries have the largest Native American populations, and although they were the most important centers of the region during and before the colonial era, their current levels of development measured according to standard economic scales are lower than most of the rest of the SSSA nations. Further south are the so-called "Southern Cone" nations of Argentina, Uruguay, Chile, and Paraguay. These countries today are members of the regional trade organization, MERCOSUR (Chile is an associate member), along with Brazil, and are considered to be the "most European" and "least Indian" of the continent. In the case of Argentina and Uruguay, this is indeed true, but Chile and, particularly, Paraguay have significant mestizo and indigenous populations. Nonetheless, the dominant cultural patterns of these southernmost nations of the hemisphere are decidedly more Caucasian than Native American.

Each of the country chapters will follow the same format: all begin with a brief look at the most important geographical features of the country and then move to an examination of several key cultural characteristics that serve to define and delineate many of the mores of the nation's residents. Communication patterns, including both verbal and nonverbal aspects, will also be discussed and, finally, the chapters close with a summary about what it is like to live and work in that country.

Argentina: Tangos and Cafes

Skye Stephenson

Ser algo que nadie puede definir...un argentino.
—Jorge Luis Borges

To be something that nobody can define, an Argentine.

Although Argentina is the largest Spanish-speaking South American (SSSA) nation, bordering half the countries of the region, many contend that it does not truly belong where it is geographically situated. They say that it should be in Europe instead. Judging by surface appearances, this seems to be true. The populace* is the second most "European" of the SSSAs both ethnically and culturally, leading to a popular description of an Argentine as "someone who gestures like an Italian, talks like a Spaniard, is educated like a French person, and copies British fashion." The nation's capital, Buenos Aires, is commonly referred to as the "Paris of the Americas" because of its notable resemblance to the Gallic city.

* Actually, Uruguay has the most European populace, with Argentina following closely behind. Throughout this chapter, many comments made about the Argentines also apply to the Uruguayans, since the two nations have much in common both ethnically and culturally due to similar historical experiences. Nonetheless, there are significant, and noteworthy, differences between them as well, particularly in the political arena (see chapter 17, "Uruguay: The Buffer State," for more details).

More familiarity with the nation and its people begins to reveal the fallacy of this widely held supposition. Argentina today is definitely not a European country, and the belief (or, for some, fervent hope) that it is has played a key role in its current woes, inculcating a seemingly perpetual identity crisis at both the micro- and macrolevels. It also serves to make the country among the most puzzling and enigmatic of the region; many of the events that appear to spring spontaneously from Argentine soil surprise and, at times, appall observers and participants alike.

The Argentine saga seems almost unbelievable. How could a country with some of the most fertile lands anywhere and a populace that is among the best educated in the region fare so badly? Many economists, political scientists, and sociologists have thrown up their hands in defeat trying to "fit" the Argentine phenomenon into any conventional model. Even the Argentines, among the most articulate of the SSSAs, find it a tall task to make sense of their own homeland. Perhaps the legion of acclaimed Argentine writers, such as Jorge Luis Borges, Julio Cortázar, Ernesto Sábato, and Adolfo Bioy Caceres, come the closest in their myriad stories of apparently fantastic dimensions. As one literary critic put it, "To write fantasy literature in Argentina is the surest way to present reality" (Teitelbaum 1998, 97). Consider the following:

- Argentina began the twentieth century with a higher per capita income than Canada but finished it with a per capita income on a par with Chile's.
- Despite the fact that Argentines (along with the Uruguayans) are the best educated and have the largest middle class of the SSSAs, a peaceful transfer of political power between two civilians of differing parties did not occur in twentieth-century Argentina until the 1980s.
- Argentines number among the most secular and least religiously devout of the SSSA nations; nonetheless, their way of relating to important national figures often borders on the reverential, as can be noted in their treatment of the Peróns as well as many other individuals throughout their history.

How can we approximate a more incisive understanding of both the glamour and the pain that is Argentina? In this chapter, we will make an attempt, looking at the geographic and regional influences, keys to Argentinean culture (including the theater of life, the tango, and the zero-sum game), communication patterns, and the Argentine workplace.

Geographic and Regional Influences

The eighth largest nation in the world, Argentina is truly a land of superlatives within whose continental borders can be found a wide variety of terrain and climatic conditions. If its alleged Antarctica territory is also included, which ostensibly extends all the way to the South Pole,[†] then there is even greater diversity.

The country's northeastern regions are sultry and humid, with rivers a prime feature. Argentina, Paraguay, and Brazil all claimed this area in earlier eras, and it was the site of several belligerent confrontations, including the infamous War of the Triple Alliance. These days, however, the three neighbors cooperate in numerous ways, including sharing access to the world-famous Iguazú Falls as well as to the electricity generated at the enormous Itaipù Dam located nearby.

Argentina's western flank is dominated by the soaring peaks of the Andes Mountains, the second highest mountain chain in the world. Its long border with Chile is delineated by the highest points of these mountains, which serve as a looming barrier between the two neighbors, reinforcing separateness rather than commonality. Located just inside the Argentine border is Mount Aconcagua, the tallest mountain in all the Americas.

---

† Argentina, along with neighboring Chile, both claim large wedges of the Antarctic, based on their geographic proximity. Argentina has gone so far as to arrange for a woman to give birth at their base, thus enabling them to say that Argentina is the only nation to date that has had a national actually born in the "white continent."

The country's northwestern corner abuts Bolivia. These two nations, which seem so different, were in fact jointly ruled during the colonial era. Previous to the European incursions, this was part of the Inca empire, and even today there is a larger percentage of indigenous people here than anyplace else in the nation.

Argentina's southern realms have a markedly different physiognomy; Patagonia and, below it, Tierra del Fuego are flat and low-lying, a windswept and frigid domain that seems to bring out the hardiness in both people and wildlife. The southernmost city in the world, Ushuaia, is located here, as is the only continually moving glacier in South America, Perito Moreno. Although sparsely populated, this area has been a bone of contention between Chile and Argentina for more than a century; the two countries almost went to war over control of a part of it as recently as the 1980s. Luckily, such parrying appears to be a thing of the past since recent diplomatic initiatives have resolved all the outstanding border disputes to the satisfaction of both parties.

Despite Argentina's incredible geographic diversity, for many the nation is synonymous with the pampas, those grassy prairies located smack in the center of the country. These lands, among the most fertile in the world, make up only about one-quarter of the national territory but are the home of three-quarters of all the Argentines, about twenty-seven million people. The pampas are also the country's greatest treasure. The livestock and crops that flourish here are Argentina's most important source of revenue, as they have been ever since cattle and horses were first introduced during the early colonial period. However, the significance of the pampas extends far beyond the demographic and economic. These lands seem to have worked themselves into the Argentinean soul, and it is truly impossible to understand the contemporary Argentines without taking these seemingly endless and forever bountiful lands into consideration.

At the most basic level, the Argentines seem to personify the pampas' spaciousness in their own communication style; they are renowned for their wide gait, uninhibited movements, and straightforward gazes. Argentines' eating habits also reflect the abundance of the pampas; they are the greatest consumers of beef anywhere, and many claim that Argentinean beef is the best in the world. The Argentines' carnivorous diet seems to affect their physiognomy, making them taller and broader on average than most other SSSAs, characteristics that may contribute to their resounding success in soccer and other competitive sports. Unfortunately, Argentines also have high rates of digestive disorders and heart disease, which many claim are due to their dietary patterns.

Some allege that the apparent limitlessness of both the land and the sky in the pampas imbues the Argentines with the sense of solitude one feels as an apparently minuscule human dwarfed by the dimensions of the terrain. As Ezequiel Martínez Estrada, in his seminal work, *X-Ray of the Pampa,* puts it,

> The vastness of the horizon, which always looks the same as we advance, as if the whole plain moved along with us, gives one the impression of something illusory in this rude reality of the open country. Here prairie is expanse, and expanse seems to be nothing more than the unfolding of the infinite within, a colloquy of the traveler with God.... It is the pampa, the land where man is alone, like an abstract being that will begin anew the story of the species—or conclude it. (1971, 7)

This metaphysical inclination is expressed through secular queries and a deep-seated search for some sort of meaning and purpose in life that extends beyond the material. As a general rule, Argentines are natural philosophers, and nearly all have an ability to express abstract ideas with a force and clarity that astound many an outsider. Indeed, some of the most thought-provoking Spanish-language writers of various genres are Argentines. One of them, Ernesto Sábato, wrote, "The weight of the infinitude of the pampa invites one to create myths, like the Russian steppe" (Teitelbaum, 261).

Some claim that this metaphysical tendency can be carried to an extreme, making many Argentines more concerned with the abstract and suprareal than with the concrete realities of their own daily life. One such critic is the acclaimed Argentine author Julio Cortázar, who described the main character in his renowned novel *Hopscotch* as follows: "He would not defend himself with the rapid and anxious accumulation of culture, the favorite dodge of the Argentine middle class to avoid facing national reality, or any other reality for that matter, and to think [of] themselves as safe from the emptiness surrounding them" (Cortázar 1966, 19).

Another criticism commonly raised regarding the pampas' influence on the Argentine people is that their sheer fertility is as much a curse as a blessing, inculcating a sense that resources can be had without excessive exertion of time or effort, which leads many to opt for the easy way. After all, if a decent living can be had by partaking of the pampas' abundance, then why work any harder? This nonchalant attitude toward work and planning helps to explain, at least in part, why the pampas have never been as efficiently or productively exploited as they could be.

On the eastern fringe of the pampas, fronting the Atlantic Ocean, is the province of Buenos Aires, the most populated and economically important of the country's twenty-three provinces. The city of Buenos Aires is the nation's capital, with a population of twelve million, which makes it not only the most important city in the nation but also the biggest city in SSSA and the tenth largest in the world. Despite its size, the city feels spacious and open, like the pampas; its principal avenue, the 9 de Mayo, is reputed to be the widest in the world, measuring 450 meters (1,476 feet) across. The city was justifiably named for the *buenos aires* (good airs) that blow through it. Despite urban traffic and congestion, there is little pollution.

What Buenos Aires does have is humidity, due to its location on the sea and its proximity to the Río de la Plata. This all-important river marks the city's northern boundary, and it seems to mirror the pampas' expanses, since it is the widest river in the world. Even on the clearest of days, it is impossible to see the opposite shore, where the Uruguayan city of Colonia is located.

Buenos Aires' port location has played a key role in much of the city's and, indeed, the nation's history. In popular language, the residents of Buenos Aires are nearly always referred to as *porteños*, from the Spanish for "port," which is *puerto*. Like many other port city residents, porteños are famed for their openness to foreign ideas and peoples, cosmopolitan ways, and fast pace. Many also contend that porteños can be pompous and snobbish; actually, porteños are probably the least liked group in the continent, and jokes abound regarding their alleged self-aggrandizing ways.

Many associate the Argentine exclusively with the porteño, a stereotype that does not do justice to the Argentines' linguistic and cultural diversity but does reflect quite accurately national dynamics, for the porteños are wont to exert their power over the *provincianos* (people from the provinces). This dynamic began in the late colonial era, when Buenos Aires was designated capital of the newly created Viceroyalty of Río de la Plata in 1776. Previously, the entire area had been a dependency of far-off Peru, and all trade had to be conducted through Lima, a policy that favored the interior cities and encouraged a booming contraband trade along the Atlantic coast. When Buenos Aires became the capital and the city began to prosper, many of the elites from the interior regions began to resent this upstart city and its inhabitants who were eclipsing their power. Independence intensified these tensions, and centralist forces and regional strongmen fought bitterly for nearly half a century until the issue was finally resolved in favor of Buenos Aires.

Today, power and control in Argentina are apparently quite centralized; the issue of regionalism has not reared its head for more than a century. Nonetheless, the extended conflict, with its accompanying distrust and even dislike between porteños and provincianos, is one of the causes for contemporary Argentina's notably weak sense of "nationhood." While there are certain specific events such as World Cup soccer that serve to unite the Argentines, at a more fundamental level the Argentine people are not sure what exactly it means to be an Argentine and often find it extremely challenging to figure out how to work together for the betterment of their nation.

Keys to Understanding the Argentines

The Theater of Life

The saying "Life is but a stage" fits Argentina perfectly, since much of its national history seems to be a series of vignettes of heroic and, oftentimes, tragic dimensions with charismatic leading characters. The Argentine people, for the most part, have often gravitated, whether in admiration or loathing or perhaps a combination of the two, to these strong personalities, as if searching for something that transcends the merely mundane in their connection with these seemingly "superhuman" figures. This penchant for the theatrical is concretely demonstrated in a deep and abiding love for the theater and cinema that characterizes most Argentines. Sometimes, the boundary between the actual stage and the national stage is hard to define.

Such theatricality began even before Argentina was a nation. During the colonial era, the nascent Argentines successfully defended themselves against British incursions in 1806. Empowered by their victory, they were the first to declare their independence from Spain. Led by General José de San Martin, the nation's greatest hero, the Argentines won their independence and then moved on to help Chile and Peru with their struggles.

In the newly won Argentinean terrains, three very different groups coexisted, oftentimes uneasily: the landed aristocracy, the gauchos, and the Indians. The owners of large landholdings had enormous ranches, known as *estancias*, which could reach thousands or even, in some cases, hundreds of thousands of acres in size, many having been granted as rewards for military actions. Most of these elite landholders tried to extract as much from their rural holdings as possible with the least personal expenditure of energy, opting, when feasible, to spend their time in Buenos Aires or, better yet, Europe, enmeshed in the affairs of high society. The Spaniard José Ortega y Gasset made the following comment, based on his observations of some of these Argentine aristocrats in the Old World: "The Argentine is a marvelously gifted man…who has never devoted himself to the activity he carries out, who has never accepted it as his vital goal, who never considers it to be definitive but a rather transitory stage on the way to his idea: advancement in wealth and social status" (1983, 188). It is said that many contemporary Argentines, whatever their social status, exhibit this characteristic, dedicating themselves more to a sophisticated social life than to hard work.

The gauchos who resided in the unfenced regions had a very different lifestyle—an almost nomadic existence, unfettered by possessions and even family in many cases. The wild horses and cattle that proliferated in the pampas provided the gauchos with nearly everything they needed: transport, sustenance, and even shelter. Corn, when available, and the ever-present *yerba maté*, or "maté tea," augmented their predominantly carnivorous diet. Each gaucho was truly a law unto himself, shunning restrictions or rules of any type:

> …independent, brave, athletic, a bold warrior, and loyal…. Of all these idealized qualities, personal independence was perhaps the most important—acting solely of one's own free will and being willing to stand up and take the consequences. To take orders from somebody else was considered undignified and weak." (1999, 2, www.invertir.com/argentina)

Although present-day Argentina was not heavily populated at the time of the Spaniards' arrival, there were at least ten different Indian tribes inhabiting the region. In fact, the first European attempts to settle Argentina were roundly thwarted by the local Indians, and it took several expeditions before the area that was to become Buenos Aires was successfully colonized.

Even centuries later, during the independence era, Indians made up about half of the entire Argentine populace; recent scholars have suggested that the original gauchos probably spoke the Indian language Guaraní as their mother tongue. Today, very few of these Argentine Indians survive, fewer than 100,000 in total. While some merged into the mainstream populace through *mestizaje*, many more were exterminated in the nineteenth century by caudillos and their gaucho soldiers, who sought to "free" the lands of Indians so that they could be more "productively used."

Despite their active participation in the Indian campaigns, by the late nineteenth century the gauchos were faring only a little better than the Native Americans, usually being looked on with disdain by their more settled contemporaries. The increasing encroachment of "civilization" into the outlying parts of the pampas occasioned the demise of the gauchos' freewheeling ways. Some remained in the rural areas, adjusting their lifestyle by becoming more "settled cowboys," while others drifted to the cities where they eked out a meager living, oftentimes as butchers at the many slaughterhouses.

Today, the gaucho memory is revered much more than the actual gaucho ever was in his heyday. He is the central character of national folklore and is oftentimes presented in a very romanticized way, lauded for all that he was once criticized for. The gaucho's independent ways and his disdain for any type of authority are commonly cited as his most endearing characteristics, and many contemporary Argentines, most of whom have no gaucho ancestry, nonetheless seem to manifest a similar inclination to exert their will whenever possible, oftentimes with little regard for rules and their enforcement. In contrast with most other SSSAs, Argentines, for the most part, shun taking orders and will try to make it appear, whenever possible, that they take orders from no one, even if the actual reality may be quite different. Argentine sociologist Guillermo O'Donnell has dubbed this the "intolerable equality of Argentine society" and uses the example of traffic behavior to demonstrate how it works.

> In the United States, traffic lights are respected and the general rule of entering a busy intersection is that the driver who arrives there first, enters first. In Argentina, in contrast...the rule is that if there is no policeman in sight, each person should go first, which involves impeding that the other person passes... the result is that the cars that are crossing advance until they almost crash....taking advantage of the most minimum vacillation to enter the onslaught....resulting in monumental inefficiency, fights, insults and other crude gestures. (1985, 10)

During the same period that many Indians and gauchos were meeting their demise, a new and very different character entered the Argentine scene: the European immigrant. The increased exploitation of the pampas, combined with technological changes that enabled Argentine beef to reach European markets, fueled an economic boom that propelled the country into the ranks of the wealthiest of the world. For many Europeans, relatively sparsely populated and increasingly prosperous Argentina functioned like a magnet, drawing them to try their luck. Between 1857 and 1926, more than six million such immigrants arrived in Argentina. Italians, primarily from northern Italy, composed the largest group, numbering about three million, followed by the Spaniards, at about two million. The remainder was made up of numerous nationalities including Polish, Turkish, French, Russian, Austro-Hungarian, and German.

Many arrived hoping to acquire land in the pampas, but most found that despite the country's vast expanses, there was little to be had, since most of the best land had already been apportioned. Interestingly, the immigrant group that had the most success obtaining rural holdings was the Jews. Prior to the rise of Zionism, influential Western European Jews, spearheaded by the Rothschild family, had the idea of creating Jewish agricultural colonies where there were "empty lands" to provide a new and more secure home for some of the Eastern European Jews then encountering severe antisemitism. Various sites around the world were considered, and Argentina was selected as the best. Jewish philanthropic organizations purchased large tracts at various sites in Argentina, and European Jews soon began arriving at these agricultural colonies, leading to the incongruous phenomenon of Yiddish-speaking gauchos! Several of these colonies functioned successfully for decades; over time, however, most of the colonists and/or their offspring ended up moving to the cities, where many became professionals. Today, there are more than half a million Jews in Argentina, giving the country the largest Jewish population in SSSA and one of the most significant in the world.

The vast majority of the newcomers ended up in the cities, especially Buenos Aires, which had a population that was over three-quarters foreign-born during the height of the immigration. One can imagine what Buenos Aires must have been like during this era, with its polyglot of languages, teeming tenements, and interface of cultures. These immigrants, for the most part, had a very different attitude toward life and work than the native Argentines did; they were desirous of improving their lot and willing to work long hours at whatever work was available to achieve their goals. Aristotle Onassis was one of the luckier ones; his initial fortune was made in Argentina as a youthful Greek immigrant.

Even though only half of the immigrants, about three million in total, remained permanently in Argentina, at the time they far outstripped the number of native-born Argentines, which was only about one and a half million. In concrete terms, this meant that Argentina during the heyday of immigration inflows had a population that was decidedly more than one-half foreign-born, a percentage that far surpasses anything that ever occurred in the United States.

The impact of these Europeans on Argentina cannot be overemphasized; they transformed the country in many ways, playing a large role in forging the modern-day nation. Through both demographics and hard work, the immigrants contributed to making Argentina the primarily middle-class society that it is today. After Uruguay, Argentina has the flattest social structure in the region, and social mobility occurs more often here than in most of the rest of the region. The nation's strong public education system, which reaches all the way to the university, was created primarily at the urging of the immigrants. It has helped many talented youth "rise up" from meager family circumstances to positions of importance.

The European influence can be noted in many other aspects of Argentine life and culture—in the nation's architecture and urban layouts, for one. Most Argentine cities and towns, most notably Buenos Aires, look and feel much like France, Spain, or northern Italy. And just like Mediterranean Europe, cafes are omnipresent throughout Argentina, no matter the size of the city or town. These public places for meeting and chatting are usually chock-full of people simultaneously sipping coffee, oftentimes smoking, and discussing politics, art, philosophy, and life in general.

Of all the immigrant groups, Italians predominate; their influence is most notable in contemporary Argentina, which some claim almost seems like a transplanted Italy. Like the Italians, the Argentines are renowned for their sense of style, and Buenos Aires is considered the fashion capital of the region. Image is important here, and both men and women are known for the attention they give to personal appearance and presentation. Also like the Italians, the Argentines have a deep appreciation and reverence for the arts in all forms. The Italian influence is ever present in the national cuisine as well. Almost as ubiquitous as beef are pastas, pizzas, and Italian-style pastries and gelatos. Some say that the Italian flair can even be seen in the nature of male-female relationships: Argentine men can be quite assertive in their pursuit of women, and are renowned as true romantics. They are also typically more willing to roll up their sleeves and help with the cooking than many other SSSA males are.

Although the local elite welcomed the sorely needed labor provided by the immigrants, they were nonetheless deeply concerned about the impact of these "hordes" on the nation, especially in the political arena. They were most worried about the supposedly radical ideas of the newly transplanted Europeans, many of whom were indeed familiar with the ideas of communism, socialism, and anarchism that were then in vogue among some sectors in Europe. As a consequence, the local Argentines prohibited all immigrants from participating in the nation's political life and strongly opposed the formation of any kind of labor organization. This meant that at least half of the productive adult population had no legitimate political channels through which to articulate their concerns, an outcome that contrasted sharply with what was happening in Uruguay, where under the leadership of President José y Ordóñez Batlle the nation became the continent's first welfare state, and in Chile, which had strong unions and leftist parties.

This disturbing reality goes far in explaining the phenomenon of Juan Domingo Perón, the most significant as well as the most controversial character in twentieth-century Argentina. The Perón saga is so spellbinding and, at times, so seemingly implausible that it has provided the raw material for many a story, novel, and play; the most well known, is, of course, Andrew Lloyd Webber's musical *Evita.*

Perón came from the military ranks. He emerged into national prominence in 1944, when he parlayed his supposedly unimportant position as Minister of Labor during a period of military rule into a personal power base by permitting labor to organize under his banner, thus ensuring their unflinching support. He rapidly became so popular among the marginalized sectors of Argentine society that all efforts to stall his rise to power, which included jailing him, proved ineffectual. In 1946, he was democratically elected president. During his term, he accomplished a considerable amount: changing the direction of national policy, stressing indigenous industrialization, and focusing government attention and resources primarily on the lower classes in the urban areas. Organized labor swelled in number from 400,000 when he took office to more than four million only three years later.

His new wife, former actress Evita Duarte, had a higher profile than most presidents' wives. She dedicated herself to helping the disenfranchised, whom she called the *descamisiados* (shirtless ones), in a way revenging herself for the taunts she had received as an illegitimate child of humble origin. The couple's popularity came to border on the religious, and many considered them saintlike. Their critics were equally vociferous in their condemnation.

Perón handily won reelection in 1951, but his military supporters thwarted his bid for Evita to be his vice president. A year later, before she was even thirty, Evita died of cancer.‡ Perón's power declined from then on until he was removed by a military coup in 1955, by which time he had been excommunicated by the Catholic Church and discredited by many of his former supporters. By the time he was exiled, national revenues had fallen by about 70 percent during his nine-year tenure as president.

Despite his downfall from power and clear personal transgressions, Perón still remained wildly popular among many segments of Argentine society, leading to an ideological battle between those desirous of bringing Perón and his kind back to power and those bent on eradicating all traces of Peronism from Argentine society. A stalemate of sorts ensued. Attempts were made to call elections, but the Peronists, who were still the strongest political force in the nation despite their leader's exit, prohibited them from occurring. When the desired elections did not take place, Perón's opponents, who numbered among many of the Argentine elite as well as the military, intervened to "stabilize" the situation.

Finally, after two decades of such maneuvering, a decision was made to legalize the Peronist party and invite Perón himself back from exile in Spain. The intention on the part of his opponents was that the "real" Perón would finally disillusion his many and

‡ Evita's remains were embalmed, and their location changed several times for fear of the formation of a cult. The remains finally ended up in a cemetery in Europe, their location revealed only when one of the individuals involved in the transfer told the truth on his deathbed. Finally, Evita's remains were returned to Argentina and were reburied in the nation's most renowned cemetary, Recoleta. For a fascinating book on this macabre subject, see *Santa Evita* by Tomás Eloy Martínez.

increasingly ideologically diverse supporters, thus providing the framework for finally ridding the nation of Peronism once and for all. Perón returned to Argentina in the early 1970s with his third wife, dancer Isabel Martínez, and handily won the 1973 election with more than 70 percent of the vote. This time he got his way, and Isabel was designated his vice president. The ironic twist is that this time Perón was the one to die, just a short time after his victory.

Isabel took over the reins of Argentina, to become the first woman president in South American history. Unfortunately, she proved disastrously inept, with none of Evita's political savvy; her astrologer/adviser Jose Lopez Rega was the true power behind the scenes. During her short period as president, Argentina literally began to fall apart; inflation hit 335 percent and guerrilla violence increased dramatically. Finally, on March 25, 1976, a coup toppled Isabel's government.

Perón is not the only twentieth-century Argentine political figure to engender both love and loathing. Argentine-born Ernesto (Che) Guevara, the communist guerrilla and Castro's right-hand man who died in Bolivia during his ill-fated attempt to start a continental revolution, is another such mythic figure. His face can still be seen, decades after his youthful "martyrdom," emblazoned on many a poster, T-shirt, and on street graffiti throughout the world, and he is considered a true hero by many, whatever their actual political inclination may be.

Despite their ideological differences, both Perón and Guevara (though the latter fought under the Cuban banner) illustrate a very Argentine perspective on international affairs, which is that the region would do much better without the intervention and interference of outside powers, particularly the United States, whose inter-American policies have been and are still considered heavy-handed and self-serving. Accompanying this is the sense, or perhaps hope, that the Argentines themselves, due to their nation's size and level of development, should assume the mantle of regional leadership. This widely supported viewpoint helps to explain many of the actions of the country's leaders in the international arena over the decades, including the enmity of many of Argentina's leaders toward U.S. policies and plans for Latin America, the nation's program for developing nuclear weapons, and its recent participation in MERCOSUR, the regional free trade zone for the Southern Cone nations.

The Tango

For many Argentines, the most revered twentieth-century hero was not a politician, but a showman: tango singer Carlos Gardel, whose mysterious origins (some say he was born in France, while others contend he was Uruguayan by birth) and tragic death in an airplane crash at the height of his fame added to his mythic stature. This veneration seems most appropriate because the tango is so symbolic of Argentine culture.

The tango's origins reflect the nation's eclectic history. Its first appearance was in the brothels and other locations of ill repute in Buenos Aires and Montevideo; its unique sounds and rhythm were shaped by a variety of musical influences, including the Cuban *habañero* (a genre brought by Caribbean sailors who passed through the port), the music played by the local black Argentines known as *candombé*, the gaucho *milonga* sung in the rural areas, and the German concertina-like *bandoneon* instrument. The first tangos were solely instrumental and usually danced by two males or by a male with a female paid to accompany him. Most "decent" Argentines shunned this music as well as the people who played and danced it. All this changed in 1911, however, when the tango was introduced in Europe, where it became the rage. By this time lyrics and orchestral accompaniment had been added. Once the Europeans fell for the tango, mainstream Argentines began to reappraise it and soon embraced it as their own.

More than a century after its birth, tango music's popularity is still increasing not only in Argentina but throughout the world. There are dance schools on all continents dedicated to the teaching of its rather demanding footwork, so "Argentine" with its stylistic flair and slightly jaded air. The melancholic tonalities of the songs, with their common theme of loss—lost loves, lost hope, even lost lives—seem to poignantly express the Argentinean pathos. As Jorge Luis Borges put it, "I come from a sad country."

The Zero-Sum Game

Indeed, the Argentine people have much to feel sad about at both a personal and a collective level, due in large part to their own choices, which have been heavily influenced over the centuries by a "zero-sum attitude," a winner-take-all mentality in which all sides believe that they hold the "exclusive truth." Not infrequently, those in power have attempted to convince others with differing perspectives of "the truth" through strong-arm measures, leading to confrontational and often bloody clashes. As Alicia Frohmann, herself an Argentine of immigrant German-Jewish parents, puts it, "Argentina has an underlying violent streak that is terrible...it is hard to explain or put into words" (author interview 2000).

This approach reached its apogee during the eight-year period of military rule (1976 to 1984) that succeeded the overthrow of Isabel Perón. During these years the various military heads of state in their quest for a permanent solution to the nation's problems of hyperinflation, political instability, and homegrown groups using guerrilla tactics, waged war against all their opponents with a ruthlessness unmatched by any of the other authoritarian regimes then reigning in much of the region. While exact figures are hard to come by, somewhere between 20,000 and 30,000 Argentines, mostly young people between the ages of twenty and thirty-five, lost their lives during this period of terror. Innumerable others were arrested and tortured and/or had to flee into exile.

It was in Argentina that the Spanish word *desaparecido*, which means "disappeared," began to take on a specific meaning to describe individuals who were arrested by military forces and never seen again, with no trace of their whereabouts or remains. Many of the desaparecidos could never be located because they had been unceremoniously pushed from military aircraft into the cavernous Río de la Plata. While their physical bodies may be missing, memories of them are not. The mothers and grandmothers of many peacefully parade every Thursday morning, as they have for more than two decades, in front of the Casa Rosada, the Argentine presidential palace, asking what happened to their loved ones. Argentine Adolfo Perez Esquivel received the Nobel Peace Prize for his efforts on behalf of the many victims of this "internal war on subversion."

The Argentine military did not stop at defeating their internal enemies; they also turned their gaze outward, setting their sights on the long-contested Malvinas/Falkland Islands located two hundred miles off Argentina's coast but populated by staunch Brits known as Kelpers, most of whom originally came to these rather remote isles during the whaling era. Grossly miscalculating their international support and their own military prowess, the junta leaders launched an attack on the islands in the early 1980s, only to find themselves rapidly embroiled in a direct war with the United Kingdom. This time, in striking contrast to the colonial era outcome, the Argentines were soundly defeated, with over a thousand enlisted soldiers' deaths a tragic consequence.

While the military's blatant excesses seem to have inured the Argentines against new attempts at nondemocratic governance, a winner-take-all mentality nonetheless persists in the nation today, manifested primarily in the economic arena. Even though the country has far less corruption than neighboring Paraguay, payoffs and other types of shady financial transactions (such as not paying taxes, depositing undeclared capital in overseas accounts, speculating on the basis of insider knowledge, and using personal connections for profit) are nonetheless widespread, particularly on the part of those in positions of power. These Machiavellian maneuverings have played a large role in the nation's current economic woes.

The greatest irony of all is that this zero-sum attitude of key players over the course of Argentina's history has produced exactly what Argentines most feared: shrinking available revenues and fewer resources for all, an apparent anomaly in this land of plenty. Over the course of the twentieth century, Argentina fell from the sixth largest economy in 1924 to 63rd place in 2002, according to the Global Competitiveness Report of 2002–2003, a decline unmatched by any other nation. One Argentine comic has half-jokingly proposed that one possible solution to the nation's current economic crisis might be to hire themselves out as consultants on how not to run a country!

This harsh reality propels Argentines these days to look inward and to examine themselves as a people and a nation as they try to figure out what went wrong in the past and what might be done better in the future. The vast majority are deeply concerned and pessimistic regarding both their own future and their children's. This is especially true for many members of the large middle class, who have seen themselves slipping downward and don't know what to do to halt this slide. As someone said, the problem with contemporary Argentina is that it "has the income of the lower class and the taste of the upper class." This discontent and anomie may explain the exceedingly high rate of psychiatric visits in Argentina, reputed to be the highest in the world. Argentina also leads the SSSA nations in the number of suicides, a figure that has, not surprisingly, increased in recent decades.

Due to the many problems besetting their country, many children and grandchildren of immigrants who once left Europe to try their fortune in a more promising Argentina now want nothing more than to leave, oftentimes returning to the homelands of their ancestors. Others have chosen to forge new paths; in this regard the United States is a particularly popular destination. These days, the Miami area is chock-full of Argentines. Tomas Eloy Martínez, himself an Argentine residing in the U.S., describes this phenomenon: "We live jumping towards the outside world, leaving, which implies that whatever is within is inhospitable, hostile or, at the least, repels us. In fact, one of the few manifestations we seem to have of being Argentinean is, precisely, this uncomfortable feeling towards our own homeland" (1999, 17).

Communication Patterns

Argentine communication modes reflect much of the nation's history and cultural patterns. There is a marked theatricality in how many of the Argentines speak and gesture. Argentines also attempt to bring down barriers rather than erect them when conversing with others, in contrast with most of the other SSSAs. This reflects the nation's relatively middle-class social structure as well as its gaucho penchant for equality. Probably the best approach to understanding Argentinian communication patterns is to consider how conversations unfold at cafes, since much of the best of Argentine life transpires in these locales. Argentines are, for the most part, open and friendly in their linguistic style. "The Spanish of the Argentine is that of confidence, of the discussed friendship" (Argambide 1996, 104). Whenever possible, the informal rather than the formal second-person pronoun is used, even between people of different social classes and positions. In fact, one of the most distinguishing features of Argentine Spanish is an idiosyncratic variation of the informal *you*. Instead of using *tú*, they (along with the Uruguayans and Paraguayans to a lesser extent) employ *vos*,[§] modifying the verb declination as follows: the standard Spanish *tú tienes* (you have), becomes *vos tenés*.

Argentine Spanish has many other unique features. Due to the strong immigrant presence in Argentina, the contemporary language has incorporated some of the tonalities and even vocabulary of its myriad European ancestors. Not surprisingly, the Italian influence is most notable. Argentine Spanish has the lilt and musicality of the Italian language as well as some of its flamboyance. Argentines, for the most part, are extroverted and demonstrative when they speak, and their voices are often a notch louder than many other SSSAs. There are some pronunciation differences as well. For instance, the letters *y* and *ll*

[§] This form is a much-modified adaptation of an relatively archaic term *vosotros*, which was originally used as a formal second-person plural pronoun in Classical Spanish.

are said with an "sh" sound, rather than the typical "y" sound employed in the rest of the Spanish-speaking world.

There is even a special type of slang, known as *lunfardo*, that is characteristic of the porteños, although other Argentines also employ it. Lunfardo was created more than a century ago by urban ruffians to communicate their illicit activities without more law-abiding folks understanding them. They took terms from many of the languages then spoken in the tenements, including Genovese, French, and Yiddish, and oftentimes reversed the order of words to increase their cryptic nature. In time lunfardo was adopted by mainstream Argentines for colloquial use, and today there are entire dictionaries dedicated to lunfardo, which is continually changing with the addition of newly coined words and phrases. One of the newest is *trucho*, which was first used to describe a pirated CD or computer game but has now become a common term to describe a corrupt politician or businessperson.

There are many other uniquely Argentine words. Perhaps the most well known is *ché*, which is hard to translate accurately. It is employed as an exclamation in a variety of circumstances: to indicate interest, exasperation, and/or a desire to get attention. Another typical Argentine word that reveals much about the nature of life in the country is *bronca*.

> An Italo-Spanish fusion, like most Argentines themselves, the word [*bronca*] implied a fury so dangerously contained as to end in ulcers. People felt bronca when they waited for an hour to be served at a bank, and then the service was bad because the cashiers all had bronca too.... Everyone had bronca. [Even] the weather, with its cruel regime of heat and thunderstorms, had bronca. (France 1999, 58–59)

Living and Working in Argentina

While it is possible that some sojourners to Argentina will have episodes of bronca during their stay, occasioned by some of the complexities of daily life in the country, nonetheless the many positive aspects of life there will most likely more than compensate. Since Argentina is such an immigrant society, Argentines are more comfortable than many other SSSAs interfacing with peoples of different cultural backgrounds and linguistic skills; consequently, one feels less conspicuous there than in most of the rest of the region. In addition, Argentines often treat foreigners, at least those from English-speaking North America (ESNA) and Europe, better than their own compatriots, so some of the more trying aspects of Argentine society impact foreigners less than they do the natives themselves.

Argentines usually make a clearer distinction between visitors (based on nationality) than many other SSSAs do, and they are nearly always extremely well versed in the politics and cultures of other peoples and places. They typically call citizens from the United States "yanquis," pronounced "janquis." This term can be used both pejoratively or, as is more common, in a friendly way. People from other parts of the English-speaking world are usually addressed based on their national affiliation, such as *canadiense*, *australiano*, and the like.

Another arena in which the Argentines clearly demonstrate their sophistication is in their survival skills. Due to the numerous crises that have beset the country in recent years, nearly all have a finely honed ability to figure out how to best cope with whatever reality the nation is currently encountering and how to work the system to their own advantage. People planning to live and work in Argentina are well advised to acquire some of this Argentine savvy as soon as possible upon arrival. They should also acquire some knowledge regarding the fine line between paying tips to expedite matters (*propinas*), which is legal under Argentine law, and bribing (*coimas*), which is not, (but is nonetheless not uncommon in some circles). If a foreign businessperson has any doubts in this regards, it is always best to seek local advice.

Another distinctive feature of life in this largest SSSA country is the greater stress on individualism here than in most of the rest of the region, a cultural attribute that holds true in both the domestic and the business realms. Cross-cultural studies have corroborated this reality.[||] This means that Argentine employees, for the most part, are more comfortable working on their own and pursuing individual rather than group goals than are many of the other SSSAs.

Despite these cultural differences between the Argentines and others from the region, in many ways the Argentines are similar to their neighbors. Hierarchy is still important in the workplace, albeit to a lesser extent perhaps than in other places on the continent. For instance, it is not customary for higher management to mingle with the employees. The Argentines also seem to prefer a strong and charismatic leadership style, and a boss with a strong and colorful personality is usually more highly regarded than a lower-key and more collegial type of leader.

Argentina's time management is also markedly Hispanic. Even by regional standards, they are nocturnal folks. The Argentine workday typically begins and ends later than almost anyplace else on the continent; many executives schedule meetings as late as 8:00 P.M. Nightlife has very late hours as well. Restaurants often don't fill up until midnight, and many nightclubs don't start "rocking" until the wee hours of the morning.

Even more than in other SSSA countries, the correct attire, as mentioned earlier, is important in the Argentine business world, and how one presents oneself plays a large role in how one is perceived. Argentine business fashion tends toward the traditional for both men and women, the understated London style usually being preferred.

* * * * * * *

The Argentina that has entered the twenty-first century is very much a nation absorbed in figuring out what went wrong in the twentieth century and what might be done differently in the fu-

---

[||] In Geert Hofstede's well-known study of IBM business managers in over fifty countries, the Argentines were clearly the most individualistic of the SSSA nationalities.

ture, the depth of their current crisis forcing them perhaps more than ever in their history to confront themselves as a people and a nation, without illusions or delusions. Most Argentines today realize all too clearly that they are indeed SSSAs, not Europeans somehow transplanted to an uncivilized and inhospitable continent. Decades of political polarization and upheaval, economic decline, and military defeat emphatically remind them of this reality. Despite all their travails, however, the Argentines continue to number among the most sophisticated and intellectually competent of all the SSSAs, and with concerted collective action they have the potential to create within their borders a society that combines the very best of the New and the Old Worlds, thus achieving, perhaps differently from the future they once imagined, a truly heroic destiny.

References and Selected Bibliography

Aherns, Mario. 2000. *Argentina Tapestry*. Olympia, WA: Pampa Publishing.

Argambide, Pedro. 1996. *Ser Argentino*. Buenos Aires: Editorial Planeta.

Borges, Jorge Luis. 1988. *Labyrinths: Selected Stories and Other Writings*. New York: W. W. Norton and Company.

Borinsky, Alicia. 1993. *Mean Woman: Mina Cruel*. Omaha: University of Nebraska Press.

Calderon, Fernando, and Mario dos Santo, coord. 1990. *Hacia un Nuevo orden estatal en América Latina: Inovacíon cultural y actors socio-culturales*. Buenos Aires: CLASCO.

Catterberg, Edgardo. 1989. *Los Argentinos Frente a la Politica: Cultura Política y Opiníon Pública en la Transicíon Argentina a la Democracia.* Buenos Aires: Editorial Planeta.

Chatwin, Bruce. 1988. *In Patagonia*. New York: Penguin USA.

Cortázar, Julio. 1985. *Blow-up and Other Stories*. New York: Random House.

———. *Hopscotch*. Translated by Gregory Rabassa. Reprint, 1987. New York: Pantheon Books.

Crassweller, Robert. 1988. *Perón and the Enigmas of Argentina*. New York: W. W. Norton and Company.

Feitlowitz, Marguerite. 1999. *A Lexicon of Terror: Argentina and the Legacies of Torture*. Oxford, England: Oxford University Press.

Foster, William David, Melissa Fitch Lockhart, and Darrell B. Lockhart. 1998. *Culture and Customs of Argentina*. Westport, CT: Greenwood.

France, Miranda. 1999. *Bad Times in Buenos Aires*. Hopwell, NJ: The Ecco Press.

Gassett, José Ortega y. 1983. "El Hombre a la defensiva." In *Obras Completas*, vol. 2. Madrid: Alinza Editorial. Article originally published in 1929.

Levine, Lawrence W., Kathleen Quinn, and Frank Ortiz. 2001. *Inside Argentina from Perón to Menem: 1950–2000 from an American point of View*. Ojai, CA: Edwin House Publishers.

Martínez Estrada, Ezequiel. 1971. *X-Ray of the Pampa*. Translated by Alain Swietlicki. Austin: University of Texas Press.

Martínez, Tomas Eloy. 1999. *El Sueño Argentina*. Buenos Aires: Edición Planeta.

———. 1998. *The Peron Novel*. Translated by Helen Lane. New York: Vintage International.

———. 1996. *Santa Evita*. Translated by Helen Lane. New York: Vintage International.

O'Donnell, Guillermo. 1985. *Y a mi, que me importa? Notas sobre sociabilidad y politica en Argentina y Brazil*. Buenos Aires: El Centro de Esudios de Estado y Soceidad.

Partnoy, Alicia. 1998. *The Little School: Tales of Disappearance and Survival in Argentina*. Reissue edition. San Francisco: Cleis Press.

Plotkin, Mariano Ben. 2001. *Freud in the Pampas: The Emergence and Development of a Psychoanalytic Culture in Argentina*. Palo Alto: Stanford University Press.

Rock, David. 1989. *Argentina, 1516–1987*. Berkeley: University of California Press.

Shumay, Nicolas. 1993. *The Invention of Argentina*. Berkeley: University of California Press.

Sorensen, Diana. 1996. *Facundo and the Construction of Argentine Culture*. Austin: University of Texas Press.

Teitelbaum, Volodia. 1998. *Los Dos Borges*. Santiago: Editorial Sudamericana.

Thornton, Lawrence. 1991. *Imagining Argentina*. Reissue edition. New York: Bantam Books.

Vezzetti, Hugo. 1996. *Aventura de Freud en el pais de los argentinos: de Jose Ingenieros a Enrique Pichon-Riviere*. Buenos Aires: Paidos.

11

Bolivia: Rooftop of South America

Linda Greenow* and Skye Stephenson

El alma de estos montes se hace hombre y piensa.

—Franz Tamayo

The soul of these mountains is transformed into man and thinks.

In Bolivia, the Native American presence is more palpable than anywhere else on the continent, or perhaps in all the Americas. Approximately six of the eight million Bolivians are of Native American lineage. Almost half of the populace speaks the indigenous languages of either Quechua or Aymara as their mother tongue, many of these being monolingual speakers who do not know much Spanish at all. Perhaps it is not surprising then that for many non-Bolivians, this landlocked nation is synonymous with the indigenous world. Countless visitors to Bolivia come to the conclusion that they have found the "real" and "untainted"

---

* Linda Greenow is associate professor and chair of the Department of Geography at the State University of New York at New Paltz, where she teaches courses in geography and Latin American Studies. She has published articles and book reviews in such journals as *Journal of Historical Geography*, *The Professional Geographer*, and *Hispanic American Historical Review* as well as textbooks and textbook units for K-12 social studies. She received a Ph.D. in geography from Syracuse University and is currently codirector of a U.S. Department of Education Title VI grant for Latin American Studies at SUNY New Paltz.

America here. Others give a different interpretation to the strong indigenous imprint in Bolivia—imputing the nation's low levels of development (the lowest in the continent, according to most standard measurements) to their "Indianness," which they claim makes Bolivians somehow "less civilized." Sometimes, Bolivia is even used as a point of comparison by other Spanish-speaking South Americans (SSSAs) to demonstrate that at least they are better off than the poor Bolivians.

Both the excessively romanticized and the excessively denigrating visions of Bolivia are equally incorrect, because the cultural dynamics in this nation are more complex than either vision represents. Bolivia is much more than just its indigenous peoples, who themselves have been strongly influenced by the Spanish. The strong Spanish imprint is due in part to Bolivia's importance during the colonial era; also there are many Bolivians, including most of the national elite, who have little affiliation with the indigenous people.

It is probably this juxtaposition of the Native American and the Caucasian cultures in Bolivia that is its single most noteworthy cultural characteristic—the contrast between modern, Western lifestyles and the Quechua or Aymara traditions that are visible nearly everywhere. Although the people belonging to these two contrasting cultures may appear to be worlds apart, contact between them is frequent and intense, sometimes resulting in collision or conflict, and sometimes leading to cooperative interaction. This multidimensional cultural dynamic serves as the backdrop and ultimate point of reference for much of what occurs in this fourth largest of the SSSA countries. Consider the following about Bolivia:

- Bolivia was at one time the richest part of the Spanish empire but is now the poorest nation in South America, despite its important twentieth-century revolution that brought about a significant redistribution of resources and power among the country's citizens.
- Bolivia at independence was one of the larger of the SSSA countries, but in the ensuing period about half of its territory

was usurped by its neighbors, leaving Bolivia as one of only two landlocked nations on the continent.

- Bolivians are noted for their willingness to protest in order to achieve social change, and the country is even named after the eminent freedom fighter Simón Bolívar (1783–1830). However, when Ernesto (Che) Guevara attempted to launch a continent-wide communist revolution from Bolivia, he did not receive very much local support, eventually being hunted down and killed on Bolivian soil—an event that transformed him into a martyr for many around the world.
- Despite the clear Hispanic influence in Bolivian culture, Bolivians are reputed to be among the least "Latin" of all the SSSAs in temperament, and many have a rather introverted, reserved, and melancholy demeanor.

In this chapter, the following themes will be useful in getting to better know the lands and people of Bolivia: geographic and regional influences, keys to understanding the Bolivians, communication patterns, and living and working in Bolivia. The key cultural characteristics that will be discussed include the indigenous imprint, exploitation and revolution, and dignity and loss.

Geographic and Regional Influences

Altiplano. The heart of Bolivia's land and its people is to be found in the high and cold plateau known as the *altiplano*, which is located 4,000 meters (13,200 feet) above sea level in the western portion of the nation, nestled between the eastern and western ranges of the Andes Mountains and ringed by some of the highest peaks in the hemisphere. In this bleak and windswept terrain live 70 percent of all Bolivians, even though the altiplano makes up only 10 percent of the national territory. This contemporary demographic reality follows historical settlement patterns, for the altiplano has been one of the most important centers of human life in this part of the continent since long before the arrival of the Spaniards, despite its apparently inhospitable terrain and frigid climate.

The altiplano landscape, which has been described as "monotonous only to those unable to perceive its subtle and infinite variations of form and color, its rare intensity of light" (Anstee 1970, 55), seems to reverberate within many of the native people, imbuing them with characteristics that mirror the altiplano itself, such as a paucity of words and an austere and reserved manner. The zone's almost limitless vistas, both vertically and horizontally, can be awe-inspiring; and, when clear, the night sky is resplendent, providing some of the best views of the heavens to be found anywhere and giving the sensation that one can almost touch the stars. Perhaps this sensation of being a part of the celestial bodies themselves helps to explain the reputed mysticism of many Bolivians, most particularly those of Native American lineage. Bolivian healers and mediums of various types are famed throughout the continent for their wisdom and powers.

The zone's rugged terrain also contributes to making communication and transportation within Bolivia quite arduous in many places, thus reinforcing local affiliation and isolating many Bolivians, especially those residing in the rural sector, in a quite circumscribed area. Even though this isolation has changed somewhat in recent years, getting around Bolivia can be a challenge. Many Bolivians still do not venture far from their birthplace throughout their lives.

Crucial to life in the region is Lake Titicaca, which is located on the northern end of the plain and is shared between Peru and Bolivia. This lake is the second largest in South America and is the highest navigable body of water in the world. It acts as a very important climatic regulator in the altiplano by releasing humidity and warmth into the air during cold nights, thus contributing to a unique ecosystem which has permitted farming and raising livestock in this otherwise inhospitable area.

In fact, humans have exploited the area around Lake Titicaca for millennia, and several of the most important food products in the world today, including potatoes, corn, and the increasingly popular grain quinoa, are reputed to have their origins here. Currently, more than 250 types of potatoes and tubers of various types and colors are grown in the altiplano, forming the basis of most of the locals' diet.

The herding of llamas and alpacas is also central to the lifestyle of the native peoples here, providing them with wool, meat, milk, fertilizer, and draft labor. Vicuñas, wild animals related to the llama, and the alpacas, whose hair is considered among the finest in the world, also reside in the altiplano, as well as throughout much of the Andes. They had been hunted nearly to extinction but have made a comeback since being legally protected in the 1960s and are now the focus of experiments to provide poor farmers with supplemental income by shearing these wild animals on a scheduled basis.

Also important for understanding the centrality of the altiplano in Bolivian national life are the vast mineral reserves (most notably silver and tin) in many of the surrounding mountains, the exploitation of which has affected much of Bolivia's history.

Bolivia's largest city and de facto capital, La Paz, is located not far from Lake Titicaca. Located at an elevation of about 3,780 meters (12,500 feet), La Paz is the highest capital in the world. Above the city, at 4,018 meters (13,260 feet), is the airport, known appropriately as El Alto, which is the highest commercial airport in the world. Situated in a steep canyon 2,000 meters (6,600 feet) deep and ringed by numerous snowcapped mountains, including the famed Nevado Illimani, which is something of a cultural icon for all Bolivians, La Paz's topography is dramatic, to say the least.

The capital's human scenery can also be very dramatic, and the contrast between the indigenous and the European is omnipresent. Businesspeople and professionals go about their day as they do in many other cities around the world, but here they are alongside women of Quechua or Aymara descent who run the many stands that line the steep streets and busy plazas, selling products including a wide variety of local herbs and other items (such as llama fetuses) that are widely employed for both medicinal and ceremonial purposes.

Coca leaf is one of the most common of the herbs for sale at these stands and, indeed, throughout Bolivia.[†] This mildly narcotic plant has been employed from time immemorial by the locals to calm hunger, alleviate cold, and help with oxygenation. Many visitors to Bolivia soon come to appreciate the medicinal qualities of this herb, because it is one of the best remedies for altitude sickness, a quite common ailment for people not accustomed to living at such heights. Coca leaves can be consumed in one of two ways—as an herb tea, known as *maté de coca,* or by chewing the leaves, which is the preferred method of most locals. Many Bolivians of indigenous extraction chew coca leaves, and a coca break in many places in Bolivia is common practice.

Oriente. Bolivia, however, is made up of more than its fascinating altiplano region. In fact, Bolivia's greatest land area is not in the highlands but rather in the lowlands, a realm that is very different in both environmental and human characteristics. Lowland Bolivia is known as the *oriente*, because it lies in the eastern portion of the country, beyond the Andes Mountains. This area actually comprises about three-fifths of the country's territory, although only 15 percent of the population resides here. The oriente is a zone marked by diverse terrains that range from dry grasslands to tropical forests, through which numerous rivers course along their trajectories from their sources high in the Andes to their outlet into the extensive Amazonian or Río de la Plata waterway systems located further downstream.

Historically, the oriente has been of marginal interest to the dominant highlanders, although a war was conducted with neighboring Paraguay in the early twentieth century over control of the Chaco area, which lies along the two nations' borders and is among the most impenetrable and inhospitable terrains in the continent. However, the peripheral status traditionally accorded to the oriente has changed dramatically in recent decades, due in

---

† Cocaine and all such narcotic drugs are illegal in Bolivia, and a clear distinction is made by the Bolivian legal authorities between coca leaf and processed cocaine.

large part to the discovery of petroleum in the zone, which has led to oil and natural gas production, pipeline construction, and the concomitant growth and change that this brings about.

The capital of the oriente is Santa Cruz, which has now become the second largest city in Bolivia, thus significantly affecting the balance of power and influence between the highlands and the lowlands, both politically and economically.

> The expansion of Santa Cruz brought a profound change to national and regional power groups...for the first time in national history there existed an important source of economic and political power outside the traditional intermountain and valley regions, the old heartland of the pre-Columbian and post-Conquest populations. (Klein 1982, 254)

This marked shift in regional influence within Bolivia has served to exacerbate the already notable cultural and ethnic distinctions that have historically existed between the more indigenous highlanders, known euphemistically as *kollas*, and the lowlanders, called *cambas*, who are primarily mestizo or Caucasian in lineage. Such clear differences between residents from the two regions have led to certain stereotypes that each group has of the other, stereotypes that in some cases even extend into outright antagonism. One can easily visualize the cultural tensions between kollas and cambas, with the more traditional highlanders, secure in their historical preeminence, confronting the upstart, fast-paced culture of Santa Cruz.

> Within Bolivia, the highland kollas have developed stereotypes for the cambas. Kollas believe that cambas are arrogant regionalists. Cambas believe that kollas are slow-witted and backward. Cambas are joyful, while kollas, they say, are melancholic. Like most stereotypes, the ones that float around Bolivia are partly true but mostly fictitious, with all human varieties found in each region. In any case, each group feels somewhat alien in the other group's physical and cultural world. (Cramer 1996, 62)

Yungas and Valles. Finally, there are two smaller regions in Bolivia, the *yungas* and the *valles* (valleys), both of which form a transition zone between the highlands and the lowlands. The yungas lie just north of the altiplano and have a dramatic topography of extraordinarily steep slopes and canyons alongside narrow basins. Roads into and out of the area wind along the edges of cliffs and hairpin curves; and the route from La Paz to the yungas is so dangerous it has been dubbed "the road of death." On average, one or two people are killed on this route *every day* in traffic accidents, and the Inter-American Development Bank has classified it as the most dangerous road in the world.

These geographic realities have served to keep the yungas both remote and sparsely populated, transforming the area into a sort of refuge or frontier for hardy souls of various types. In the yungas reside many of the Bolivians of African ancestry who came here after their emancipation in search of warmer climates and available lands. In more recent times, thousands of landless peasants from the highlands have relocated here under government auspices as colonists. The region's isolation combined with good climatic conditions for the growing of coca have made it a magnet for a very different type of personality, the drug lord; and this part of Bolivia is one of the most important coca growing regions in the world today.

The last of Bolivia's regions is the valles, an area located in the middle of Bolivia and nestled between the altiplano and the oriente. This relatively compact zone is perhaps the most pleasant place to live in Bolivia from a climatic perspective, and its towns are popular vacation destinations for highlanders because of their Mediterranean-like climate in which it rains in the summer, instead of in the winter as it does in the highlands. Many crops are grown here, including olives, grapes, and wheat, and the success of commercial agriculture lends these towns an air of prosperity and natural abundance that is missing on the cold, bleak altiplano.

Keys to Understanding the Bolivians

The Indigenous Imprint

It is impossible to understand modern-day Bolivia without stepping back into the nation's precolonial history, for even more than in the other SSSA countries, it is the indigenous peoples and their cultures, as well as the legacy of the confrontation, conflict, and acculturation that occurred between them and the European colonizers, that shape much of the nation's current lifestyle and culture. Understandably, many Bolivians feel great pride in their nation's importance during both the pre-Incan and the Incan periods, and it is hard not to contrast the historical importance of the area during those times with its more peripheral status, at least from the standpoints of economic development and regional influence today.

Many of the indigenous peoples from the Andes region believed that life was created from Lake Titicaca, including the entire human race. The Incas traced their origins to this body of water as well; many people, both locals and visitors, claim that there are very powerful energies in the Lake Titicaca area and, indeed, throughout the entire altiplano. One Bolivian spiritual healer commented on this aspect of her homeland as follows:

> Most visitors to Bolivia do not realize the tremendous spiritual forces that are present in the altiplano; that is the reason that a lot of people get sick when they visit because the forces are too powerful for their bodies. What they need to do is to visit the magic groups when they first arrive, and learn how to protect themselves, then they will be fine.

Even before the emergence of the Incas in the twelfth century, the altiplano region had been a magnet for important civilizations, the most well known being the Tiwanaku empire that occupied this zone for nearly two millennia. The first reliable records of the Tiwanaku people can be traced back to around 1600 B.C., and the civilization reached its peak from the sixth century B.C. to the ninth century A.D., encompassing half of southern Bolivia as well as areas in present-day Peru, Chile, and Argentina. The capital of this far-flung empire was the city of Tiwanaku, located near the southern shore of Lake Titicaca. At its apogee, this city had more than twenty thousand residents, making it one of the largest in the world at the time.

In many ways the Tiwanakus' level of sophistication rivaled that of ancient Egypt. Many impressive stone buildings, sacred temples, and monuments were built, and stone blocks weighing as much as 145,000 kilos (160 tons) were hauled over long distances to the construction sites. Finished edifices were frequently gilded and covered in hieroglyphs that even today remain undeciphered. The Tiwanaku people also excelled in ceramics, textiles, and metalwork and had an extensive trading system that included settlements in the tropical lowlands to the east and along the Pacific coast to the west.

Nobody has ever been able to definitively explain why this dynamic civilization declined dramatically sometime around A.D. 900 Whatever the cause, however, by the twelfth century, when the Quechua-speaking Incas moved into this region and consolidated their control over it, they found a rival indigenous group from the west, known as the kollas, or Aymaras, occupying Tiwanaku, living among ruins they could not rebuild or even explain.

Eventually, the Aymaras were incorporated into the vast Inca empire, which at its height extended much further than the Tiwanaku empire ever did, reaching 2,500 miles from north to south. Nevertheless, during nearly the entire period of Inca domination, the Aymaras kept their language and culture intact because of their fierce and independent spirit. The cultural and linguistic differences between the Quechua- and the Aymara-speaking peoples persist in Bolivia today; about one million Bolivians, mostly residents of the northern portion of the altiplano, speak Aymara, and another three million speak Quechua.

While to many outsiders the lifestyle of many of these Bolivians of Native American lineage seems to be very "authentic," in point of fact even the most apparently Indian of the Bolivians live in a manner very different from that of their predecessors prior to the arrival of the Spanish; they incorporate elements of both the Native American and the European in their lifestyle and beliefs, giving rise to a cultural amalgam that is neither one nor the other. This dynamic is apparent in many aspects of life in the Bolivian highlands, including cuisine, medical practices, spiritual beliefs, and the clothing and hats worn by many altiplano females, which is a combination of certain European styles and traditional indigenous attire.

While there are clear distinctions (based on ethnicity, origin, residence, and lifestyle, etc.), among the Bolivians of Native American ancestry, they pale in comparison with those between Bolivians of primarily indigenous extraction and those of more European lineage. Just as in neighboring Peru, the Spanish colonists established a very hierarchical social and economic structure in Bolivia. A small number of Europeans and, later, Creoles held nearly total control, exploiting the labor of the Native Americans and frequently viewing them with disdain. In fact, during the centuries of colonial control, the Native Americans were even prohibited from using Spanish, thus crystallizing even more the already marked differences between the two groups.

In order to have a ready and inexpensive supply of labor, the Spanish colonial leaders revived and modified an Incan system of forced labor known as the *mita,* whereby indigenous communities were required to provide a certain number of laborers on a continuing basis and to pay for most of their upkeep and transportation. A parallel phenomenon was the growth of a semifeudal type of sharecropping system involving dispossessed Native Americans who were forced to provide labor and other services to the large landowners in order to obtain access to small plots of lands that were allotted them to raise their own food. By the mid-1800s, there were literally hundreds of thousands of *yanaconas* throughout highland Bolivia.

As a consequence of these economic and social dynamics, miscegenation was not as well accepted in Bolivia as in nearby Paraguay or other more peripheral areas of the Spanish colonies.

This situation reinforced the marked distinctions between the "red" and the "white" in Bolivia, differences that even now are still a predominant characteristic of Bolivian society. It has been said that many whites in Bolivia "perceive themselves as the embodiment of the best in Hispanic tradition, the refinement of European cosmopolitan cultures" (Morales 1992, 17). Given this European mindset, many Bolivians of Native American ancestry tend to be rather reticent with strangers and people they do not know very well, due in part to their centuries-long struggle to maintain their own way of life in the face of cultural imposition from the dominant elites.

However, the supposedly subservient and downtrodden position of Bolivia's Native Americans should not be overestimated. In fact, many of the indigenous Bolivians are quite politicized and can be very vocal in pushing for their rights and prerogatives in society, especially in recent decades. For instance, the market ladies of La Paz are quite powerful merchants in the local economy and have been described as

> redoubtable ladies [who] conduct much of the country's retail trade and are distinguished not only by their distinctive clothing but also by their political influence...(and) their reputation for sharp bargaining.... Their acquaintance with the general populace is wide, and they are strategically located to make known their discontent with policies and personalities of the regime currently in power. More than one government in recent decades has learned to its regret the danger of arousing the concerted opposition of the market women of La Paz. (Alexander 1982, 10)

The place of Indian culture in Bolivia's national identity has been seriously debated. On one side of the argument, Bolivian writers such as Alcides Arguedas, in the early twentieth century, acknowledged the country's indigenous roots and then blamed these people for many of Bolivia's difficulties. The indigenist school of literature, which developed in opposition to Arguedas' views, was spearheaded by Franz Tamayo and was based on the belief that Bolivia's true identity was to be found in the land and in Indian beliefs. A number of Bolivian writers and philosophers have followed Tamayo's lead and manifested, in various degrees, a respect and admiration for the indigenous core of Bolivia's culture and identity.

Whatever the official view of the Native American in Bolivia may be, it cannot be denied that much of what is considered most symbolic of Bolivia has strong indigenous roots. This is true of Bolivian music; its haunting melodies, dominated by woodwinds of various types, evoke the sounds of the wind and/or the spirit of the altiplano.

Bolivians are probably most famous for their beautiful woolen weavings and knitted goods, the typically muted earth tones of which also seem to reflect the tonalities of the altiplano region. It should not be surprising that these textiles are world renowned, for they have at least a three-millennia tradition. Nearly all the work that goes into the production of these pieces is done by hand, from the shearing of sheep, llama, or alpaca wool to the execution of the weaving or knitting.

Exploitation and Revolution

Economics is also key to understanding many aspects of contemporary Bolivian society, and in fact, Bolivia is in many ways the quintessential example of a nation made poor precisely because of its riches, in this case silver and tin. It is also a vivid case of blatant exploitation of laborers over the centuries, especially miners, that eventually led to a revolution in the mid-twentieth century that transformed many aspects of Bolivian national life.

Although Bolivia is now the poorest nation of SSSA, during the colonial era, this region was the richest of the Spanish colonies, due primarily to the extensive silver vein, the most important in all the Americas, located within its domains. A Native American called Diego Huallpa revealed the presence of this mineral lode to the Spanish in 1544, and a short while afterward, mining began in earnest. Located high in the Andes, in a zone of inhospitable climate and difficult access, the mineral riches nonetheless spurred the establishment of the city of

Potosí near the mine and brought about the consolidation of Spanish control throughout the entire Andean region. During the heyday of silver mining, Potosí was one of the richest and largest cities on the continent, with a population of more than 150,000. Silver from this area became an important source of revenue for the Spanish monarchy for over two hundred years, and even now in Spain the phrase "as rich as Potosí" is commonly used to describe something of great value.

While the Spanish and Creole overlords during the boom years had very lavish lifestyles derived from silver revenues, the living conditions of the many individuals who actually mined the vein were very poor, and their working conditions were horrendous, even by the standards of the era. Many of these laborers, mostly Native Americans, perished during their labors, due to sheer physical and mental exhaustion, accidents, and/or pulmonary silicosis. As a way of increasing the stamina of the workers, the mine owners encouraged the use of coca, previously the exclusive prerogative of the Inca nobles, in order to give the laborers additional stamina and to numb their physical pain. The following anecdote from a recent Latin American visitor to the Potosí mine (where tours are now available) illustrates how the locals remember the labor conditions during that period:

> I told my guide in Potosí that I had heard that so much silver had been mined in Potosí that it could have built a bridge entirely of silver from the mine all the way to Spain. My guide looked at me and replied that what is more important to remember is that so many people died working the mines that their bones, if laid end to end, would reach around the entire world several times!

By the mid-seventeenth century, the situation went from boom to bust as the silver lode was depleted simultaneously with the discovery of other sites rich in silver elsewhere in the Spanish colonies. Wealthy Potosí began an abrupt decline, and within a few short years it was a near ghost town, causing severe economic hardships not only for the residents of the mining city but also for the many people throughout the entire region who had provided food and supplies to Potosí. However, even with the decline in importance of the Potosí reserves, silver mining did continue in Bolivia, albeit at a slower pace, and it is still carried on in some places today.

Tin began to eclipse silver in importance in the early twentieth century, to become Bolivia's major export. In most cases, tin was found in the same region and oftentimes even in the same mines from which silver had been extracted. The exploitation of tin in Bolivia is linked with the name Patiño, a Bolivian family that at one time came to dominate more than half of all the nation's tin mining and was reputed to be among the wealthiest in the world. These days, natural gas and zinc are more important natural resource exports from Bolivia, and make up about half of the nation's export earnings.

The economic structures and social patterns created from the Bolivian mining development continued into the twentieth century. Although the mita practice was discontinued with independence, most of the miners continued to be indigenous people who worked under very exploitative conditions for a pittance. In the agricultural sector, vast disparities of land distribution were the norm, and the 1950 census showed that 92 percent of all arable land was in the hands of only 6.3 percent of landowners, who often cultivated only a tiny fraction of their lands.

All of these aforementioned factors—the legacy of mining and economic exploitation of all types, the blatant inequalities of resource distribution, the often interlinked issues of racism and classism—contributed to setting the stage for the all-important 1952 Bolivian revolution, which is considered to be among the most significant twentieth-century revolutions in the hemisphere, along with the Mexican and Cuban revolutions. This monumental event served to shake many structures and institutions in Bolivia and affected everyone in powerful ways.

The Bolivian revolution was a relatively bloodless one, peaceful and democratic in large part. It has been described variously as a "revolution in a hurry, revolution by proclamation, revolution without blueprint" (Herring 1968, 631). Spearheaded by reformist politician Victor Paz Estenssoro, who led a movement known as the Movimiento Nacionalista Revolucionario (MNR) that had the support of a broad coalition of labor groups, university students, and civilian groups as well as the national military police, the revolution resulted in many far-reaching reforms over the course of twelve years. Some of the reforms included extending suffrage to all adult men and women, nationalizing mines and evicting the tin barons, and carrying out an extensive land reform in which large landholdings were seized and turned over to landless workers, who were typically Indian. In addition, education and health care were made more accessible to Bolivians, especially in the rural sectors, increasing the nation's literacy levels from only one-third of the populace prior to the revolution to two-thirds by 1976.

Despite these laudable reforms, Paz Estenssoro and the MNR were not able to raise living standards or improve agricultural production as much as they had expected; by 1964 his government began to lose popularity and was deposed by a military coup. Now, more than three decades later, critics point out the many unmet goals of the revolution: Bolivia still remains the poorest nation in South America, and life for many Bolivians, especially those of Native American ancestry, is still precarious. Despite strides forward, racism is still deeply entrenched in Bolivian culture and society, and as some point out, "the Indian question has not been resolved: Bolivia's majority is still psychologically, socially, and legally bereft of full citizenship, and Hispanic elitism remains the dominant myth" (Morales, 29).

Even the working and living conditions of the miners, who were among the strongest supporters of the revolution, are far from ideal today. Several books, based in part on oral history, provide an interesting window into the world of the Bolivian miners. Especially well known are *Let Me Speak! Testimony of Domitila, a Woman of the Bolivian Mines* and June Nash's *We Eat the Mines and the Mines Eat Us*, which takes its title from a miner's saying. The novels of Julian Cespedes and Roberto Leiton also describe the exploitation of miners in some detail and the effects of the brutally punishing physical labor on the miners' lives.

Despite its many shortcomings, the Bolivian revolution did serve to partially free workers and peasants from the mind-numbing serfdom left over from colonial days, and it also raised both the volume of discourse and the complexity of social and political interaction. This legacy continues into the present, and political discussion is both heated and frequent, as are marches, demonstrations, speeches, strikes, work slowdowns, and other forms of more active political protest. Occasionally, curfews are imposed to maintain order. On Friday nights after work, many bars and restaurants are filled with students, workers, business associates, and friends (mostly men), noisily debating, discussing, and arguing about national politics over beer or drinks as part of *viernes de soltero* (bachelor's Friday night).

Dignity and Loss

At its deepest level, the Bolivian revolution was about gaining respect and dignity for the Bolivian nation and people, especially the poorer members of society, and for many who benefited from changes brought about by the revolution, especially the agrarian reform, "the return of their land has meant much more…than the improvement of their material lot…. It has signified a return to human dignity and has had immeasurable psychological effects, restoring the individual's estimation of himself, and making him feel that he belongs to his country" (Anstee, 51–52).

This sense of dignity is of particular symbolic importance for many Bolivians, not only because of the marked social and economic disparities within the nation but also because of their collective history of losses to their neighbors, which are vividly etched in the national psyche. In fact, Bolivia has had to cede territory to every one of its five neighbors, losing over one-half of its former territory since independence, which reduced the country to its current size of about one million square kilometers (625,000 square miles), and made it one of only two landlocked nations on the continent.

The first and most significant territorial loss was to Chile as a result of the disastrous War of the Pacific, which took place from 1879 to 1884. This war was fought over control of the arid Atacama Desert region, which belonged to Peru and Bolivia but was being exploited by many Chileans, as well as by British interests. Particularly coveted were the prized areas where nitrates were being extensively mined at the time.

In 1879, using the issue of supposedly unfair taxes levied by the Bolivians and Peruvians, the Chilean leaders, with their superior navy, launched an offensive against their two northern neighbors. In the end, the Chileans emerged as the decisive victors, gaining full control of the contested region. The Bolivians, for their part, had to accept the greatest losses, including not only the Atacama Desert region with its vast mineral riches but also their outlet to the Pacific Ocean. In this way, Bolivia became the landlocked nation that it is today.

To some extent, the Bolivian people have never totally reconciled themselves to this defeat, neither practically nor psychologically; even today, more than a century later, animosity toward Chileans is bitter. Even without control over coastal land, Bolivia maintains a navy that carries out its military exercises on Lake Titicaca, and national leaders continue to push for an outlet to the sea through diplomatic channels of various types.

In the ensuing years after the War of the Pacific, Peru, Brazil, and Argentina all usurped additional Bolivian territory, thus reducing the weakened country's size even more. Finally, tired of such pillaging, Bolivian leaders in the early 1930s decided to take the offensive. Shifting their attention to the remote, inhospitable, and never clearly demarcated Chaco area jointly held with Paraguay, they decided that expanding control in this zone could be another way to gain the ocean access they longed for, since the Atlantic Ocean can be reached via the Paraguay River that runs through the contested area. The rumor that there were important petroleum reserves located in the zone provided yet another incentive for Bolivian leaders to fight for the Chaco.

The Bolivians' initial calculations proved woefully incorrect, and the outcome of the three-year-long War of the Chaco (1932–1935) was devastating for the country. Not only did Bolivia lose its hoped-for access to the Atlantic Ocean, but it was also forced to cede a large amount of territory to Paraguay. It has been estimated that about 65,000 Bolivian soldiers perished as a result of this bloody conflict, a very high figure considering Bolivia's relatively small population. The impact of this war was even greater than its battle losses, however, because it transformed numerous aspects of the Bolivian nation, and many historians believe that it contributed in significant ways to setting the stage for the later revolution of 1952.

> Bolivia entered the Chaco War as a highly traditional, underdeveloped, and export-dominated economy and emerged from that conflict with the same characteristics. But it changed from being one of the least mobilized societies in Latin America, in terms of radical ideology and union organization, to one of the most advanced. The war shattered the traditional belief systems and led to a fundamental rethinking of the nature of Bolivian society. … From these perspectives, the Chaco War, like the War of the Pacific before it, would prove to be one of the major turning points in Bolivian historical development. (Klein, 187)

These territorial losses and the concomitant shrinking of national borders have all served to reinforce Bolivia's relative isolation. Its borders—extremely high peaks along the western border, the Amazon basin to the east, and the almost impenetrable Chaco to the south—make transportation into and out of Bolivia difficult, thus increasing the nation's appeal to individuals and/or groups looking for a safe haven. Among such characters can be counted Butch Cassidy (of *Butch Cassidy and the Sundance Kid* fame), reputed to have died there in 1911, as well as former SS Colonel Klaus Barbie, who lived in Bolivia for thirty years before he was eventually repatriated to France.

The most famous person to use Bolivia for clandestine activities was the communist revolutionary Che Guevara. This

Argentine was one of the principal figures in the Cuban revolution of 1959, and he fervently believed that the conditions throughout South America in the mid-1960s were "ripe" for a communist victory and that Bolivia was the ideal spot from which to launch this struggle. He and his band of guerrillas found out the hard way how mistaken their initial assumptions had been. Following the "Cuban model," they located their *foco* (insurgent group) in a remote rural area in Bolivia. Much to their dismay, they discovered that most of the local Bolivians were uninterested in participating in the communist struggle, perhaps due in part to their own revolution not so long before. To make matters worse, communication was nearly impossible with many of the peasants because a significant number did not speak Spanish—and nobody in Che's group spoke either Quechua or Aymara. With little local support, dwindling supplies, and infrequent (at best) communication with Cuba, Che and his band of insurgents became increasingly isolated. Eventually, they were discovered by the Bolivian military, and Che himself was shot and killed, his death transforming him into a heroic figure for many around the world.

These days, a very different type of extralegal character—the drug baron—is exploiting Bolivia's relative inaccessibility. In recent decades, Bolivia has become an increasingly important center of the drug trade, and many peasants have shifted to growing coca exclusively because it is much more lucrative than any other crop. Other Bolivians, needless to say, are involved in different aspects of coca production and distribution. The drug trade has so permeated Bolivian society that some estimates claim close to one-third of the entire Bolivian workforce has been involved in some form of coca production and/or trafficking. According to Herbert Klein, in 1989 the growing, processing, and sale of coca leaf and cocaine paste generated an annual income of $1.5 billion for the nation (18). Luckily, however, the illegal drug trade has not produced in Bolivia the level of violence and disruption that it has in Colombia and in some areas of Peru.

Some contend that Bolivia's geopolitical future is somewhat uncertain. Analysts point out that potentially Bolivia could lose even more territory to its neighbors, considering its small population and lack of physical integration. Whenever such claims are made, however, with some pundits even going so far as to state that Bolivia is a "geographic mistake," Bolivians' fierce nationalism comes to the fore, leading in more than one instance to protests and demonstrations that clearly show the depth of loyalty among Bolivians for their country, despite it all.

Communication Patterns

The Native American prominence in Bolivia profoundly influences communication patterns and mores. Bolivians often appear quiet and subdued (some have even said melancholy) on the surface. The reputed openness and gregariousness of many other SSSAs is, for the most part, missing among Bolivians and is generally attributed to the Native American background of many Bolivians. Some even claim that Bolivians are the "least Latin" in temperament of all the SSSAs. As a general rule, Bolivians attempt to maintain a certain smoothness or equilibrium in their relationships, avoiding loud, confrontational encounters whenever possible. Many, especially those of Native American ancestry, may be reticent about talking with strangers, and some do not even want to have their photograph taken, believing that it somehow steals their soul.

Since Spanish is not the first language for about half of the nation's populace, many terms for places and objects in Bolivia are of Native American origin. Perhaps more significantly, some contend that the linguistic structures of these Native American languages have influenced the mindset of many Bolivians, imbuing them with a nonlinear way of perceiving and behaving within the workplace. For instance, in Aymara there are three distinct responses to any inquiry: yes, no, and maybe, the latter of which is considered just as valid as either an affirmative or a negative. It is rumored that a group of Japanese computer scientists have been studying the Aymara language in an attempt to incorporate a category similar to the Aymara "maybe" into current binary computer language. If such a category were realizable, it would greatly expand the possibilities for computers to represent intermediate categories and/or indefinite status.

Numerous terms are employed to describe people of Native American ancestry in Bolivia, and they evoke various perceptions and responses among listeners. For instance, the Spanish term *indio*, meaning "Indian," is an extraordinarily offensive term and should never be used. In an anthropological or historical context, *los indígenas* might be a preferable term; but in ordinary speech, most Bolivians refer to people of Native American descent, especially those in the rural areas, as campesinos, or peasants. *Cholo* is often used as well, although it has mixed and sometimes confusing connotations. The term *cholo* originally referred to people having both Indian and European ancestry, but its use has changed, and today it suggests a person of mixed ancestry who is moving up socially from an indigenous culture and environment to an urban setting by adopting the Spanish language and mestizo dress and customs.

The Spanish spoken in Bolivia is quite neutral in accent, and it can be difficult to distinguish Bolivian from Peruvian or Colombian spoken Spanish. As in many countries that have both highland and lowland regions, Bolivia's highlanders tend to speak more slowly and formally than do lowlanders. In La Paz, people are generally calm, speak quietly and thoughtfully, and are easy for nonnative Spanish speakers to understand. In Santa Cruz and other lowland areas, the speech is somewhat more relaxed and faster.

Bolivians are generally quite courteous with each other, and there is a marked formality in Bolivian speech patterns and forms of address, which is due to the strong hierarchical structure of Bolivian society. When in doubt, it is always better to err on the side of formality when talking with Bolivians. On first meeting people, the formal forms of address, "Señor" and "Señora," are most appropriate; and the use of "Don" and "Doña" is appreciated for older people or for those who are more distinguished or respected.

Greetings are usually a handshake for men and a quick kiss on each cheek between women. Men who are good friends often give each other a quick hug as well. Female friends and relatives are often seen holding hands, and older women often take the arm of a companion, male or female, in the street.

A person's demeanor and dress are considered very important in Bolivia, as these communicate one's status. In La Paz and other highland cities, suits and ties are customary for men, as are suits or nice dresses for women. Shoes should be shined. There is no lack of shoe-shine boys on the plazas, and they may call out an amusing sales pitch: "*Una vez al año no te hace daño!*" ("Once a year won't hurt!").

Living and Working in Bolivia

Despite the omnipresence of the Native American in much of Bolivian society, most foreigners' contacts in the workplace will be with the white or mestizo groups, due to the cultural and linguistic differences as well as to the almost segregated social worlds of the Native Americans and the Caucasians or mestizos. This does not mean that foreigners in Bolivia will not interact with Bolivians of Native American extraction. In fact, such contact will most likely be quite frequent, for example, in the markets, in commerce, and oftentimes as domestic help within one's own household. However, such relationships will most likely remain rather superficial in nature. Nonetheless, for many visitors to Bolivia, just observing and learning more about the Quechua- and Aymara-speaking Bolivians often prove to be the most rewarding aspect of their sojourn.

One of the legacies of Hispanic colonization in Bolivia is the nation's bureaucratic procedures, which are among the most convoluted and time-consuming of all the SSSA nations. Careful attention must be accorded to the details of required stamps, seals, signatures, witnesses, and copies of documents in all paperwork.

Even many Bolivians commonly experience great disappointment after assembling all the necessary paperwork for a project, only to be turned down because one signature or document is supposedly missing, which often leads to missed deadlines and delays of other types, not because of incompetence or laziness but because of bureaucratic inflexibility. Supposedly, bureaucratic processes have recently been streamlined, and Bolivia has adopted a simplified taxation system and a new investment code, which is designed to provide a "stable and open environment for foreign investors." Nevertheless, traditional bureaucratic practices still persist.

Time use at meetings and other business endeavors is yet another way in which the Hispanic legacy has left its mark on contemporary Bolivia. In general, Bolivian businesspeople are not the most punctual, and many meetings neither begin nor end on time. It is customary for higher-ranking officials to be tardy more often than lower-ranking associates, and such delays are common practice.

Procedures and documentation are only half of doing business in Bolivia; the other half is *personalismo*, the nurturing and use of personal contacts. Personal relationships begin in Bolivia with acknowledgment of a person's status in the working world, and particularly with respect for colleagues' and co-workers' titles. Rarely are first names used, except among intimate associates. Professional titles are many and precise: *licenciado* (economists and accountants), *doctor* (both attorneys and physicians), *ingeniero* (engineers), *arquitecto* (architect or planner), and *profesor* (teacher) are a few of the titles used. These titles are granted through official licenses, certificates, or diplomas, and in many cases, Bolivians will not take suggestions seriously from someone who does not have a title and official position. A Bolivian recalls the case of a construction worker and craftsman who had worked for many years in the United States, eventually becoming a building contractor in business with an associate. Upon returning home, he was unable to find any equivalent work until he received the degree and certificate of ingeniero, regardless of what he had actually accomplished and knew how to do.

The formality of bureaucracy and titles carries over to written correspondence and documentation. Contracts and agreements in Bolivia are explicit, precise, and complete. Nothing is assumed, all contingencies are spelled out, and authorization is given for specific purposes. For nonnative Spanish speakers, an additional challenge is posed by written communication. English is not spoken as widely in Bolivia as in some other SSSA countries, and attempts to speak Spanish will be appreciated.

Beyond the importance of titles and official positions, personal contacts are vital to a foreigner's success. In the business and professional world, few things distress Bolivians more than a patronizing attitude by people from other countries. As one Bolivian puts it, "People think that since we are from a Third World country, we have no education. In fact, many Bolivians have degrees from universities abroad, or at least a strong education in our own universities and institutes." Admission to Bolivian universities is highly competitive, since the openings are few compared with the number of candidates; and some fields that are considered less desirable for business in the United States, like sociology, are very rigorous programs of study in Bolivia, in which only those with the best minds can successfully graduate. In addition, most Bolivians in the professions, government, and business have had some experience working with companies and individuals from other countries, and Bolivia in recent decades has become an eager participant in economic globalization. Considering the importance of *dignidad* in this culture, an appreciation of what Bolivians have accomplished under difficult circumstances can only enhance working relationships.

The hierarchical system of relationships dating back to the Inca empire and reinforced by the Spaniards is still of great importance in Bolivia; individuals of a higher social rank are expected to be generous in tangible ways, for example with compliments, invitations, the exchange of favors, and assistance for the needy. An often-puzzling custom for English-speaking North Americans (ESNAs) is the array of individuals typically called upon in Bolivia to contribute to weddings, baptisms, and other ceremonies. For example, most weddings have a number of *padrinos* or *madrinas*, who function as sponsors to pay for the wedding cake, the bride's gown, the reception, or other specific items. This is a method for sharing the expenses as well as a way of cementing and expressing relationships and creating ties of mutual support that may have practical benefits in the future. The indigenous counterpart to this is the many local fiestas, some of which date back to pre-Incan times, in which the most prosperous members of a community provide a feast and celebration of grand proportions.

The distinct separation between public and private lives typical of the SSSA nations holds true in Bolivia as well. In urban residential neighborhoods, homes are located behind high walls that do not permit the interior to be seen from the street, with rooms usually arranged around a private courtyard or patio. Protection of the family and the home—in both practical and symbolic terms—is a strong sentiment in Bolivia, and an invitation to someone's home is something of an honor, since generally business or professional contacts are first entertained in restaurants or cafes. Once invited to a Bolivian's home, however, guests are treated with great generosity and warmth. It is customary for guests to bring a small gift of flowers or candy to the hosts.

Much of one's comfort in Bolivia, particularly in the mountains, depends on wardrobe. The sun is quite warm at noon, but nights can be very cold, and there is little or no central heating. Even at noon you will see that people prefer the sunny side of the street and avoid shade or the shadows of buildings. Layers of clothing that can be adjusted to the changing temperatures through the day are most convenient. Bolivians are cautious about the cold, for example, taking a warm blanket on an overnight bus or car trip and ordering cold drinks without ice.

Bolivian food is hearty, with plentiful vegetables, legumes, and grains but small quantities of meat. Breakfasts are often just coffee and rolls, but the later coffee break for *salteñas*, spicy meat pies, makes up for the slim breakfast. The main meal of the day is usually served in early afternoon and often includes soup and a potato dish. Watch out for *ají*, a spicy pepper, and its even more fiery cousin, *rocoto*. In early evening, a treat called *humitas* is available, a sort of corn pudding wrapped and baked in corn husks. Pizza, Chinese food, and other international favorites have always been available on a limited basis in La Paz, but recently fast food has also moved in. Outside of La Paz, the cuisine is more traditionally Bolivian except in the cosmopolitan atmosphere of Santa Cruz.

* * * * * * *

Bolivians have much to lament historically, including significant territorial losses and military defeats, but they also have much to be proud of, such as their peaceful twentieth-century revolution and their multicultural society. While Bolivia may rank near the bottom of many indicators of social and economic welfare in the hemisphere, the nation has incredible riches of other types—especially in the cultural and artistic realms. From an anthropological perspective, this nation, located in the heartland of South America, is one of the most fascinating in the hemisphere, and there are few visitors who are not deeply affected by the visual images of the lands and peoples of Bolivia. Bolivians themselves staunchly believe in their country and its future. Perhaps more than any other place in the western hemisphere, Bolivia has been able to balance its traditional cultures with the modern world, creating myriad blendings of these two very different ways of life. The fruits of these efforts can be seen in many aspects of life in contemporary Bolivia, including the fact that in 1993 Bolivians were the first people in South America to elect a Native American as vice president of the country.

References and Selected Bibliography

Alexander, Robert J. 1982. *Bolivia: Past, Present and Future of Its Politics*. New York: Praeger.

Anstee, Margaret Joan. 1970. *Bolivia: Gate of the Sun*. New York: Paul S. Eriksson.

Antonil. *Mama Coca*. 1978. London: Hassle Free Press.

Barios de Chungara, Domitila, with Moema Viezzer. 1978. *Let Me Speak! Testimony of Domitila, a Woman of the Bolivian Mines*. New York: Monthly Review Press.

Benner, Susan E., and Kathy S. Leonard, eds. 1998. *Fire from the Andes: Short Fiction by Women from Bolivia, Ecuador and Peru*. Albuquerque: University of New Mexico Press.

Cramer, Mark. 1996. *Bolivia: Culture Shock*. Portland, OR: Graphic Arts Center.

Ferry, Stephen (photographer), Eduardo Galeano. 1999. *I Am Rich Potosi: The Mountain that Eats Men*. New York: Monacelli Press.

Guevara, Ernesto (Che). 2000. *The Complete Bolivian Diary of Ernesto Che Guevara*. Edited by Mary-Alice Walker. Translated by Michael Taber. London: Pathfinder Press.

Guise, Anselm Verener Lee. 1997. *Six Years in Bolivia: The Adventures of a Mining Engineer*. West Lafayette, IN: Purdue University Press.

Harris, Richard L. 2000. *Death of a Revolutionary: Che Guevara's Last Mission*. New York: W. W. Norton & Company.

Herring, Hubert. 1968. *A History of Latin America from the Beginnings to the Present*. 3d ed. New York: A. Knopf

Klein, Herbert S. 1982. *Bolivia: The Evolution of a Multi-Ethnic Society*. Reprint, 1992, Oxford, England: Oxford University Press.

McFarren, Peter. 1988. *An Insider's Guide to Bolivia*. La Paz: Fundación Cultural "Quipus."

Morales, Waltrand Queiser. 1992. *Bolivia: Land of Struggle*. Boulder, CO: Westview Press.

Nash, June C. 1993. *We Eat the Mines and the Mines Eat Us: Dependency and Exploitation in Bolivian Tin Mines*. New York: Columbia University Press.

Reyes, Sandra, and John DuVal, eds. 1998. *Oblivion and Stone: A Selection of Contemporary Bolivian Poetry and Fiction*. Fayetteville: University of Arkansas Press.

Ross, John F. 2000. "Mountains of Pain," *Smithsonian* (November): 142.

Saldana, Rodolfo, and Mary-Alice Waters. 2001. *Fertile Ground: Che Guevara and Bolivia*. London: Pathfinder Press.

Santos, Rosario, ed. 2000. *The Fat Man from La Paz: Contemporary Fiction from Bolivia*. New York: Seven Stories Press.

Velasquez, Sofía. 1996. *The World of Sofía Velasquez: The Autobiography of a Bolivian Market Vendor*. Translated by Hans C. Buechler and Judith-Maria Buechler. New York: Columbia University Press.

12

Chile: A Continental Island

Skye Stephenson

> *Los chilenos creemos que somos el ombligo del mundo, siempre estámos mirando hacia adentro, estudiandonos, analizandonos, comparandonos con nosotros mismos.*
>
> —Isabel Allende
>
> *We Chileans think that we are the center of the world, we are always looking within, studying ourselves, analyzing ourselves, comparing ourselves with ourselves.*

Many characteristics of Chile distinguish it from the other Spanish-speaking South American (SSSA) nations, including its geography. On maps, long and narrow Chile appears to cling precariously to the southwestern portion of the American landmass. Stretching about 4,000 kilometers (2,500 miles) from north to south (the equivalent of the distance from southern Alaska to Baja Mexico) but with a breadth of only between 160 (100) and 400 kilometers (250 miles) from east to west, there is truly no nation anywhere shaped like it. Cartographers even have difficulty "fitting" the nation into conventional map format, and commonly present it in two or three segments.

The Chileans' cultural patterns and communication style seem to mirror their homeland's unique character, and while all the other SSSAs have a strong cultural affinity with at least one of their neighbors, the Chilean people stand alone; neither the Argentines to the east nor the Peruvians and Bolivians to the north have much in common with the Chileans. Among the savvy, Chileans are rarely confused with anyone else.

Although Chile is geographically and culturally separate from the other SSSA countries, it has often received more international attention than its neighbors, despite the fact that it is the fourth smallest country in the region in both size and population. This international renown is due to numerous factors, including its fascinating political saga and its innovative economic policies. The legion of lauded writers, poets, and songwriters who hail from this string bean of a country is yet another reason for Chile's fame. Most of these verbal artists find much of their inspiration in the awe-striking natural beauty and epic events of their homeland.

What explains the fascinating constellation of occurrences that have made Chile what it is today? Perhaps some explanation can be found in the nature of the Chilean people themselves. Consider the following:

- Chileans have been characterized as both the most innovative of the SSSAs and the most conservative. For example, Chile was one of the first nations in the region to recognize labor unions, legalize the Communist Party, and enact certain social welfare policies; yet today it is the only nation in the Western world that still prohibits divorce.
- Most Chileans consider themselves classist and give great importance to where each person fits in the social hierarchy. At the same time, most Chileans would define themselves as middle class.
- Chile is one of the least corrupt nations in South America, yet Chileans tend to have little confidence in one another.

In this chapter the most noteworthy cultural patterns of the singular Chileans will be explored, including their geographic and regional influences, key cultural characteristics, and patterns of communication as well as aspects of living and working in Chile. Among the cultural characteristics that will be discussed are the love (and control) of the land, British influence, and innovation, conservatism, hypocrisy, and indirectness.

Geographic and Regional Influences

Chileans make much of the fact that they are literally located at the "end of the world" and like to point out that their country is a terminal destination, since "nobody comes here on their way to anyplace else." Even the nation's rather unusual name alludes to this reality, for *Chili* means "the land beyond" in Aymara, a Native American language spoken in northern Chile, southern Peru, and Bolivia.

The nation's remoteness is exacerbated by the natural features that form its boundaries. The country's northern border is the Atacama Desert, the driest in the world, with places where no rain has fallen for more than a century. This region was, at one time, the southernmost reach of the Inca empire. Today, the remains of some of these Incas as well as much earlier peoples can still be found in caves and other burial sites. These remains are remarkably well preserved due to the arid conditions and a sophisticated mummification process that was first employed by a local tribe in Chile known as the Chinchorros more than two thousand years before the Egyptians.

Chile's southernmost border has the opposite character: a relatively flat and cold place known as Patagonia, across which pass winds that commonly exceed one hundred miles an hour and where daily rain is the norm. Although now sparsely inhabited, the biggest city here, Punta Arenas, was among the most important in the continent prior to the building of the Panama Canal. It was a place of rest for sailors who had successfully traversed the treacherous passage to the Pacific; many others were literally "put to rest" in the turbid offshore waters when their ships did not make it through.

The Coast. The vast Pacific Ocean emphatically marks Chile's entire western border, and crashing surf pounds the entire coastline. Offshore, the frigid Humboldt Current attracts many kinds of marine life, making Chile one of the most important fish-producing countries on the continent, along with neighboring Peru. A visit to any Chilean fish market attests to the sea's bounty, and among the plethora of fish and shellfish available for purchase are *corvina* (Chilean sea bass), *congrio* (a more meaty fish usually served in soup or fried), razor clams, sea urchins, mussels of various sizes, abalone, and *picoroco* (a kind of barnacle that is added to fish soup).

Until the advent of air travel, water was the best way to reach Chile, and several of the nation's most important cities are ports. The most well known is Valparaiso, which is located about two hours directly west of Santiago, the capital. Dubbed the "Pearl of the Pacific," it has invariably been compared with San Francisco due to a similar hilly topography abutting the sea. Though this city is now the seat of the National Congress, which was moved in the 1980s as part of an effort to decentralize power, as well as the headquarters for the nation's navy, considered one of the best in the region, it nonetheless has an air of faded glory. In earlier periods, it was one of the most booming ports of the South American Pacific. During the California Gold Rush, those who chose the sea route to reach California would invariably stop over in Valparaiso, inculcating a kind of affinity between the two places. These days, adjoining and more touristy Viña del Mar is a sister city to Sausalito, California, and the two places are remarkably similar in look and feel.

Chileans, for the most part, do not venture into the sea for recreation, since the cold waters and strong offshore currents make serious swimming and/or boating a challenging task for the novice; nonetheless, they still fervently "feel the sea" within them, and most urban dwellers, when given the chance, will joyously escape to one of the many beaches that line the coast. Even more than as a place for rest and recreation, the Pacific seems to pound within the Chilean soul, and many national writers and artists laud these watery domains, expressing the collective sense of the nation. Poet and Nobel laureate Pablo Neruda is perhaps the best example. Although he admitted to getting seasick and being a poor swimmer, Neruda found the Pacific Ocean to be one of his greatest sources of inspiration. He resided for years right on the coast, in his unique house now turned museum at Isla Negra; he adopted the fish as his symbol and even called himself a "*marinero en tierra*" ("sailor on land").

The Andes. Chileans' eastern gaze takes them to the second highest mountains in the world: the jagged and looming Andes. The nation's entire boundary with Argentina is defined by the highest peaks of this range. While the hemisphere's tallest mountain, Aconcagua, stands just over the Argentine border, Chile nonetheless boasts many snowcapped peaks, several of which are prime ski resorts. These rocky giants are omnipresent in most Chilean vistas and simplify finding one's bearings, as they emphatically mark out the eastern direction. While esthetically breathtaking, they can also be harsh, spewing forth air that lends a frigid evening and morning chill to most of the nation, even during the summer months. The mountainous presence in Chile is not confined to the Andes; a parallel but lower string of mountains known as the Coastal Ranges runs parallel to them throughout most of the central area of the country, providing yet another series of peaks along the horizon.

For many visitors, their first and most enduring image of Chile is of its mountains, which they glimpse from the airplane window as they fly into Santiago, some so awestruck by the mountains' raw beauty that they have literally broken into tears. Indeed, these peaks are unforgettable, and they seem to "change personality" during the course of the day and the seasons, depending on the light, climate, and visibility. Many contend that Chileans are primarily a "watery people," but others maintain that they are, at a deeper level, truly a "mountain people." Chile's other Nobel laureate poet, Gabriela Mistral, represents this in her own works, for she lauds above all else the Chilean mountains that were so omnipresent in her childhood home in the Elqui Valley. As she put it,

In mountains I was born,
With three dozen peaks uplifted.
And it seems to me that never, never did I lose them,
Even when I had to march to other places. (2001, 587)

These mountains are not just part of the landscape; they are also visible evidence of the various tectonic forces at work in Chile. Indeed, the entire Chilean nation falls along the so-called "ring of fire," and the country is full of bubbling hot springs and active volcanos. More ominously, it is racked by earthquakes, and several of the most monumental national events revolve around this reality. One of the strongest earthquakes ever recorded, measuring more than 9.0 on the Richter scale, hit the southern coastal city of Valdivia in 1960, destroying much of the city in less than two minutes. When the earthquake subsided, residents of a nearby fishing village discovered to their pleasant surprise that the entire bay was exposed, and they ventured out into the mud to pick up floundering fish. All of a sudden, a gigantic tidal wave bore down on the bay and took almost the entire village away in one fell swoop.

These daunting natural realities serve to reinforce Chilean isolation in numerous dimensions, even the biological. Many of the plants and animals here have evolved in unique ways over time, a verity that in at least one instance had important international repercussions. In the late nineteenth century, Chilean grapes were the only ones unaffected by the phylloxera blight because the fungus could not cross the Andes; consequently, they were used to breed the phylloxera-resistant hybrids now cultivated worldwide.

The Cental Valley. As if eschewing their imposing borders, Chileans turn their gaze inward rather than outward, concentrating their energies and attention on a 640-square-kilometer (400-square-mile) zone known as the Central Valley, located in the middle of the country. In this fertile area, over three quarters of the entire populace of fifteen million reside. This valley is much more than just the physical home of most Chileans; it is also, in many ways, the heart and soul of the nation, and it is from this zone that most mainstream Chilean cultural modalities spring.

The Central Valley is an agricultural zone par excellence, and many crops flourish here, including grapes, peaches, nectarines, and raspberries as well as other lesser-known fruits such as orange-colored *nisperos*; a small variegated and melonlike fruit known as *pepinos;* a verdant green-skinned and orange-fleshed fruit called *lucuma;* and a favorite of all known as *chirimoya*. Avocados, corn, and tomatoes number among the most important vegetables, the former so ubiquitous in the Chilean diet that McDonald's had to incorporate avocado (known locally as *palta)* into its condiment offerings in its Chilean stores. Not surprisingly, the Chilean cuisine reflects this abundance of fruits and vegetables, with salads and stews of different types predominating, changing seasonally depending on what is being harvested.

Much more than just its food comes from this Central Valley; the most important Chilean folk figure hails from here as well. Known as the *huaso*, he is a more rooted and community-oriented cowboy than the Argentine and Uruguayan gaucho. His garb differs as well: the huaso typically dons a black flat-rimmed hat, a white shirt, and black or brown trousers topped with a short striped poncho known as a *manta*. His most distinguishing attire is his boots, which are tall, black, and have a particular type of spiked spurs that are even sold as souvenirs. Using these boots, the huaso dances the Chilean folk dance known as the *cueca*. This rather flirtatious dance is said to be patterned after the mating ritual between a rooster and a chicken and is characterized by both the male and female waving white handkerchiefs as they carry out their staccato footwork.

Of the approximately ten million Central Valley inhabitants, about half reside in Santiago, which is located right in the middle of the area. Wedged between the Andes and the Coastal Ranges, the city's layout makes it a rather "tight" place, with nothing like the expanses found in the other Southern Cone capitals of Buenos Aires and Montevideo. More ominously, Santiago's valley location exacerbates the problems of air pollution, particularly in the winter months, and affects the health of many of the local residents. Other than this, Santiago is a pleasant city that has many of the advantages of an important urban area but nonetheless still feels quite manageable.

This concentration of people and cultural emanations in the Central Valley region contributes to making the Chilean people, despite their nation's great geographic diversity, among the most homogeneous and unified of all the SSSAs both linguistically and culturally. The nation's form of organization plays a part as well, as Chile is extremely centralized, even by SSSA standards. The country's flag, so similar to the Texas state flag, concretely represents this unitary thrust in its single white star, said to represent the Chilean people.

Such national cohesiveness, however, should not be overestimated. As one moves out from the Central Valley, some cultural differences emerge that increase the farther one goes in either direction. In the far north, along the border with Peru and Bolivia, many of the Chileans are of indigenous origins and speak Aymara. At the other extreme of Chile, the locals are renowned for their myths and lore, especially the inhabitants of the island of Chiloe, many of whom believe that they share their misty and verdant homeland with magical inhabitants. Among these are a dwarf that can make a woman pregnant if she looks at him; the *tue-tue*, a bird whose sighting is a harbinger of bad tidings; and a ghost ship that sweeps people away forever.

The Islands. Even more distinctive are another group of Chilean island residents, the natives of Easter Island. Located more than 2,000 miles off the mainland on one of the most remote of all archipelagos, Easter Island truly belongs to Oceania. The 3,000 natives who reside there call their home Rapa Nui, which in their Polynesian language means "naval of the world." Easter Island is most well known for its 600 or more monumental volcanic rock statues, known as *moais*, that were raised here centuries ago and whose meaning is still shrouded in great mystery and debate.

The Juan Fernandez Islands are another group of Pacific islands that also belong to the Chilean nation. Located about 650 kilometers (four hundred miles) off the Chilean coast, they were uninhabited in 1704 when a British sailor known as Alexander Selkirk was unceremoniously dropped here as punishment for improper conduct. He spent the next five years alone on this island, eventually being rescued by a passing ship. His story became the basis for the famous novel *Robinson Crusoe*, written by Daniel Defoe. Today, the main island is known as Robinson Crusoe in homage to this literary masterpiece, and about five hundred people make this site their home.

Antarctica Holdings? Many Chileans contend that their nation does not stop with its South American and oceanic holdings. They say that they have territory in a third continental zone, that of Antarctica. Many Chilean maps present the nation with its alleged Antarctic territory included, a large wedge of the "white continent" that extends all the way to the South Pole, and weather reports on the nightly news often refer to the blustery conditions there.

Keys to Understanding the Chileans

The Land: Love and Control

The land of present-day Chile seems to bewitch and enchant many who enter its realm, frequently causing visitors and locals alike to fall under its spell by becoming deeply attached to this special place with its incredibly diverse and often very challenging terrains. Chilean poet Nicanor Parra expressed this feeling when he wrote, in his typically tongue-in-cheek style, "*Creemos ser pais, y la verdad es que somos apenas paisaje*" ("We believe we are a country, but the truth is we are just our countryside").

Love of the Land: Mapuches and Spaniards. The largest indigenous group in Chile, the Mapuches or, as they are sometimes known, the Araucanians, manifest love of the land emphatically in their own culture and history. Their homeland originally covered most of central and southern Chile (down to the Patagonia region) as well as parts of Andean Argentina. In fact, their name means "people of the land" in their native tongue.* Although the Mapuches shared a common language and similar cultural attributes, numerous subgroups functioned quite autonomously, each having its own distinctive leadership. For the most part, authority was loosely exercised, and the Mapuches were markedly more egalitarian in their social organization than most of the Andean tribes, such as the Inca. Among the most important members of each group, along with the *lonko*, or chief, was the *machi*, a healer and usually a female.

Most often peaceful, the Mapuches could, if circumstances warranted, be fierce and tireless defenders of their lands. When attacked, various groups would band together and choose the strongest and most able among them to serve as the *toqui*, or military chief, in battle. This strategy, as well as the Mapuches' remarkable ability to adopt the same techniques used by any would-be invaders, made them resoundingly successful warriors. They managed to repel both the Incas and the Spanish, keeping the latter at bay for more than three centuries, at least in the southern realms of present-day Chile. In fact, the Iberian conquerors considered the Mapuches their most formidable adversaries in the entire continent. The first important piece of Spanish colonial literature, *The Araucana*, penned by Alonso de Ercilla, attests to these Native Americans' bravery.

The Mapuches weren't the only ones who deeply loved the lands of Chile, so too did the Spanish conquistador Pedro de Valdivia, who was cut from different cloth than most of his contemporaries, being relatively well educated and from one of the higher classes. According to popular legend, he fell in love with the beauty of the Central Valley region and was undeterred by the fact that there was no gold or silver to be had. The white men would not discover until long after Valdivia's time

---

* The term *mapu* is usually translated as "Earth"; a mapuche healer, however, told the author that actually *mapu* means much more: "space" or "cosmos," and there are different levels of mapu, one of which is Earth.

the many mineral riches that lay hidden in Chile's subsoil, the most important being copper. Today, Chile is the largest copper exporter in the world, and although national leaders have made serious efforts in recent decades toward lessening the nation's dependence on this metal for revenues, copper is still crucial to the Chilean economy.

Control of the Land. From the start, the Mapuches fiercely fought the Spanish aggressors; in fact, Pedro de Valdivia himself was felled by a Mapuche chieftan. After decades of skirmishes following Valdivia's death, at last a tacit understanding was reached whereby the white people would confine their activities to the north of the Bio-Bio River and the Mapuches, to the south. Neither side totally abided by this division, however, and there were sporadic clashes between the two groups until the late nineteenth century, forcing the Spanish and, later, the Chileans to maintain a special frontier army as well as a series of forts along this conflicted border.[†] For several centuries, life in Chile was more like the Wild West in the United States than the other centers under Spanish control, and the roots of some of the cultural characteristics of the modern-day Chilean people can be traced to these formative years of conflict and colonization when two very different cultures collided.

One resulting trait is the Chileans' decidedly militaristic streak, which has been unleashed not only against the Mapuches but also against all of their current neighbors. In the late nineteenth century, Chile won much of what now constitutes the northern third of the country from Bolivia and Peru in the War of the Pacific (see chapter 11, "Bolivia: Rooftop of the World,"

[†] There was even one episode, during the 1860s, in which a quixotic Frenchman named Orelie-Antoine de Tounens attempted to create an independent kingdom of Araucania, with himself as the emperor. He did manage to garner significant support from some of the Mapuche chiefs before he was expelled from the continent by Chilean authorities. He eventually passed away in France without his dream coming to fruition; nonetheless, he established a hereditary monarchy, and his closest descendant, a nephew, is currently the pretender to the title!

for more details). During a nearly two-decades-long period of military rule from 1973 to 1989, some of Chile's militarism was turned against its own people. In those repressive years, at least three thousand Chileans were killed at the hands of the military (many more were imprisoned and/or exiled).

The Mapuches were eventually brought into the national fold, in part through military action. In 1898, fresh from their victory in the War of the Pacific, the Chilean military marched south into Mapuche territories and forcefully took control under the banner of fervent nationalism. Technically, however, the Mapuches were never "formally" defeated, and the centuries-long stalemate was ultimately resolved with the signing of a peace treaty between the Chilean authorities and the Mapuches.

Love of the Law. This event epitomizes another aspect of the Chileans' approach to problem solving, which is clearly stated in the country's motto: *por la razón o la fuerza* (by reason or force). Just as the Mapuches were legally incorporated into the nation rather than exterminated (as occurred in neighboring Argentina), a legalistic approach (*la razón)* to problem solving is as characteristic of Chilean culture as is its more aggressive side. Rules and regulations abound for nearly everything, from the most mundane to the most complex, and Chileans are, for the most part, very well informed regarding their rights and responsibilities. The Colombian writer Gabriel García Márquez once commented that Chile was the only place he had ever been where legal codes are widely sold at newspaper stands, and people actually bought them as reading material! In fact, as of 1999, Chile had 19,642 official laws, which is a very high number for any nation, especially one of its size. For comparison, countries with much longer legal traditions, such as France or England, are estimated to have only about 11,000 laws (*El Mercurio*, 4 October 2000, 3).

The importance accorded to rules and regulations in Chilean society helps to explain the nation's strong democratic traditions. Along with Uruguay, it boasts the greatest number of years of democratic governance in the region. In fact, Chile's infamous period of military control was not at all characteristic of Chilean politics, and in the twentieth century it was the only time that the armed forces took control of the nation (except for a very brief interlude right at the start of the 1932 Depression).

Ethnicity and Class. Although the conflict between the Native Americans and the Europeans has ostensibly been over for more than a century, it continues to exert a profound influence on modern-day Chile, manifesting itself in deeply seated and fervently held beliefs regarding both personal and group identity, albeit many times this crucial issue is not openly discussed or, in some cases, even consciously recognized. Although official statistics place the country's Native American population (the great majority of which are Mapuche) at between 8 and 12 percent, actually the Chilean populace is primarily mestizo, a concrete manifestation that the interaction between Native Americans and white Europeans extended beyond mere belligerence.

Chileans of the "popular" classes, as the poorer segments of society are euphemistically called, embrace their indigenous ancestry, for the most part. Those of the middle and upper sectors of society, however, usually stress their "whiteness," and many look disparagingly upon those who appear Indian and even upon those countries that have large indigenous populations, such as Peru and Bolivia, considering them as "less civilized." As a consequence, even more than in other SSSAs, the Chilean elite accord great status and prestige to people who are light-skinned. Chilean Jaime Valdivieso describes this reality as follows: "We, the *huincas* (Mapuche name for white Chileans), live a myth of being European. We declare ourselves white, all the while not admitting the racial mixture we actually carry, because we are embarrassed to look at ourselves in the mirror to discover signs of racial mixing" (in Segovia 1999, 20).

In a sense Chilean society in the twenty-first century is still divided into two clearly marked camps, although the division these days is ostensibly based on class rather than ethnicity, as was the case in the frontier era. In reality, however, class and race are inextricably linked in Chile, as they are elsewhere throughout the

SSSA region. Chile is a profoundly classist society, and everyone is keenly aware of both his or her own place in society and that of others. This is even reflected in Chilean Spanish, which has many terms to define social class. For instance, there are at least twenty different possible designations for someone of low class, the most common being *roto*, which literally means "broken" or "torn." For most Chileans from the middle class upward, to be roto or to mix with rotos is to be avoided at all costs.

There are also many words to describe those from the upper class, each with a slightly different connotation. For instance, a *cuico* is somebody who is snobby in attitude and conservative in political inclination, typically a nouveau riche; a *pituco* belongs to the Chilean elite and is of "old money." Both of these terms are used pejoratively by people from the lower classes and/or the left wing of the political spectrum to describe people who are elitest and often stuck-up. Thus, in some circles, being cuico or pituco is considered much worse than being roto.

Social segmentation in Chile even has spatial implications, with many of the urban areas having clearly marked sectors for the "different types" of Chileans. This phenomenon is most clearly demarcated in Santiago, where an invisible but profoundly important dividing line runs through Plaza Italia in the center of the city, separating the "popular" classes from the upper classes. Residential differentiation can be even more specific. Just like in frontier times, Chileans gravitate toward living in tight groups, surrounded by people of similar backgrounds and approaches to life. They tend to be suspicious of people they do not know well, especially if they look, think, or act differently. In fact, several surveys have found that Chileans have decidedly low levels of confidence and trust in one another, even though the country is one of the safest in the region.

Lack of Trust; Trickery. Perhaps one explanation for this suspicious attitude can be found in the nature of the Caucasian/Mapuche interactions over the centuries, which were characterized by trickery and even sabotage by both parties. Even when the Mapuches were "pacified" and began to integrate into mainstream Chilean society, they would oftentimes carry out minor acts of disobedience as a way, perhaps unconsciously, of demonstrating that they could still exert their will and wield at least some degree of power. Typically these actions would, in turn, be met with heavy-handed methods of control to "keep the Mapuches in their place."

Such trickery and misbehavior—on both sides—have even been given a name, *picardía chilensis*, which is a uniquely Chilean version of picardía and is commonly manifested by people seeing what they "can get away with." This can sometimes be done quite humorously, and much interaction between people revolves around this theme. One of the most beloved of Chilean figures, the cartoon character Condorito, personifies this very Chilean behavior in his escapades.

A Lasting Bond. Despite class differences and a suspicious nature, Chileans maintain a deep attachment to their homeland, a bond that seems to transcend whatever divisions there may be among them. This bond to the homeland contributes to Chilean nationalism, which seems to be stronger than in most of the other SSSA countries. Chileans resoundingly sing their national anthem at many events, routinely compare themselves with their neighbors (oftentimes finding themselves the better of the lot, especially these days), and usually miss their country deeply whenever they are away.

Other factors also account for the strong ties Chileans feel to one another and their land. The rural lifestyle still strongly influences the nation's cultural patterns, and despite the trend toward urbanization in the last half century, the country has a "small-town" flavor. Even Santiago, with its five million inhabitants, has an intimate feel to it. Just as in a small town, people are connected and know what is happening to one another, and family names can carry great weight. In the 1994 presidential race, for instance, the son of one former president and the grandson of another former president faced off against each other. The media also reflect this interest in local happenings in their reporting; the most widely read newspaper in the country, the well-respected *El Mercurio*, routinely dedicates about one third of its front section to society pages.

Chileans' love of their land and the enlightened actions over the centuries of several key members of the Chilean elite, who willingly (up to a certain limit) accommodated the needs of the lower social classes, have benefited the country. Despite strong social segmentation, Chile is predominantly (60 percent or more) middle class today. In recent decades, due to the country's economic prosperity, the number of Chileans below the poverty line has actually decreased, a phenomenon that has not occurred in any other SSSA nation.

The British of South America

Because Chile's natural isolating features make it seem almost like an island, it is perhaps not surprising that the Chileans have been equated with another island nationality—the British. While this comparison is not very accurate from a genealogical standpoint (Chileans of British ancestry are far outnumbered by those of Iberian, Yugoslavian, and/or German descent), nonetheless, Chileans do have certain cultural commonalities with the British. Not only does the country's greatest revolutionary hero, Bernardo O'Higgins, have a decidedly Irish name (he was the illegitimate son of an Irish viceroy of Peru and his Chilean lover), but also British influence can be noted in the architecture of some of the coastal cities as well as in the nature of many of the elite private schools in the country. Also Chileans, like the British, have teatime every day between five and six in the afternoon, a habit that they call, oddly enough, *tomando onces* (having elevenses).[‡]

In their sense of style, there is also a similarity with the Brit-

[‡] The alleged derivation of this term comes from a type of brandy, known as *aguardiente*, which has eleven letters. The story goes that some Chilean husbands wanted to go out drinking in the late afternoon and, in order to avoid their wives' wrath, told them that they were having elevenses, as a euphemistic way of telling the women that they were planning to imbibe brandy.

ish. In Chile the bright colors of the tropics give way to muted tones of gray, blue, and brown. Similarly, Chileans usually look disparagingly upon people who wear clothing that is too colorful or distinctive, which they disdainfully call tropical.

At a deeper level, Chileans have probably been dubbed "the British of Latin America" due to their approach to work and life, which seems to be almost Anglo-Saxon in certain ways. Of all the SSSAs, Chileans are said to be the hardest working. An International Labor Organization survey found that Chileans worked the most hours of any country polled, surpassing even the Koreans.

Chileans tend toward sobriety as well. This can be noted in most of the well-known Chilean political figures, from General Augusto Pinochet to the Christian Democratic Frei family, whose rather austere behavior and sobriety contrasts sharply with the flamboyant style of some of the Argentine political leaders like Juan Perón and Carlos Menem. Mónica Echeverría describes her fellow Chileans as follows: "We are without eroticism and sensuality, we are discolored and tense" (in Segovia, 17).

Perhaps the most important cultural trait that the Chileans and the British share, however, is the islandlike vantage point from which they view the world. Like other island nationalities, Chileans have a strong sense of "insider" versus "outsider." Although Chileans usually feel very comfortable with each other, knowing the proper rules of behavior within their national boundaries, they often seem ill at ease with outsiders and self-consciously concerned with what others think of them and their country.

Innovation, Conservativism, Hypocrisy, and Indirectness

In many ways Chileans' attitude toward foreign things is similar to yet another island nationality, the Japanese. Like the Japanese, Chileans are known for looking abroad for innovations and introducing them at home. One consequence of this is that Chileans often seem to be the most innovative and future oriented of the SSSA countries. For example, Chile is currently among the leaders in the region in number of computers and cell phones as well as volume of Internet use, and it even has a software industry.

This willingness to experiment goes far beyond the technological realm. Politically, the nation has had a tumultuous and fascinating history. In the last half century, Chile has gone from being one of the strongest democracies in Latin America to having been the first country in the world to democratically elect a Marxist president (Salvador Allende—1970 to 1973). This political experiment was cut short by the violent intervention of the Chilean military in 1973, followed by sixteen years of military rule by Augusto Pinochet. Democracy was restored again in 1989, and in 2000 a Socialist—Ricardo Lagos—was elected, representing yet another twist in Chile's political saga.

Chile is also well-known for its economic innovations. Chileans were the first in the region during the early 1980s to open up their economy after undertaking massive privatizations and a decrease in government spending. As a consequence, and despite several initial years of hardship, the country has experienced decidedly more economic growth than any of its neighbors in recent years. This prosperity has brought about far-reaching changes in many aspects of contemporary Chilean society that extend way beyond the economic.

However, like the Japanese, the Chileans are usually quite careful about adapting foreign innovations to their own cultural realities, which are often profoundly conservative. Chile is the only nation in the Western world (at the time of this writing) that still does not have a divorce law. Topics such as homosexuality are taboo for many sectors of the population, and abortion is illegal even if the mother's life is at stake. One North American journalist, Clifford Krauss of the *New York Times*, went so far as to juxtapose contemporary Chilean norms with those of Victorian England.

Several factors account for Chile's conservative bent. The country's isolation and its recent history of authoritarian rule have both played a part. More important, however, is the role of the Catholic Church, which emerged from the Pinochet years with great moral strength because of its support of human rights during the dictatorship. As a consequence, the Church plays a prominent role in Chilean society; for example, two of the country's three major television stations are strongly Catholic in orientation, and censors have banned more than fifty films and censored over seven hundred videos in recent years, one prime example being Martin Scorsese's 1988 film, *The Last Temptation of Christ*.

One of the most puzzling aspects of Chilean culture is its tendency to be simultaneously very conservative and very innovative in its ideas and policies. Although some people like to label certain sectors in Chilean society as "conservative" and others as "innovative," the reality is actually more complex; most Chileans of whatever class and political inclination hold both very open-minded attitudes and quite conservative ones, a fact that helps to explain many apparently paradoxical aspects of life there.

This conservative public discourse in Chile encourages hypocritical behavior. People appear to follow socially accepted conventions while often behaving quite differently in their private lives. For example, despite the illegality of divorce, the number of annulled marriages in Chile is exorbitant, and over one-third of all Chilean children are technically illegitimate. Extramarital affairs abound, as do clandestine abortions. Mariana Alywin, herself from the elite, has the following to say in this regard: "Our social elite is very conservative, but I don't know a city in the world with more motels and infidelity. This is a very hypocritical country" (in Krauss 1999). Others claim that such behavior is not actually hypocrisy but rather a uniquely Chilean way of resolving conflicting morality. As Alfredo Jocelyn-Holt sees it, "Chile is traditional, but it is not an orthodox conservative country. It is a morally flexible country. If there is a gay person in the family you accept it without ever talking about it" (in Krauss).

Such an oblique approach to dealing with conflict illustrates yet another Chilean cultural characteristic—its fondness for indirectness. It is as though the Chileans, getting their inspiration from across the vast Pacific Ocean, have adopted an almost Asian approach to dealing with conflict and dissension. This mode of communication can be interpreted as either politeness in its concern with avoiding confrontation or as rudeness in its lack of clarity and honesty. As Esther Edwards sees it,

> The Chileans don't lie more than other nationalities. The North Americans can be more brutal, more direct,...but the Chilean is cautious. It is not a lie; it is that Chileans do not like to contradict....
>
> After traveling all over the world, one comes to Chile and says, What charming people! How sweet! How nice! That is because the Chilean will never say a brutal truth. An Argentine friend said to me,..."How good are those Chileans that say to you, I can't go because I have to take my daughter someplace. An Argentine would say, There is no way you can make me go."
>
> Another friend from the United States commented that the Chileans are big liars, and *lie* is a heavy word in the United States. I told this person that [this is a matter of] codes, manners. You have to learn to navigate in these verbal waters. We are very Oriental. (1998, 10)

Communication Patterns

Influenced by their nation's insular character, Chileans have a distinctive way of speaking Spanish that disconcerts many when they first hear it. John Brennan and Alvaro Taboada, in their dictionary of Chilean slang, explain the reasons for this as follows:

> Chilean Spanish is not typical Spanish. It is an idiomatic language that perhaps stems from two contradictory characteristics. The first is Chile's history of immigration and close-knit immigrant communities and thus the frequency of words and expressions from other languages (primarily Italian, Yugoslavian, German and English).... The second characteristic is Chile's island-like

> character. This has led to an internal, almost incestuous, linguistic development, which occurs in a very playful sense. (1998, 10)

There are innumerable examples of uniquely Chilean words and variations, a stellar one being the ubiquitous term *huevón* that has evolved from its original, rather lewd meaning to becoming one of the most widely employed terms in informal exchanges, particularly among men. From this one word, at least twenty or more variations have spun off, with implications ranging from "buddy" all the way to much stronger language implying male genitals. In fact, one linguist dedicated an entire book just to the etymology and evolution of the term.

When discussing Chileans' communication style, it is hard to avoid comparing them with the Argentines. Although the two nationalities share a large border, they have quite different ways of expressing themselves. Argentines are self-confident, direct, and verbal, while Chileans are usually more self-effacing and restrained in both body language and speech patterns. One unpublished study found that the average Argentine uses about 2,000 words a day, while the average Chilean uses only 700. As one Chilean in this study explains, "We are not as outgoing as you might imagine, and usually don't start talking to just anybody…in a sense we are quite timid."

Chileans' speech patterns reflect this tentativeness and can often be recognized merely on the basis of their frequent use of the diminutive *-ito/a*, which is added to the ending of words as a way of "softening" them. Thus, *guagua* (Chilean way to say baby) becomes *guaguito/a*, *tomar te* (to drink tea) becomes *tomar tecito*, and so on. This habit is strongest among females, but males use the diminutive as well at times. Some contend that these speech patterns give the impression of insecurity and/or lack of confidence, and certain Chileans in the business sector have expressed a concern that such practices do not mesh well with an increasingly globalized world where directness and assertiveness are accorded greater value.

Living and Working in Chile

These days Chile is probably one of the easiest of the SSSA countries for English-speaking North Americans (ESNAs) to live in; recently Santiago was ranked the number one city in South America for expatriate living. Due to the nation's level of economic development and recent economic boom, most of the larger urban sectors (as well as some of the rural areas where agro-industry and/or mining is practiced) are quite modern in amenities and infrastructure, leading some visitors to complain that the nation does not seem "exotic" enough.

However, initial impressions can sometimes be deceiving in Chile's case. Despite the superficial appearance of modernity and globalization, there is much that hasn't changed and that is profoundly Hispanic, including a proliferate bureaucracy, a strongly marked hierarchy in human interactions, and a pace of life and use of time that is markedly different from that of ESNA. Among the most challenging issues for many long-term residents is the marked insularity of Chilean society, which can make it difficult for outsiders to feel accepted as an equal by many Chileans. While foreigners—usually called gringos—are invariably treated hospitably, they sometimes find it hard to establish real friendships with the rather reserved and cliquish natives.

Due to Chile's unique cultural patterns, working in this country can differ from the initial expectations of some expatriates, even those who have worked in other parts of the region. Chileans, at least when conducting business, are among the hardest working and most punctual of the SSSA nationalities. Many of the professionals are well trained, and quite a few have advanced degrees from universities abroad. One of the most pleasant aspects of doing business in Chile is that the business sector is well organized, with numerous active associations and Chambers of Commerce. For the most part, business practices are relatively straightforward. Further facilitating the process is the low level of corruption, about on par with that of the United States.[§]

Despite all these positive characteristics of the Chilean business sector, workplace efficiency is markedly lower than in ESNA. Several different explanations have been put forward to explain this phenomenon. A Chilean undersecretary of labor maintains that inefficiency prevails because "Chileans tend to put things off…and…do not administer their time wisely" (Roraff and Camacho 1998, 141). Others attribute this trait, at least in part, to the enormous amount of time and energy that is typically dedicated to establishing and maintaining relationships in the Chilean work setting. Geert Hofstede, in his well-known study of IBM business executives from around the world, ranked the Chileans among the most concerned of all the Spanish-speaking nationalities with the maintenance of human contacts.

The importance accorded to relationships is noticeable within the office environment and in the business sector as a whole. People frequently employ friends and/or people who are recommended by friends, a practice known as using a *pituto* (a personal contact), and many Chilean businesspeople know each other from their university days, if not before. As a consequence, foreigners sometimes find it difficult to "establish their credentials" with Chileans. As one businessperson commented in a questionnaire by Maria Isabel Mizon, "Chile is a very tight business society." Another pointed out that "It took some successes for Chilean colleagues to begin to have faith in me."

In Chile, as in all the SSSA countries, one's physical presentation and attire are extremely important for success, especially in the business sector. In keeping with the Chileans' preference for understatement, both men and women prefer rather conservative business clothes in subdued tones, and in many offices

---

[§] In the 1988 Transparency International survey, Chile was placed right below the United States in its level of corruption (19th and 18th, respectively), making it the least corrupt Latin American country included in the survey.

secretaries and other junior staff wear uniforms. Even Chileans' taste in business cards leans toward the austere—usually quite simple in tone and design.

* * * * * * *

Chilean culture has gone through vast transformations in the last thirty years, propelled in large part by political and economic events. Consequently, the Chileans of today tend to be less parochial and more concerned about "getting ahead" than earlier generations. Nonetheless, many of the fundamental characteristics of Chilean cultural patterns persist: the Chilean people have as strong a sense of identity as ever and clearly differentiate themselves from all others, and they continue to present, at first impression, a sober and cautious demeanor, oftentimes communicating rather indirectly. Perhaps most important of all, Chileans are still trying to figure out their own identity and where they fit in the world as they struggle to maintain a delicate equilibrium between their traditional ways and the many forces of profound change swirling around them.

References and Selected Bibliography

Allende, Isabel. 1986. *House of the Spirits*. New York: Bantam Books.

Antonio de la Parra, Marco. 1999. *La Mala Memoria*. Santiago: Editorial Planeta.

Bengoa, Jose. 1996. *Historia del Pueblo Mapuche*. Santiago: Editorial Sur.

Constable, Pamela, and Arturo Valenzuela. 1993. *A Nation of Enemies: Chile Under Pinochet*. New York: W. W. Norton & Company.

Dorfman, Ariel. 1998. *Heading South, Looking North: A Bilingual Journey*. New York: Farrar, Straus, and Giroux.

Edwards, Esther. 1998. "No somos mentiroso, solo inexactos." *Ya*, 3 March.

Fleet, Michael. 1985. *Rise and Fall of Christian Democracy*. Princeton, NJ: Princeton University Press.

Krauss, Clifford. 1999. "Victoria Would Not Be Amazed by Chile Today." *The New York Times*, 24 October.

Loveman, Brian. 2001. *Chile: The Legacy of Hispanic Capitalism*. Oxford, England: Oxford University Press.

Márquez, Gabriel García. 1995. *Clandestine in Chile: The Adventures of Miguel Littin*. New York: Henry Holt.

Mistral, Gabriela. 2001. *Poesia Completa*. Santiago: Andres Bello.

Montecino, Sonia. 1996. *Madres y Huachos: Alegorías del Mestizaje Chileno*. 3d ed. Santiago: Editorial Sudamericana.

Moulian, Tomás. 1997. *Chile Actual: Anatomia de un Mito*. Santiago: LOM.

Paley, Julie. 2001. *Marketing Democracy: Power and Social Movements in Post-Dictatorship Chile*. Berkeley: University of California Press.

Peralta, Ariel. 1999. *El Mito de Chile*. Santiago: Editorial Bogavante.

Roraff, Susan, and Laura Camacho. 1998. *Culture Shock! Chile*. Portland, OR: Graphic Arts Publishing.

Segovia, Pilar. 1999. "El Estupidario Chileno." *Ya*, 5 October.

Smith, Brian, and Michael Fleet. 2000. *The Catholic Church and Democracy in Chile and Peru*. Notre Dame, IN: University of Notre Dame Press.

Spooner, Mary Helen. 1999. *Soldiers in a Narrow Land: The Pinochet Regime in Chile*. Berkeley: University of California Press.

Subercaseaux, Bernardo. 1996. *Chile: Un Pais Moderno?* Santiago: Grupo Editoria Zeta.

Toloza, Cristian, and Eugenio Lahera, eds. 1998. *Chile en los Noventa*. Santiago: Dolmen Ediciones.

Valenzuela, Arturo. 1979. *The Breakdown of Democratic Regimes: Chile*. Baltimore, MD: Johns Hopkins Press.

Wheeler, Sara. 1999. *Travels in a Thin Country: A Journey through Chile*. New York: Modern Library.

Zapata, Celia Correas. 1998. *Isabel Allende: Vida y Espiritus*. Barcelona: Plaza y Janes, Editores.

Colombia: A Nation of Nations

*Kevin G. Guerrieri**

*El pobre surrealismo se estrella en
añicos contra la realidad de Colombia.*

—Fernando Vallejo

*Poor surrealism is smashed to
pieces by the reality of Colombia.*

The third largest of the Spanish-speaking South American (SSSA) nations, Colombia is a land of contrasts and extremes of many types, some of which are quite exceptional. Perhaps most noteworthy is the nation's notoriety as one of the most violent places in the world today; nevertheless, it has one of the longest standing democratic political systems in the entire continent. This violence affects much of life in contemporary Colombia and is reflected on many fronts, including political conflicts, guerrilla warfare, drug trafficking, and urban strife.

---

* Kevin G. Guerrieri is Assistant Professor of Spanish and Latin American literature at the University of San Diego. His M.A. is from the University of Colorado at Boulder and his Ph.D., from the University of California, Riverside. He has coauthored the book *Culture and Customs of Colombia* and has served as a Fulbright scholar (2000–2001) in Colombia.

Oftentimes ignored in this emphasis on Colombian violence is the fact that this nation and its peoples embody so much more than just the conflictual proclivity of a minority of its citizens. Some of the most well-known SSSA products hail from Colombia, including many of the fragrant flowers that deck homes and businesses throughout English-speaking North America (ESNA), as well as some of the best coffee to be found anywhere. As if reflecting their country's great natural bounty, Colombians are reputed to have a strong aesthetic sense and artistic proclivity. They have long been considered among the most "cultured" of the SSSAs, which can be noted in all the artistic disciplines. Several of the most popular performers in the international Spanish language music scene these days are Colombians, such as Shakira and Carlos Vives. One of the most well-known Latin American authors, Nobel laureate Gabriel García Márquez, also hails from Colombia. All of these creators have drawn their inspiration in large part from the cultural richness, ethnic diversity, and glaring incongruities of their homeland, all of which can be related to the following aspects of this nation:

- Colombia is the only South American country that has coastlines on both the Pacific Ocean and the Caribbean Sea; however, most of the important areas of settlement are clustered in mountain valleys located in the inland region of the country.
- Colombia has a diverse economic base and has fared better than most SSSA countries in recent decades. Although this nation has abundant natural resources, its most famous (or infamous) export is illegal drugs.
- Paradoxically, Colombia has traditionally been considered one of the most "cultured" of all the SSSA countries, and yet at the same time it has had more civil wars and internal conflicts than almost any other nation in the continent.

In order to better understand the Colombian nation and its peoples, the following topics will be discussed: geographic and regional influences; key cultural characteristics, including grand illusions and harsh realities, making sense of Colombia's violence, and artistic creation and the legacy of the regeneration; communication patterns; and living and working in Colombia.

Geographic and Regional Influences

Regionalism has profoundly marked the character and identity of Colombians to an even greater extent than it has its neighbors; in many ways, Colombia is more a "nation of nations" than a single, united country. There are numerous factors that account for the strength and persistence of regionalist sentiments among Colombians, one of the most important being the nation's geography. While other countries in the region can also boast great geographical variety, what makes the Colombian case unique is that this landmass serves as a bridge or linkage point between several very different topographical and climatic zones, each one represented within its own national boundaries.

Colombia is the only South American country that borders Central America, and, in fact, Panama and Colombia were one country until the beginning of the twentieth century. Colombia is also the only nation in South America to have coastlines on two different bodies of water—the Pacific Ocean and the Caribbean Sea. The easternmost region of the country is characterized by a place of vast grassy plains, called the llanos, which are shared jointly with Venezuela. This area is also often referred to as the "región de la Orinoquía," due to the presence of the Orinoco River, which marks part of the boundary between these two countries. Moving south from the llanos, Colombia transforms into an Amazonian country with important downstream linkages with Brazil. Finally, and perhaps most important of all in terms of the locus of settlement patterns, Colombia is an Andean nation with high mountains and numerous, fertile valleys within which live and work the majority of Colombia's population.

The flora and fauna found in Colombian terrains are as diverse as the nation's ecosystems: this country boasts the greatest diversity of animal species per unit of area of any country in the world and the second greatest number of total species after

Brazil. This includes over 1,700 different recorded species of birds and over 3,000 types of orchids. In fact, Colombia is one of the world's major exporters of flowers. The wealth of natural resources that are found in this country is remarkable, from innumerable plant and animal species to precious stones, coal, petroleum, and other products.

The Colombian people are also a diverse lot, and differential settlement patterns based in part on ethnicity have been yet another factor in the shaping of regional distinctions. As in most of the other SSSA countries, the three major groups that interfaced in Colombia were the Native Americans, Africans, and Spaniards; however, the mixture that emerged over the centuries was somewhat different from that found in either of its Andean neighbors, Peru and Ecuador, or its eastern neighbor, Venezuela. In contrast with the former two nations, most of the territory that eventually became present-day Colombia was not included in the vast Inca empire; instead, numerous tribal groups, with a total population of about three million at the time of the Spaniards' arrival, inhabited the area, each group with its own language and cultural patterns. The Chibcha, renowned for their gold work, were among the most prominent of these groups. The vast majority did not survive the colonial period, and today only about 400,000 tribal peoples hailing from approximately eighty different linguistic dialects or families remain. To make up for the paucity of Native American workers, Spanish conquistadores imported Africans in significant numbers, giving this nation, along with neighboring Venezuela, the largest black population of the SSSA countries. However, in contrast with Venezuela, the European presence was much stronger in the area of present-day Colombia due to the fact that it was the capital of the Viceroyalty of Nueva Granada and an important center of Spanish power in the continent.

The strength of Colombian regionalism is partly attributable to political factors that have shaped the nation throughout its history. In contrast with most of the other SSSA countries, Colombia was organized in a rather decentralized manner throughout much of its early postindependence existence. Under the extremely liberal Constitution of 1863, for example, the country was named the Estados Unidos (United States) de Colombia, and the political power and administration of the country was redistributed, prioritizing local and regional interests over national ones. Toward the end of the nineteenth century, however, the conservative party took control of the country, and the regime known as the Regeneration, spearheaded by the presidency of Rafael Núñez, initiated a project of national consolidation based on the centralization of power. In spite of the efforts of the Regeneration and the accelerated modernization of the country in the first half of the twentieth century, the legacy of regional identification and differentiation has remained strong even today.

Colombia's regionalism is typically subdivided according to five principal geographically designated regions, most of which, in turn, contain a wide diversity of peoples, climatic conditions, topographical features, and products.[†] These are the Caribbean coast, the Pacific coast, the Andes, the llanos and the Amazon. It is important to emphasize that these regions cannot be seen as clearly definable and homogeneous within. The Colombian Andes, for example, contain several subregions that are distinctive due to geographical features, economic structures, and sociocultural configurations.

[†] Colombian regionalism is a well-researched topic with an extensive bibliography, and many different strategies for the regional division have been developed. For a graphic illustration of the regional differences in the mid-nineteenth-century Colombia, see Guillermo Hernández de Alba, *Acuarelas de la Comisión Corográfica: Colombia 1850–1859*, Litografía Arco (Bogotá, 1986). The ever-growing number of studies that focus on specific regions of Colombia highlight the fact that it is a "nation of nations"; these studies include *Colombia: Territorial Rule and the Llanos Frontier* by Jane M. Rausch, *The Colombian Caribbean: A Regional History, 1870–1950* by Eduardo Posada-Carbó, *Blackness and Race Mixture: The Dynamics of Racial Identity in Colombia* by Peter Wade, and *Colombia amazónica*, among many others.

Coastal Regions

Colombia's Caribbean coastal region comprises primarily a low, flat plain that runs along the approximately 1,600 kilometers (1,000 miles) of national territory that fronts the Caribbean Sea. Several rivers snake through these warm and humid lowlands in their journey to the sea. In some places the current is so slow that swamps and lagoons form in the near-stagnant waters, while in other areas local flooding occurs annually during the rainy season. Rising above this very tropical terrain, almost incongruously, stands the highest coastal mountain range in the world, the Sierra Nevada de Santa Marta, whose tallest peaks are permanently snowcapped. The primary port, as well as the commercial and industrial center of this region, is the city of Barranquilla, which has over a million inhabitants.

As is true of residents from other coastal regions of SSSA, the Colombian Caribbeans—known as *costeños*—are reputed to be quite receptive to new and different peoples and ideas. The black presence is especially notable here; there are some villages, called *palenques*, in this part of Colombia that were originally founded by rebellious African slaves during the colonial period, and remained semi-isolated for centuries.[‡] This region, known simply as the Costa, is characterized by this dynamic mixture of ethnicities, which also includes a strong Hispanic presence and that of more recent immigration from other parts of Europe and the Middle East. This heterogeneous region provided some of the first stimuli to the imagination of young Gabriel García Márquez, who was born along this coast, in the town of Aracataca, in 1927.

There is a true Caribbean flair in the cultural patterns of the zone's residents, who are reputed to be the most fun-loving and gregarious of all Colombians. Music provides a constant backdrop, and dancing, joking, and socializing are highly valued. In fact, both Shakira and Carlos Vives were born here, the former from Barranquilla and the latter from Santa Marta. Much plea-

‡ See William W. Megenney's book on the language spoken by this population, *El palenquero: un lenguaje post-criollo de Colombia*.

sure is derived from enjoying the present moment, a trait that Colombians from other regions of the nation claim makes the costeños rather lackadaisical toward planning and/or working toward the future.

Residents of Colombia's other coast, the Pacific, share many ethnic and cultural similarities with the costeños; however, they exhibit some noteworthy differences as well, related to climatic and economical factors. This zone is a challenging place to live because of the nearly daily torrential rains and major storms of various sorts that often wreak havoc on the adjoining coastal lands. Due to these conditions and also to the historical predominance of the Caribbean port cities as primary international trade routes, Colombia's Pacific coast is decidedly poorer than its Caribbean neighbors; in addition, in some of the more isolated villages, the poverty is even more severe. While there seems to be a more cohesive identity uniting the costeños of the Caribbean coast, the residents of the Colombian Pacific coast are typically referred to according to their more local origins, such as *chocoano* (from Chocó) or *tumaqueño* (from Tumaco), for example.

The Andes

Despite Colombia's extensive and diverse coastal regions, it is the country's mountains with their ensuing valleys that are the strongest forces in shaping national life and culture. The Colombian Andes Mountains are made up of three principal ranges that run north and south: the Cordillera Occidental, the Cordillera Central, and the Cordillera Oriental. In the southernmost part of the country these three ranges merge together and continue onward, extending over the entire length of South America. Of the fourteen most important population centers in the country, eleven are to be found in the valleys and intermountain plateaus that are located along and between the three cordilleras. Over the centuries, each of these settlements developed quite separately from the others due to difficulties in communication and transportation, resulting in quite distinctive local cultures and a marked insular attitude toward outsiders:

the most important of these areas are the sugar-growing zone, the coffee region, the industrially and commercially oriented Antioquia, and the Colombian altiplano, where the nation's capital, Bogotá, is located.

The sugar-growing zone is located in the southwestern portion of the nation, primarily in the department (an administrative unit) of Valle del Cauca, but also in the department of Cauca. The most important city in this region is Cali, with a population of about two million. Also located on the Cauca River, Buenaventura is Colombia's primary seaport on the Pacific coast. The semitropical climate and fertile conditions of the Cauca River valley make it ideal for growing a wide variety of crops, the most important of which is sugarcane. Some general distinctions can be drawn among the different populations of the Valle del Cauca and the neighboring department of Cauca. While the Valle is considered *tierra caliente* (hot lands) and the *caleños* (people from Cali) are known for their lively spirit and preference for salsa music, the department of Cauca—in addition to its sugar-growing and coastal areas—includes a prominent mountainous zone where the cooler climate is reflected in the more reserved temperament of its people. Cauca also has the largest indigenous population of any department of Colombia.

The *zona cafetera* (coffee zone), primarily concentrated in the area known as the "golden triangle" between Bogotá, Medellín, and Cali, is somewhat higher in altitude and further inland, between the Cordillera Occidental and the Cordillera Oriental. The impact of coffee cultivation and exportation on the Colombian economy and the rise of a rural middle class during the first half of the twentieth century were factors of great significance in the future development of the nation as a whole. In fact, it has been suggested that coffee was the catalyst to Colombia's becoming a capitalist society.[§] Nonetheless, in spite of being the capitals of their respective departments, four

---

§ See James D. Henderson's book *Modernization in Colombia: The Laureano Gómez Years, 1889–1965* and also the study by Marco Palacios, *El café en Colombia, 1850–1970: Una historia económica, social y política*.

of the principal cities of the zone—Manizales, Pereira, Armenia, and Ibagué—are quite provincial, and this area in general has retained a predominantly rural character.

Colombia's coffee is world renowned, and for many the words *Colombian* and *coffee* are practically synonymous. This idea is continually reinforced by the appearance of the internationally recognized figure of Juan Valdés, the romanticized version of the coffee-bean picker. The regional distinctions of the "golden triangle" were highlighted in the Colombian soap opera *Café*, which was extremely successful in the 1990s, both within the country and abroad. This program depicted many different aspects of the zona cafetera and served a didactic function with respect to Colombian coffee production in general. Not surprisingly, Colombians are, for the most part, avid coffee drinkers—and not just those who live in the zona cafetera. In urban areas, for example, innumerable coffee shops and coffee stands dot the streets. Likewise, most offices hire a worker (usually a woman) whose duties include serving coffee to the rest of the staff throughout the day; she is typically referred to as *la señora de los tintos*.

Antioquia. The department of Antioquia, the most highly populated area of the Colombian Andean region after Bogotá and located to the north of the zona cafetera, has established itself as a primary commercial zone of the country. This region traditionally had a high percentage of *criollos* (Creoles, or Caucasians of Spanish bloodlines born in the colonies) and is still popularly referred to as Colombia's "whitest" department. The *antioqueños*, also known as *paisas* and whose accent is easily identified by other Colombians, are widely admired for their strong work ethic and entrepreneurial tendencies. Medellín, a city of more than three and a half million inhabitants and the capital of Antioquia, is recognized as both the "Industrial City of Colombia" and the "City of Eternal Spring." This city has historically been a primary base for the country's textile industry, which also serves to explain its fame as the Colombian fashion center. Medellín boasts the country's only subway system and is regarded as a clean and pleasant tourist destination. Whereas the caleños tend to be *salseros*,

Medellín is the "Capital of Tango"; it was here that Carlos Gardel, the legendary tango singer, died in an airplane crash in 1935. In general, the paisas take great pride in their origins, with which they continue to strongly identify themselves, even when living in other parts of the country.

Colombia's altiplano, located in the center of the country on the Cordillera Oriental and adjacent to the eastern llanos, is the highest part of the country, although its altitude does not reach that of the altiplano in Bolivia and Peru. This region is the coolest place in the country, with moderate temperatures that rarely exceed 80 degrees Fahrenheit. The residents of Cundinamarca and Boyacá, the two departments within the altiplano, reflect the temperate climate of their home with a "cooler" and more introverted nature than Colombians from other regions.

Bogotá, the nation's capital and officially renamed "Santa fé de Bogotá" in the 1990s, is located on the altiplano in Cundinamarca. Founded by the Spaniard Gonzalo Jiménez de Quesada in 1538, Bogotá came to be one of the most important colonial cities of the Spanish empire and was the capital of the Viceroyalty of Nueva Granada, which encompassed most of modern-day Colombia, Venezuela, Ecuador, and Panama. Despite the marked regionalism of Colombia, Bogotá constitutes the economic, political, and cultural center of the nation. Internal migration and continual urbanization have turned this city with over eight million inhabitants (Colombia's total population is more than forty million) into a microcosm of the nation, emblematic of its heterogeneous character. The contrasts found in Bogotá can be alarming—extreme poverty and opulent prosperity, often immediately juxtaposed. In spite of the diversity of peoples who have come to reside in the capital, the personality of the *bogotanos*, also known as *cachacos*, predominates. They are generally considered to be arrogant and aloof compared with other Colombians.

The Llanos and the Amazon

To the east of the Andes Mountains lies half of Colombia's territory: the Llanos and the Amazon; yet only about 5 percent of the population live in this part of the country. The llanos is a zone of grassy plains that lies along the Venezuelan border that is shared by the two nations (see page 345 in chapter 18, "Venezuela: The Tropical Beat," for a more in-depth description of the region); the region of the Amazon is the least populated part of the country. In the Colombian Amazon there are only small islands of human settlements, most of which can only be reached by air or river, as land transportation into or out of this region is extremely limited. These two regions are vividly depicted in the Colombian canonical novel *La vorágine* (*The Vortex*), published by José Eustasio Rivera in 1924. In more current times, the sparse population and remoteness of both of these regions have made them attractive for the cultivation of illegal crops and also for guerrilla and paramilitary activity.

Keys to Understanding the Colombians

Grand Illusions and Harsh Realities

The region that is now Colombia has long been a theater for the making and breaking of human dreams, many of which have been notably quixotic in character. More than half a millennium ago, the initial encounters between indigenous groups and Spanish conquistadores led to the legend of El Dorado. Upon landing at Cabo de la Vela on La Guajira Peninsula in 1499 and coming into contact with members of the Tairona indigenous group, the Spaniard Alonso de Ojeda soon heard the story of a king who submerged himself in a lake after covering his entire body with gold dust. From this tale arose the legend of El Dorado, which consequently prompted the invasion, conquest, and subsequent colonization of much of the interior Andean region of Colombia. In fact, the Colombian city of Santa María la Antigua del Darién served as one of the first bases for the colonization of South America by the Spanish.

The search for El Dorado eventually proved fruitless; no such extensive treasure trove of gold has ever been discovered in

Colombia, at least not in the same dimensions as imagined by the early conquistadores and adventurers, who were willing to decimate indigenous populations in their search to fulfill grandiose dreams of wealth. Nonetheless, Colombia is in reality a very rich land, the subsoil of which yields many types of minerals, including gold and platinum. Emeralds are particularly plentiful, and 95 percent of all these precious green gems in the world come from Colombia. Emerald trading businesses dominate an area of downtown Bogotá, and the *esmeralderos*—emerald traders—can be seen congregated on the street dealing in these precious stones.

In addition, large reserves of coal and petroleum also figure among this country's natural resources. Some of the largest coal deposits in South America are found on La Guajira Peninsula on the Colombian Caribbean coast, an accessible source U.S. energy companies have not overlooked. As briefly noted in these few examples, Colombia's abundant natural resources have long produced dreams of wealth.

Smuggling contraband has been a widespread practice in Colombia dating back to the colonial period. This clandestine activity can be related as much to dreams of wealth and adventure as to the cruel reality of economic existence. Colombia's geographical features, with two major coasts, the Pacific and the Caribbean, and its northern border with Panama, are conducive to smuggling, and typical contraband transported out of the country has long included items such as emeralds, exotic birds, and sugar, among others. Other products are smuggled into the country in order to avoid the high import duties and value-added taxes that are placed on imported goods.

The selling of pirated editions of books and CDs as well as contraband of just about anything imaginable, which many Colombians have resorted to in their struggle to survive, has become a serious problem for the Colombian economy. Many of these products are sold in *sanandresitos*, groups of small businesses where people go in search of bargains, or simply in the streets. In response to this, law enforcement officials periodically raid these illegal enterprises, and the national government has launched a propaganda campaign aimed at deterring both smuggling and purchasing contraband items by educating the public. In one recent commercial, a cartoon-figure camel is shown crossing the desert with a television strapped on its back. The narrator then reads, "*No pares el camello*" ("Don't stop the camel"). *Camello* is a Colombian colloquialism for "job" or "work," the lack of which is a common predicament reflected in the high levels of unemployment facing the Colombian population and worsened by smuggling.

In the last two decades, the export that has placed Colombia in the international limelight and greatly stigmatized the people of this nation is that of illegal drugs, which has created a multibillion-dollar industry for the nation's underground economy. Drug trafficking can be characterized as another of Colombia's grand illusions; it is an activity in which only a small percentage of the population participates but which has had dramatic consequences for the entire country. One figure who reached legendary proportions during his life as a drug lord was Pablo Escobar, leader of the Medellín drug cartel who, paradoxically, managed to found a newspaper, was elected to the Congress, and was known by many as El Robin Hood Paisa for his benevolent actions. Escobar came to be seen as a mythical figure of popular culture, who donated enormous sums of money to public works projects in the poorer neighborhoods of Medellín. After turning himself in in 1989, Escobar was incarcerated in a specially built prison called, ironically enough, *La Catedral*, located in his hometown of Envigado. After escaping and eventually dying at the hands of the police, this infamous drug lord was mourned by many Colombians. Such apparent paradoxes have led one sociologist to describe Colombia as a "society characterized as chaotic at best, and murderously dysfunctional at worst" (Fitch 1998, 5).

In 1996 Gabriel García Márquez published *Noticia de un secuestro* (*News of a Kidnapping*), a journalistic account of the kidnappings and violence carried out by the Medellín cartel in the late 1980s and early 1990s. He is best known for his most accomplished novel, *Cien años de soledad* (*One Hundred Years of Solitude*), published in 1967. In this novel, García Márquez juxtaposes the magical and the everyday with such masterful style that, since the late 1960s, his name is commonly associated with the literary form known as, "magic realism." *One Hundred Years of Solitude* offers many insights into Colombian culture and society as reflected in its story about the foundation of the town of Macondo by the Buendía family and its subsequent development and modernization. In this novel and others, García Márquez captures with great artistic mastery the sociohistorical circumstances of his country, exemplifying the coexistence—oftentimes conflictive—of grand illusions and harsh realities.

Simón Bolívar is a historical figure of nearly mythical dimensions in Colombia. In *El general en su laberinto* (*The General in His Labyrinth*), published in 1989, García Márquez tells the story of the final days of the legendary hero who had one of the most ambitious dreams of all: the creation of a unified SSSA. From 1550 until its political independence from Spain, the territory of present-day Colombia was known as the Nuevo Reino de Granada. Independence was achieved in the Battle of Boyacá in 1819 under the leadership of Bolívar—commonly known as El Libertador—who then forged the territory known as Gran Colombia, which consisted of modern-day Colombia, Ecuador, Panama, and Venezuela. Nonetheless, due to the enormous size of the territory, the drastic regional and cultural differences, and constant internal strife, Gran Colombia crumbled apart, losing Ecuador and Venezuela in 1830.

The nation was renamed the República de Nueva Granada, and in this same year Bolívar died in Santa Marta on the Colombian Caribbean coast. In spite of the failure of his ambitious political dream, the Liberator is still widely venerated in Colombia, and his legacy as a freedom fighter carries significant symbolic weight for many. In the 1990s, for example, some of the major Colombian guerrilla groups formed a coalition that they named the Coordinadora Guerrillera Simón Bolívar.

Following the death of Bolívar and the loss of Ecuador and

Venezuela in 1830, the Colombian nation experienced further drastic modifications throughout the nineteenth century and into the early twentieth. After several previous name changes—each indicative of distinct political dreams and nation-building projects—the country received its current name, the República de Colombia, in 1886, under the conservative government of Rafael Núñez. The name itself is a tribute to Christopher Columbus, the Genovese explorer who, ironically, never actually set foot on Colombian territory. The last major setback to Colombian sovereignty took place with the loss of Panama.

While the rest of the country was engaged in a bloody civil war at the turn of the century, Panamanian separatists, fully backed by the U.S. government under president Theodore Roosevelt, declared their independence and were granted political autonomy in 1904. The United States' actions were clearly motivated by the trade possibilities offered by the construction of and control over the Panama Canal, which was completed in 1914. Although this tragic episode in the country's national history officially ended in the early 1920s, when the U.S. paid Colombia twenty-five million dollars as compensation for the loss of Panama, the old scar remains, fueling a continuing resentment toward the U.S. for intervening in Colombian sovereignty, and serves, symbolically, as the final chapter of Bolívar's broken dream.

Throughout the twentieth century, Colombia underwent the twin processes of modernization and urbanization, bringing about far-reaching changes in the lifestyle and livelihood of most locals. Likewise, the nostalgic remembrances of *Colombia linda* (beautiful Colombia), centered around idealized images of treasured country life, have been displaced by the harsh realities of violence, which has turned much of the extraordinarily beautiful Colombian natural world into a forbidden zone, inaccessible to its own citizens.

Making Sense of Colombia's Violence

Colombia is a country marked by a long tradition of internal conflict and violence. In spite of periodic moments of peace, order, and growth, this tradition held true in large measure during both the nineteenth and twentieth centuries. One journalist has even indicated that "Colombia is the country in which 'violentology' was born as an academic subject" (Bastenier 2000, 6). The pervasive violence in Colombia affects nearly everyone to some degree, and the legacy of its long history has been stamped into the nation's collective conscience. Violence is reflected in many facets of Colombian society, but the most apparent manifestations include the armed conflict evidenced by guerrilla, paramilitary, and military action and also by drug trafficking. Added to this, Colombia's noncombat homicide rate is the highest in the world, and its crime rate is staggering.

The causes behind all of this violence cannot be easily understood, but some primary factors can be identified: the struggle for Colombia's resources (gold, emeralds, land, coal, petroleum, etc.); political and ideological differences; conditions of inequality, injustice, and poverty; and the involvement of external forces within Colombia, referring here to other countries and multinational corporations. These factors must be seen as intermeshed with various manifestations of violence in different historical moments. Near the end of the nineteenth century, when Colombia still had not reached its first centenary as an independent nation, Rafael Núñez remarked, "The general rule has been civil war, and the exception has been public order" (Ocampo López 1987, 258).

During the nineteenth century, Colombia experienced fifty-two civil wars—sometimes referred to as insurrections—in its various regions, the majority of which were provincial and small-scale, but which nonetheless resulted in violent conflicts. Between 1864 and 1885 alone, two major civil wars took place (one of which lasted two years), in addition to eight revolutions, one coup d'etat, and several internal upheavals (257). Although the various conflicts arose from different circumstances, one common cause behind many of them can be attributed to the political tug-of-war between the Liberal and the Conservative

Parties, in their multifaceted guises and denominations.[||] Since that time and up to the present day, these two parties have come to be seen by many Colombians as two sides of the same coin: the conservative wealthy oligarchy that wields the power in the political, social, and economic arenas.[¶]

Colombia entered the twentieth century in the midst of a civil war known as the Guerra de los Mil Días (War of a Thousand Days) between the liberals and the conservatives. When a peace treaty was finally signed in 1902, this war had caused as many as a hundred thousand deaths, and the conservatives remained in power until 1930. At this time, the liberals gained control of the government, and during the presidency of Alfonso López Pumarejo (1934–1938), La Revolución en Marcha, a program of social reform and modernization, was implemented. The nation did in fact experience a high degree of unification and modernization from the 1930s to the 1950s. Nonetheless, the gap between the popular masses and the upper classes continued to widen. Already in the 1920s, the arrival of socialist and communist ideologies in Colombia promoted numerous movements that sought reforms in land distribution, labor conditions, and the rights of indigenous groups. Many violent conflicts sprang from these groups, including the often-commented-upon massacre of the striking workers of the United Fruit Company by Colombian soldiers in 1928.

The war with the most devastating consequences in twentieth-century Colombia was triggered by the assassination of the liberal leader Jorge Eliécer Gaitán on 9 April 1948. This act led to what is known as the Bogotazo and eventually developed into La Violencia, a civil war which claimed the lives of some

---

|| A recently published book by Cristina Rojas, *Civilization and Violence: Regimes of Representation in Nineteenth-Century Colombia*, offers a perceptive interpretation of the relationship between the "will to civilization" and violence in this period of Colombian history.

¶ William Ospina's *La franja amarilla* deals with the conformation of political power in Colombia and illustrates the relations that exist between conservative and liberal elites.

three hundred thousand Colombians. Initially, the violence and fighting took place in Bogotá but soon thereafter was transferred to rural areas where armies formed of campesinos fought against the symbols and strongholds of Colombian conservatism. By the early 1950s, several alliances were formed between peasant *comandantes* and small bands of communist guerrillas. In order to reestablish peace and order in the country, both the liberals and conservatives supported a military coup—Colombia's only military junta of the twentieth century—that was carried out by General Gustavo Rojas Pinilla. Under the general's military regime, the liberal guerrillas were offered amnesty. While some six thousand peasant fighters handed over their arms, others were pursued by the forces of the dictatorship. The period of La Violencia is fundamental for gaining a clearer understanding of the contemporary situation in Colombia. The near anarchy that reigned during this period, largely due to the breakdown of the judicial and law enforcement systems, strongly eroded the legitimacy of the state in the eyes of the average citizen.

In 1958 the liberals and conservatives formed the Frente Nacional (National Front), an agreement that provided for power sharing between the two parties. The presidency would alternate between the two parties every four years, with essentially the same political leaders who wielded the power before La Violencia returning to their previous positions. Leftist politicians and activists—who had a strong presence in many of Colombia's social organizations such as labor unions and organizations of teachers, campesinos, and indigenous peoples—were suppressed and explicitly excluded from the official political process, which led to the further growth of guerrilla activity as an extralegal channel for pressing marginalized agendas and issues. By the 1970s several guerrilla groups, each with its own strategies, ideologies, and objectives were operating. Among the principal groups were the Fuerzas Armadas Revolucionarias de Colombia (FARC), founded in 1963; the Ejército de Liberación Nacional (ELN), founded in 1965; the Movimiento 19 de Abril (M-19); and the Ejército Popular de Liberación (EPL), among others. It was not until the 1980s that the sociopolitical instability and guerrilla warfare in Colombia seriously intensified, due to the boom of the illegal drug business.

The trafficking in emeralds and other contraband, as mentioned earlier, was a noteworthy antecedent of the more recent drug trade. Drug trafficking began in a small way in the 1960s with primitive smuggling methods and dealt primarily in marijuana cultivated on La Guajira Peninsula. By the 1970s, cocaine trafficking began to emerge as well, and Colombian traffickers often served as middlemen between cocaine producers in Peru and Bolivia and the primary consumers of the drug in the northern hemisphere. By the 1980s the Medellín cartel already dominated a significant portion of the cocaine business, and due to the enormous wealth and power it accumulated, the cartel, under the leadership of Pablo Escobar, threatened to undermine the authority of the government, its presence evident in many aspects of Colombian society.

In 1984 the Colombian police raided Tranquilandia, the largest cocaine laboratory in history (located in the llanos), and in retaliation for the crackdown, the "narcos" assassinated Justice Minister Rodrigo Lara Bonilla. This led to the policy of extraditing Colombian narcos wanted for trial in the United States. To avoid extradition, the drug lords then resorted to violence and bribes, even offering to pay off Colombia's entire thirteen billion dollar foreign debt. In 1989 the assassination of the leading presidential candidate, Luis Carlos Galán, led to an all-out war against the narcos. At this point, the Colombian government was engaged in two internal wars, one against guerrillas and another against the drug cartels.

In the 1980s the Cali cartel began infiltrating the shattered Medellín cartel markets. By the mid-1990s—following the death of Escobar in 1993—the cartel already controlled a high percentage of the international cocaine market. The profile of the Colombian drug traffickers has changed drastically since the heyday of the Medellín cartel, characterized then by exceptional media exposure and the legendary figure of Escobar. The Medellín and Cali cartels have essentially been destroyed, and many Colombian traffickers have become part of larger international organizations, such as the Mexican Tijuana and Juárez cartels. Today, the Colombian narcos operate in different ways; they tend to be midlevel, low-profile, highly technologized movers. Many have banking and business backgrounds, and it is perhaps most accurate to now speak of *cartelitos* that are less visible to the public eye.**

In the last two decades, drug trafficking has been one of the primary factors behind the strengthening of the guerrilla movements, the rise of paramilitarism, and a general ethical and moral deterioration felt in Colombian society at large. Many Colombians who previously supported the guerrillas' causes—which included their communist and socialist ideals, the revamping of the political system in order to eliminate corruption and social injustice, and agrarian reforms leading toward land redistribution, among other causes—are now questioning the guerrillas' methods of financing their operations, which largely consist of extortion, kidnapping, and "taxing" drug traffickers and growers.

Countless businesses and corporations that still operate in *zonas rojas*—areas of intensive armed conflict—are forced to pay *vacunas* ("vaccinations") to avoid being targeted. In addition to the narcos and the traditional guerrilla groups, ultra-right-wing paramilitary forces (formed under the name of Autodefensas Unidas de Colombia but commonly referred to as *paras*), who are supposedly fighting against the guerrillas, have further complicated the situation, as they, too, are involved in multiple crimes against the civil population, including torture, kidnapping, and assassination.

At the end of the 1990s, under the presidency of Andrés Pastrana, the Colombian government reopened negotiations with the guerrillas, and in 1998 a demilitarized zone (*zona de distensión*) the size of Switzerland was conceded to the FARC for the pur-

** For an interesting study of the cultural impact of the drug trade on Medellín, see Alonso Salazar J. and Ana María Jaramillo, *Las subculturas del narcotráfico*, Cinep (Bogotá, 1996). Salazar J. has also written a sociological-literary account, *No nacimos pa' semilla*, which deals with the lifestyle of *sicarios* (assassins) in Medellín.

pose of dialogue. Nonetheless, after three years of talks (during which time the violence continued) with negligible results, the Colombian military recaptured the zone. It should come as no surprise that all sectors of Colombian society have settled into a general weariness with the continuous armed conflict and a profound disillusionment with both the government, composed of "old money" and corruption, and the guerrillas, seen by many as professionalized bandits whose original political aims have been forfeited for personal interests.

The armed conflict and cultivation of illegal crops, primarily in rural areas, have had damaging consequences for the entire country. During the 1990s an estimated one and a half million Colombians—mostly rural residents—were displaced due to the activity of guerrillas and drug traffickers (*National Geographic*, February 2000). In 1999 alone, some 350,000 people were forced to abandon their homes in coca-growing regions, and the same number of Colombians emigrated abroad. This tragic displacement of the rural population is an ongoing phenomenon that has contributed to serious difficulties for society in general: insufficient infrastructure, shortage of housing, lack of public services, poverty, and unemployment. Furthermore, urban violence has reached an exceptional level, especially in areas where resources become scarcer and needs have escalated as the unequal distribution of wealth becomes more pronounced.

All of these different threads that have been woven into the fabric of the Colombian national identity over the centuries must be recognized as interrelated and complex factors that must continually be studied in order to make sense of the endemic violence that afflicts this country. Obviously, the Colombian people are not any more violent than those of any other country, but the particular political, economic, cultural, and sociohistorical conditions of the nation have combined to create the violence that is a prevalent aspect of Colombian existence. In fact, the vast majority of the general population longs for peace and a permanent end to violence more than for any other type of national project, as is evident in mass demonstrations, the creation of numerous organizations that struggle for peace, and the multitude of published studies and books aimed at understanding the different facets of this problem and proposing theories for overcoming it.

Artistic Creation and the Legacy of the Regeneration

In spite of the monumental problems it faces, Colombia boasts a national economy that has historically been among the strongest in the continent and a political system that, despite its difficulties, is often considered the longest uninterrupted constitutional democracy of SSSA. Perhaps most noteworthy of its achievements is the nation's well-deserved reputation as a cultural and artistic mecca of sorts. Colombia seems to be a breeding ground for artistic inspiration, perhaps not a surprising phenomenon, given the nation's cast of cultural characters, vivid and varied scenery, dramatic history, and current events. In any case, artistic creation and cultural expression should be viewed in the concept of Colombia as a nation of nations. The discussion here focuses on the tension between the "official" national culture formulated in the capital and the plurality of cultural expressions and regional voices, which are often marginalized by this hegemony.

Colombia has a long tradition—which goes back to the colonial period when Bogotá was the capital of a Spanish viceroyalty—of a strong relationship among politics, literature, and religion, all of which have been melded into a powerful hegemony in the hands of a conservative aristocracy. The regime known as the Regeneration, officially inaugurated by the Constitution of 1886, reestablished strong ties with the state, education, cultural expression, and the Catholic Church. In addition, this administration, under the leadership of Rafael Núñez, emphasized the principle of political centralization and administrative decentralization, while at the same time reinforcing the Hispanic tradition in the nation. Miguel Antonio Caro and José Manuel Marroquín were among the founders of the Colombian Academy of the Language, which, in 1871, was the first of its kind on the continent. These two intellectuals were among the so-called *gramáticos presidentes* (grammarian presidents), men of letters who eventually became president of the country.

These intellectuals and national leaders established both the political and the linguistic norms that were to determine exclusion or entry into the tight circle that wielded the power in the nation at the turn of the century. The legacy of the Regeneration and the gramáticos presidentes is evident in the still widespread belief, both in Colombia and abroad, that Colombians speak the most correct and pure variety of Spanish in existence today. In general, many bogotanos are quick to boast of "Colombian" linguistic purity, but it is commonly recognized that this self-proclaimed language superiority has been used to maintain the dominance of the Bogotá elite through the erroneous and prejudiced notion that their manner of speaking is the standard, superior to all regional dialects.

Bogotá's reputation as an important center of culture earned it the nickname "the South American Athens" in the late nineteenth century.[††] Members of the Bogotá elite came to be referred to as *lanudos* (woolly or fleecy) because of their dark, formal attire and their tendency to have gatherings dedicated to discussions of literature and politics. The legacy of the Regeneration for the twentieth century was the formation of an official national culture that prioritized Colombia's Spanish origins, conservative humanist values, and the church's moral tutelage. This culture functioned on the basis of exclusion—of difference, of marginal voices, of regionalist distinctions, and of dissident tendencies. Although the political dominance of the leaders of the Regeneration ended with the conclusion of the period known as the Conservative Republic (1886–1930), its legacy in the cultural formation of Colombia left traces throughout the twentieth century.

Many Colombian writers and artists have been driven to overcome the dominance of Bogotá's cultural center, either by

[††] This designation was first made by Spanish philologist Marcelino Menéndez y Pelayo, according to Javier Ocampo López, *Historia básica de Colombia*, Plaza y Janés (Bogotá, 1987), 261.

highlighting regional distinctions within Colombia's borders or by turning their focus abroad in order to incorporate techniques and worldviews from Europe and the United States. José María Vargas Vila was one such writer, and among the most iconoclastic figures in Colombian literary history. He was a best-selling author during the first three decades of the twentieth century and was widely known in the Spanish-speaking world for his sexually scandalous novels and politically charged essays.

The poet and novelist José Asunción Silva, a key figure within the Spanish American modernist movement, also promoted the modernization of Colombian literature through interaction with contemporary European works. In contrast, the novelist Tomás Carrasquilla embodies the exaltation of regional characteristics and values, in his case, those of Antioquia.

Perhaps the most significant manifestation of a literary counterculture in the first half of the twentieth century was found in Barranquilla: the avant-garde cultural magazine *Voces* (1917–1920), edited by the Catalan Ramón Vinyes, served the dual function of disseminating writings by regional costeño writers, such as José Félix Fuenmayor, for example, as well as works by contemporary writers from abroad.

The works of Gabriel García Márquez were greatly inspired by the costeño cultural atmosphere in general, and in the early 1950s the future Nobel laureate became a member of the Grupo de Barranquilla, a group of journalists, writers of fiction, and artists who opposed the elitist cultural center in Bogotá and sought to bring Colombian literature and art up to date. In addition to García Márquez, numerous other writers contributed to the effort to modernize the nation's literature in the second half of the twentieth century, including Manuel Mejía Vallejo and Álvaro Mutis, among many others.[‡‡]

‡‡ Álvaro Cepeda Samudio, Héctor Rojas Herazo, Manuel Zapata Olivella, Eduardo Caballero Calderón, Gustavo Álvarez Gardeazábal, Darío Jaramillo Agudelo, R. H. Moreno-Durán, Fanny Buitrago, and Albalucía Ángel, among others, played an important role in the modernization of Colombian literature.

The rebellious *nadaísta* literary movement of the 1960s, spearheaded by poet Gonzalo Arango, defied many of the narrow conventional beliefs and provincial values of the dominant Colombian culture of that time. In more recent years, other writers have focused their literary sights on the marginal youth culture, the popular music scene, the drug culture, different aspects of urban violence and *sicarios* (hired assassins), and other conditions of modern Colombian society.[§§]

Colombia's vast regional diversity has been a tremendous source of inspiration for many of the nation's painters and sculptors, who have gone beyond the aesthetic norms of the capital and earned international reputations as world-class innovators. Fernando Botero is perhaps Colombia's most well-known contemporary artist; his works are characterized by irreverent and satirical oversized human figures. Other important Colombian visual artists include Alejandro Obregón (a former member of the Grupo de Barranquilla who was a master at capturing the essence of the Caribbean with a personalized expressionistic style) and Enrique Grau, whose work ranges from ingeniously placed humor to minute details, in addition to numerous other artists. In theater the major Colombian figures of the twentieth century are Enrique Buenaventura and Santiago García, and in cinema, most notable are Sergio Cabrera, Lisandro Duque, and Víctor Gaviria.

The artistic expression of Colombia's regional and ethnic diversity is not limited to its literature and visual arts; the wide variety of its music constitutes one of the richest and most diverse repertoires of all the SSSA countries. These distinct regional musical traditions include the *cumbia*, the *vallenato* (played with an accordion), and the *puya* from the Costa; the *mapalé* from the Pacific coast; *la música llanera* (played on the harp) from the llanos; the *carranguera*, the *bunde*, and the *guabina* from the altiplano; and so on (Wade 2000). The costeños Shakira

---

§§ These writers include Andrés Caicedo, Manuel Giraldo Magil, Rafael Chaparro Madiedo, Alonso Salazar J., Jorge Franco Ramos, and Fernando Vallejo, among others.

and Carlos Vives as well as the rock group Aterciopelados from Bogotá, among other contemporary musicians, have each drawn from these different sources in creating their own unique musical styles and forging a niche in the international music scene.

The ongoing tension between the long-lasting cultural legacy of the Regeneration and the multitude of cultural and artistic expressions springing from Colombia's regional diversity should not be seen as simply one of outright opposition but rather as a multifaceted relation of contradictions and appropriations. This may be illustrated by a popular example of graffiti in Bogotá that parodies the capital's alleged reputation for cultural sophistication by suggesting that this city is not really the "*Atenas de Sudamérica*" ("the Athens of South America") but rather "*Apenas Sudamérica*" ("barely South America").

Communication Patterns

Colombians' general enthusiasm for language is evident in their fondness for verbal agility, wit, and debate. Colombians are typically good conversationalists and appreciate those who can respond in kind. In keeping with this love for language is the reputation Colombians have for the longest greeting rituals of all the SSSAs. Conversations typically begin rather formally with long inquiries into the health, location, and status of the speakers involved as well as of mutually known acquaintances and friends. Several explanations for such extensive greeting patterns have been proposed, ranging from indigenous linguistic influences to the geographic isolation previously experienced in and among different regions.

The importance of formality in Colombian daily life can also be noted in the honorific title of *doctor/a*, which is widely used when speaking to a social superior, whether that person has reached the distinction of doctor or not. Its use is an absolute necessity, for example, when addressing a lawyer, the most abundant of the "doctores" in Colombia. The common use of the phrase "*¿me regala…?*" ("Would you give me—as a gift—…?"), as a way of requesting an item or service in a store or when one is a guest, is yet another indicator of common Colombian formality.

In spite of these commonalities, Colombia's communication patterns are more marked by regional distinctions than by national homogeneity. Costeños, for instance, are rather relaxed and informal, frequently employing the informal *tú* and addressing people by their first name, even those in authority. In contrast, Colombians from the Andean region, especially residents of Bogotá, tend, as previously mentioned, to be quite formal in their manner and use of language. This characteristic is also reflected in the more formal attire of residents of the capital. This distinction between costeños and bogotanos, in general, could easily be related to climate: warmer climates, warmer and friendlier inhabitants; colder climates, more formal and reserved residents.

One of the most important factors in accounting for the garrulousness of many Colombians is the influence of oral culture, a phenomenon that is still common in some areas of rural Colombia today and has left a strong legacy in mainstream Colombian cultural patterns and social customs. The now-commercialized vallenato music, for example, was originally an aspect of oral culture that served as a primary source of information and news for small, isolated towns before the arrival of modern communications technology, a service that is still performed by "town criers" in some of the settlements in the Colombian Amazon region.[|| ||] It is also worth noting that at least eighty indigenous languages and/or dialects are still spoken within Colombia, and significant linguistic traces of African languages can be identified in the speech patterns of some regions.

Regionalism is also reflected in dialect variations, which often provide the raw material for good-natured teasing and mockery

|| || For a study of the interactions between oral and writing cultures in the Colombian novel, see *The Colombian Novel, 1844–1987* by Raymond Leslie Williams.

among Colombians from different parts of the country. Bogotanos, for example, are also known as *rolos* for their particular accent marked by the rolled *r*. Paisas are famed as endless and rambling talkers with an impressive list of common sayings and proverbs at the ready, and *pastusos* (persons from Pasto, in the southwestern department of Nariño) are often stereotyped as being slow or stupid and therefore become the butt of many jokes. There seems to be a different accent for practically every department, and accent and other linguistic distinctions are often used by Colombians to determine each other's regional origin.

Living and Working in Colombia

Given the present state of affairs in Colombia, the foreigner planning to live and/or work in this nation will probably be most concerned with personal safety. For some high-level business executives this concern might extend all the way to kidnapping and other types of extortion, but the primary focus for most people will be securing their home, family, and self against possible burglary, robbery, and other forms of violence.[¶¶] Almost all Colombians and foreigners who have lived here for an extended period of time have been affected by violence to varying degrees, either directly or indirectly. Travel is a primary concern for sojourners, both between towns and cities and through urban areas. Roadblocks installed by guerrilla and paramilitary forces make travel in many areas of the country unsafe. Likewise, in large urban areas such as Bogotá, both private and public transportation can present certain dangers, which foreigners may lessen by being well informed.

Despite—or maybe because of—the dangers involved in living in a violent and conflicted society, Colombians are known

¶¶ Although reaching a profound understanding of the cultural traits of a country and a people is of utmost importance, the foreigner traveling to Colombia should also consult guidebooks and other knowledgeable sources that provide practical tips and advice on "dos and don'ts" for personal safety in Colombia. The space and focus of this book do not allow for such information here.

for their natural openness and friendliness. This is related to what sociologist Kristine Fitch has identified as an "interpersonal ideology of connectedness [that] generates a tremendous human warmth" (1998, 6).

Life in Colombia—above all, in urban areas—can be physically and emotionally demanding. Exacerbating the physical challenges are bureaucratic obstacles. In both the business and government sectors, mountains of required paperwork often turn seemingly simple transactions into overwhelming tasks, even when one has the personal connections to facilitate these processes. With regard to punctuality for business meetings, the general rule is to arrive on time or early but be prepared to wait; the length of the wait often depends on your position and the nature of the meeting. Although the notion of time in Colombia revolves in large part around the demands of urban life and the business sector, Colombians in general maintain a firm appreciation of leisure time and daily social interaction.

Despite the importance of the twin processes of modernization and urbanization that have occurred during the last half century in Colombia, many traditions of rural life remain. Large numbers of urban-dwelling Colombians return to their ancestral towns to celebrate important holidays. Likewise, the regional differences that define Colombia's identity as a nation of nations extend from daily living patterns to special events and annual festivals that serve to reinforce such distinctions.

* * * * * * *

In spite of the many problems facing the Colombian nation and people in current times, Colombians have numerous achievements of which to be proud in addition to those already mentioned: these include, among many others, the scientific accomplishments of Manuel E. Patarroyo and Rodolfo Llinás; the triumphs in international sports of cyclist Lucho Herrera, baseball player Edgar Rentería, tennis player Fabiola Zuluaga, and weightlifter María Isabel Urretia; the success of the mezzo-soprano Marta Senn; and the political integrity demonstrated by Jorge Eliécer Gaitán, María Cano, and Luis Carlos Galán.

Many Colombians have a refreshingly open and honest view of their country and typically do not flaunt a grand national ego largely because of the strong regionalism described above. Colombians share, however, a collective sensitivity to the common perceptions of their country that persist abroad: drug trafficking and prevalent violence. Such stereotypes reinforce an excessively narrow perspective on this fascinating and diverse country, whose populace is characterized by creativity, vitality, and energy. Currently, Colombia is a nation at a crucial crossroads, and its future depends, even more than in many other nations, on the collective will of its citizenry.

References and Selected Bibliography

Bastenier, M. A. 2000. "La sociedad civil de Colombia reivindica su ansia de paz." *El País*, 2 de julio.

Bergquist, Charles W. 1986. *Coffee and Conflict in Colombia, 1886–1910*. Durham, NC: Duke University Press.

Bushnell, David. 1993. *The Making of Modern Colombia: A Nation in Spite of Itself*. Los Angeles: University of California Press.

Farnsworth-Alvear, Ann. 2000. *Dulcinea in the Factory: Myths, Morals, Men, and Women in Colombia's Industrial Experiment, 1905–1960*. Durham, NC: Duke University Press.

Fitch, Kristine L. 1998. *Speaking Relationally: Culture, Communication, and Interpersonal Connection*. New York: Guilford Press.

Henderson, James D. 2001. *Modernization in Colombia: the Laureano Gómez Years, 1889–1965*. Gainesville: University Press of Florida.

Henríquez, Cecilia. 1996. *Imperio y ocaso del sagrado corazón en Colombia: Un estudio histórico-simbólico*. Bogotá: Altamir Ediciones.

Hernández de Alba, Guillermo. 1986. *Acuarelas de la Comisión Corográfica: Colombia 1850–1859*. Bogotá: Litografía Arco.

Jaramillo, María Mercedes, et al., comps. and eds. 2000. *Literatura y cultura: narrativa colombiana del siglo XX*. 3 vols. Bogotá: Ministerio de Cultura.

Jaramillo de Olarte, Lucía, y Mónica Trujillo Jaramillo. 1991. *Trece danzas tradicionales de Colombia: sus trajes y su música*. Bogotá: Editorial Nueva América.

López, Javier Ocampo. 1987. *Historia básica de Colombia*. Bogotá: Plaza y Janés.

Megenney, William W. 1986. *El palenquero: un lenguaje post-criollo de Colombia*. Bogotá: Instituto Caro y Cuervo.

Ospina, William. 2000. *¿Dónde está la franja amarilla?* Bogotá: Norma.

Posada-Carbó, Eduardo. 1996. *The Colombian Caribbean: A Regional History, 1870–1950*. New York: Oxford University Press.

Rausch, Jane M. 1999. *Colombia: Territorial Rule and the Llanos Frontier*. Gainesville: University Press of Florida.

Rojas, Cristina. 2002. *Civilization and Violence: Regimes of Representation in Nineteenth-Century Colombia*. Minneapolis: University of Minnesota.

Safford, Franks, and Marco Palacios. 2001. *Colombia: Fragmented Land, Divided Society*. New York: Oxford University Press.

Salazar, J., Alonso. 1990. No *nacimos pa' semilla*. Bogotá: Cinep.

Salazar J., Alonso, and Ana María Jaramillo. 1996. *Las subculturas del narcotráfico*. Bogotá: Cinep.

Vallejo Ángel, Clemencia, coord. 1997. *Pagar el paraíso*. Vol. 10. Bogotá: Instituto Colombiano de Cultura Hispánica.

Vallejo, Fernando. 1998. *La virgende los sicarios*. Bogotá: Alfaguara.

Viviescas, Fernando, and Fabio Giraldo Isaza, eds. 1991. *Colombia: el despertar de la modernidad*. Bogotá: Foro Nacional por Colombia.

Wade, Peter. 2000. *Music, Race and Nation: Musica Tropical in Colombia*. Chicago: University of Chicago Press.

———. 1993. *Blackness and Race Mixture: The Dynamics of Racial Identity in Colombia*. Baltimore: The Johns Hopkins University Press.

Williams, Raymond Leslie. 1991. *The Colombian Novel, 1844–1987*. Austin: University of Texas Press.

Williams, Raymond Leslie, and Kevin G. Guerrieri. 1999. *Culture and Customs of Colombia*. Westport, CT: Greenwood Press.

Ecuador: In the Middle of the World

Lynn Hirschkind

Preguntan de donde soy
y no se que responder.
De tanto no tener nada,
no tengo de donde ser.

—Jorge Enrique Adoum

They ask where I'm from
And I don't know what to answer
From so much of having nothing
I have nowhere to be from

Ecuador is named for its location on the equator. Situated in the western portion of the South American continent, this midsize nation of nearly thirteen million is truly right in the middle of the world, with about a quarter of the country located in the northern hemisphere and three quarters in the southern hemisphere. The capital city of Quito nearly straddles the equatorial line.

Ecuadorian citizenship and nationality have never been defined by consensus and are subjects of ongoing contestation. Even

* Lynn Hirschkind is an anthropologist who has lived in Ecuador for twenty-three years. She teaches anthropology and directs the academic curriculum for an overseas study program in Cuenca, Ecuador. Her professional interests range from ethnoveterinary medicine to globalization.

more than in neighboring Colombia, regionalism divides Ecuadorians, as do other factors such as class and ethnicity. From an anthropological perspective, cultural and ethnic diversity in this small country is much greater than in most of the larger nations in the region. Despite, and perhaps because of, this heterogeneity, national identity has been constructed on a mestizo model with Hispanic whiteness (*blanqueamiento*) considered superior. This model is, however, emphatically rejected by a myriad of indigenous and Afro-Ecuadorian political and interest groups. For these groups, the revitalizing, reinforcing, and reinventing of ethnicity are among their main goals.

Contradictory interpretations regarding Ecuadorian identity are echoed in political, economic, and geographical spheres. Consider the following facts:

- Despite its small size, Ecuador has a greater diversity of climate, landscape, vegetation, and fauna than many larger countries. Its Amazon forests and northwestern lowlands are among the most biologically diverse in the world (Encalada Reyes 1983).
- Ecuador, after Venezuela, has the largest petroleum reserves in Spanish-speaking South America (SSSA); nonetheless it is one of the poorest nations in the continent.
- Ecuador lost about one-third of its territory to its southern neighbor, Peru, resulting in several border incidents between the two countries, the most recent in 1998. Even so, Ecuador is often called an "island of peace" compared with its northern and southern neighbors, and Ecuadorians are noted for their relatively pacific nature.
- Politeness, generosity, and humility are characteristic of Ecuadorian personalities; yet integral to their pleasant demeanor is the widespread use of lies of various types, and duplicity and trickery are considered normal.

This chapter will explore aspects of Ecuadorian culture and social structures by discussing the following: geographic and regional influences, keys to understanding Ecuadorians, communication patterns, and living and working in Ecuador. The key cultural characteristics to be examined are questions of identity, differences and divides, the sense of being Ecuadorian, and the "island of peace" versus the lack of cooperation.

Geographic and Regional Influences

Ecuador's position on the equator gives it relatively uniform days and nights of twelve hours each as well as fairly minor seasonal variations, which are marked primarily by changes in the amount of rainfall. The coast and the upper Amazon basin, to the east, are tropical in climate; the Andes Mountains, running the length of the country from north to south, give much of the nation cool to frigid temperatures, depending on the altitude. The highest point is the volcano Chimborazo, which towers 6,310 meters (20,820 feet) above sea level and lies only two hundred kilometers (125 miles) from the Pacific Ocean.

Ecuador is perched on the seismically active "ring of fire" that extends throughout the Pacific region. The country's history is punctuated by cataclysmic events surrounding volcanic explosions. In the past five hundred years, volcanos Cotopaxi and Chimborazo have both erupted, destroying nearby towns and cities. Currently, three volcanos in Ecuador are active—Sangay is permanently active but is far enough away from population centers that it bothers no one; Pichincha, close to Quito, has recently spewed ash and gases onto the capital, interrupting air traffic and causing respiratory problems; and Tunguragua, located near Baños, threatens a major eruption and has forced the evacuation of its immediate region.

A very different phenomenon, the cool Humbolt Current that runs along the southern half of Ecuador's 840-kilometer coast, is also of great significance to the nation and its people. Not only does this frigid water flow attract a great variety of fish, crustaceans, and shellfish, which Ecuadorians exploit both for personal consumption and as important export products, but it also affects weather conditions. Every six or seven years a phenomenon known as El Niño (because it happens around

Christmastime) recurs, when the Humbolt Current shifts westward and the coastal waters warm considerably, disrupting marine life cycles and causing torrential rains that inundate the coastal plain, destroying homes, infrastructure, and farms.

Ecuador's unique combination of equatorial tropical climate with high-altitude terrain produces a fantastic variety of landscapes, vegetation, microclimates, and wildlife, which can be divided into four markedly different geographic zones. The two most important regions in terms of both population (95 percent of all Ecuadorians) and economic significance are the *sierra* (highlands) and the *costa* (coast).

Sierra Region. The sierra region is dominated by the Andes Mountains, which are split into eastern and western ranges that run lengthwise along the country. In between these two *cordilleras* (ranges) lie a series of approximately ten basins or inter-Andean valleys with elevations ranging from 1,800 to 3,000 meters (6,000 to 9,000 feet) above sea level. In these basins the climate is temperate year-round, and the agricultural lands are very fertile. Quito, the nation's capital and second largest city, is located in one of these basins.

Quito is a beautiful colonial-style city, the second highest capital in the Americas (after La Paz), at about 2,727 meters (9,000 feet). It has been designated a World Heritage site by the United Nations for its classic Spanish colonial architecture, especially its rich, baroque churches and huge convents. Some of these were built toward the end of the colonial period, when Quito was an important training center for artists and craftsmen. Much of the artwork was inspired by religion and came to be known as the Escuela Quiteña (Quito School) style of art.

Most of Ecuador's indigenous people live in the sierra countryside. Agriculture is the most important economic activity, with most of the production destined for the domestic market. Also vital to the economy is textile production, which has a long history in the highlands and was a mainstay in colonial times. Woolen cloth was produced in large quantities in weaving workshops in which Indians were required to labor. The wool was then traded throughout Spain's South American colonies. Textile production continues to play an important role at the present time, with many people of Native American ancestry making cloth and clothing for their own use and for sale.

Coastal Region. The coastal region is markedly different from the sierra because it is tropical and close to sea level. Named for the area's extensive coastline, it boasts beautiful beaches and several important harbors as well as abundant marine resources. These geographic configurations seem to encourage a cosmopolitan outlook, and in fact *costeños* are reputed to be quite open to new thoughts and ideas and less tied to traditional ways than are many residents from the sierra region. Guayaquil, Ecuador's largest city and principal port, is located on the coast. Many of Ecuador's exports are produced or prepared on the coast, including bananas, cacao, coffee, fish, and shrimp, and are shipped out from either Guayaquil or Manta, another major port and center of the canned fish industry located on the central coast. Oil from the Oriente region (see below) is exported principally from another port, San Lorenzo, located near the Colombian border.

Though the indigenous presence is barely noticeable along the coastal areas, most of Ecuador's black population, which is about 5 percent of the national total, lives here, giving the region a different cultural flavor. These people of African descent were brought to Ecuador to work as slaves during the colonial era. Some of them managed to escape and to establish free black communities on the north coast, where their descendants still reside.

Oriente. The third and last mainland region in Ecuador is known as the Oriente, because it falls to the east of the Andes Mountains. Most of the Oriente is a dense, tropical rain forest and is one of the most biologically diverse places on earth, including harboring the greatest variety of hummingbirds anywhere (Encalada Reyes). Sometimes called la Amazonía, this name is actually a misnomer because Ecuador lost access to the Amazon River as a result of territorial concessions to Peru in 1941. Until recent decades, Ecuadorian leaders tended to ignore this region, which is sparsely populated, and one Ecuadorian president had even declared it "a myth."

Before the Spanish conquest, many different Native American groups lived in the Oriente, practicing shifting cultivation in combination with hunting and gathering and living in small, mobile settlements. Over the next five centuries, under the multiple pressures of disease, missionaries, colonists, commercial ranching and farming, natural resource exploitation, and even tourism, many of these native groups died out or were absorbed by their neighbors. Now only seven or eight ethnic groups remain, divided by competing interests, languages, and mutual distrust. Many Ecuadorians from the other regions stereotyped these Oriente indigenous peoples as primitive and dangerous, based on two of the indigenous groups from the zone: the famous ex-headhunting Shuar and the missionary-killing Waorani.

Government interest in and policies toward the Oriente changed dramatically in the early 1970s, when petroleum was discovered there, bringing about profound economic and social transformations, including the arrival of many technicians and other specialists, the expansion of infrastructure, and the increased penetration of national and international interests into this relatively remote and formerly isolated region.

The oil industry has led to displacement and cultural upheaval for many of the Oriente's original inhabitants, who have seen their lands occupied by colonists, their ways of life ever more entangled within the world of commodities, and their forested land destroyed on a vast scale. Forced contact with the outside world brought about by oil exploration in the indigenous territories has even led to sporadic violent clashes between some of the diverse Native American residents (sometimes supported by environmental groups) on the one hand and technicians and others involved with petroleum exploitation on the other.

Galapagos Islands. The fourth Ecuadorian region, the Galapagos Islands, is a remote archipelago located 1,000 kilometers (600 miles) west of continental South America, made up of thirteen large and many small islands. These islands are truly unique, not only in the national context but in the international view as well. They are most famed as the locale where in 1835, Charles Darwin found evidence for his revolutionary theory of evolution, based in large part on his observations of the numerous species living on these remote islands. Especially important in his studies were several varieties of finches, whose distinguishing characteristics Darwin proposed to explain by his theory of adaptation and natural selection.

These islands were actually first claimed by Ecuador in 1832, just three years before Darwin arrived there. At that time, the archipelago was uninhabited, and the remote islands were used primarily as a supply base for seafarers in the South Pacific. The giant tortoises, *galapagos*, for which the islands are named, were captured and kept alive on board to supply the sailors with fresh meat. Local legend has it that pirates also visited the islands during this period, leaving behind buried treasure still waiting to be unearthed. Once under Ecuadorian control, the Galapagos Islands served primarily as a penitentiary for much of the nineteenth and early twentieth centuries. These days, the islands receive a very different sort of visitor, the international tourist, providing revenues as well as serving as a point of pride and prestige for the Ecuadorian nation and its peoples.

Keys to Understanding the Ecuadorians

Questions of Identity

Many claim that there is no such thing as an Ecuadorian identity due to differences of culture, region, race, ethnicity, class, and even family. As one Ecuadorian intellectual explains it,

> I don't think an Ecuadorian nation exists...because historically, there are a series of economic, social, and political reasons that led to the formation of separate, isolated groups that haven't been integrated.... So in an unarticulated society, crosscut by a series of ethnic contradictions, and where the dominant classes

> have always imposed what I call simulated culture, it has been very difficult to arrive at a national identity. The nation has been instead an emblem serving certain political interests in certain circumstances. (Traverso Yépez 1998, 194)

This ambivalence regarding Ecuadorian identity is attributable to numerous factors, and divisions among the Ecuadorians can be traced all the way back to the pre-Columbian era. The fifteenth-century indigenous population in what is now Ecuador is estimated to have been about 1,648,600, split among at least twenty-five different ethnic groups, each with its own language and cultural patterns (Newson 1995). To bring order to this evidently fractured past, one school of Ecuadorian historians has described a "Kingdom of Quito," ruled by the Cara Indians, as a pre-Columbian precursor of the modern-day nation-state. However, this theory is not substantiated by archeological, historical, or ethnohistorical data.

What historians are quite sure of is that the Incas from Peru consolidated their control over most of highland Ecuador by the early sixteenth century and built a road between Cuzco, the Inca capital, and Quito, even then an important population center. When the Spanish conquistador Francisco Pizarro arrived, control of the Inca empire was in dispute between two royal brothers—Huáscar in Cuzco and Atahuallpa in Quito—and a civil war had broken out. This internal conflict greatly facilitated the Spaniards' conquest of the region, though European disease epidemics also contributed to their success.

During the colonial era, Ecuador was merely an outlying area of the oldest and most important viceroyalty in the continent, Peru. After independence, Ecuador was included in Simón Bolívar's ill-fated Confederation of Gran Colombia until its dissolution. These circumstances did nothing to create a sense of national Ecuadorian identity. Since then, Ecuador's international borders have suffered various alterations, the most recent being the border demarcation in 1998.

Traces of pre-Columbian people are faint but still present in Ecuador today. Some of the remnants of the ridged fields where crops were raised on the coastal plain can still be seen. Prehistoric earthen terraces cover entire hillsides in the highlands, and *tolas* (large earth mounds thought to be ancient burial sites), have been found in the northern highlands. In remote areas there are remains of towns and cities: building foundations, water control channels, and central squares. Scattered throughout the highlands are traces of Incan stonework, all that is left of their paved roadways, storage buildings, houses, and temples, such as the one at Ingapirca in Cañar province.

Even more significantly, the indigenous influence is still evident in the Ecuadorian people. Native groups make up anywhere from 10 to 40 percent of the population. Although no official census figures on ethnicity exist, a lower number is probably more accurate. Eight native languages are still in use in Ecuador: Quichua, Coaiquer, Cayapa, Tsatchela, Shuar-Achuar, Cofán, Siona-Secoya, and Waorani. By far the most prominent is Quichua, which is the Ecuadorian variant of the Inca language, Quechua. There are approximately 1,260,000 native speakers of Quichua in Ecuador today. Far beyond the ethnic boundaries, Native American heritage is evident in many aspects of mainstream Ecuadorian culture: Quichua vocabulary and grammatical constructions in Ecuadorian Spanish, religious beliefs and practices, native plants, cuisine, and medical knowledge and remedies.

Differences and Divides

As in the other Andean nations of Bolivia, Peru, and parts of Colombia with large Native American populations, the Spanish colonists established economic, political, and social structures that formed a simple hierarchy of disenfranchised laborers (mainly Indians and poor mestizos), artisans, entrepreneurs (mostly mestizos), and an elite (mostly white) that owned or controlled access to resources. This stratification system continues to order many aspects of social and economic life today, with the addition of bureaucrats and salaried employees to the former artisan middle sector. Many quasi-colonial relationships persist, intertwined with modern social practice. Paternalism and patron-client relations are often evident in the interactions between individuals of different socioeconomic status. The various strata making up these hierarchies are separated by firm boundaries. The elites struggle among themselves for privileges, power, and wealth; the middle sectors protect their own, more thinly spread resources; and peasants and the poor working class (mostly indigenous people) are given nominal recognition as members of society, but in practice they enjoy few of its privileges.

Class stratification can be noted in many ways. For instance, a polite person is one who is "*culta*" (refined) and "*educada*" (well-mannered), qualities attainable mainly to the upper classes. Thus, by definition the lower classes cannot be polite or "decent" because they are not cultured or educated. To be polite means knowing one's own social position and the positions of others, which requires interpreting clothes, speech patterns and usage, family connections, and employment to assign the appropriate social categories to others. Based on their relative positions, people know how to behave correctly toward each other when they interact.

One indicator of gender-marked class behavior is that upper- and upper-middle-class ladies do not sit in public parks and, in general, avoid appearing in public at all. The idea is that nothing offensive can happen to a woman in her own home. Offices and classrooms, where everyone knows each other, are also fairly respectable places, but any extended time spent in a public place, where all classes of people may mingle, is considered undesirable. It is sometimes said that the prettiest girls are never seen in public—the prettiest being of the highest class, of course.

Fictive kinship relationships such as *compadrazgo* (godparent) ties are quite widespread in Ecuador; often people from the lower strata of society ask individuals who are "higher up" to become godparents to their children. This practice serves the important purpose of establishing bonds across social class divides, thus creating networks of exchange and reciprocity. It nevertheless reinforces a rigid social and economic stratification system.

Closely related and inextricably linked to class stratification is the issue of racism, which is deeply entrenched in Ecuadorian culture: the belief in white superiority. Racist attitudes are fairly common and are often overtly manifested as discriminatory behavior toward indigenous peoples and Afro-Ecuadorians. Though many Ecuadorians of mixed ancestry may today belong to the middle class (according to income, job, and education), their social class status is nevertheless attenuated by their race. Ecuadorians themselves acknowledge racist currents in their culture. As one Ecuadorian put it in a recent survey,

> I believe there is discrimination and racism (in Ecuador) and the person who doesn't acknowledge this fact is wrong, a liar. It is found in the way we are trained; in our very education we are taught racism, unconsciously in some ways, and not only in the upper classes. There is racism among the poor too. Like when a poor person says, "Watch out for that Negro, or that mulatto, or that Indian." Even now the bus drivers make Indians go to the back of the bus, if they pick them up at all. (Traverso Yépez, 276)

Since the 1960s, when agrarian reform released highland peasants from their bonds to large landowners, there has been a proliferation of Native American organizations of different types. In recent years Ecuador's indigenous groups have been among the most vocal and politically active in the continent. Although they have quite different agendas and memberships, they all represent an organized and specific response to their perceived discrimination and/or injustice at the hands of the upper classes. Several uprisings have been staged, during which activists have blocked roads, occupied public buildings, and delivered long lists of demands to the government. These include recognition of a separate state for themselves, where they can make their own laws, speak their own languages, and choose their own leaders. Although the outcomes of such protests have fallen short of their objectives, indigenous people are, nonetheless, an important political presence in contemporary Ecuadorian politics and must be taken into account by national leaders.

The ambiguous sense of nationality coexists with and serves to reinforce the sense of regionalism in Ecuador, as in neighboring Colombia. This phenomenon is particularly strong between the two most important regions in terms of populace and power: the sierra and the costa. Each generally views the other with misunderstanding, distrust, and oftentimes stereotypical views that can even extend to the attribution of serious flaws of character and custom.

The differences among the people from the two regions are quite noticeable, encompassing not only the ethnic distinctions noted in the previous section but also different styles of communication, vocabulary, accent, and worldview. Even attire and demeanor vary: in the highlands, formality in attire is admired and preferred. Along the coast the hot climate encourages a more casual self-presentation. There the men often wear a *guayabera*, a loose, short-sleeved, hip-length garment in a lightweight material worn outside the trousers. Also, both men and women may wear straw hats. The so-called "Panama hat" originated on the central coast of Ecuador and is still worn by many people on the coast and in the southern highlands.

The personality characteristics ascribed to the residents of the two regions mimic the characteristics of their climates. Costeños are considered to be "hot-blooded" and supposedly more prone to violence and crime, whereas *serranos* (people from the sierra region) are thought to be more "cold-blooded," implying a cowardly, timid, and passive character. Miguel Donoso Pareja describes the opposing stereotypes as follows:

> While highlanders are more circumspect, formal, subdued and conservative, coastal people are flamboyant, expressive, exuberant and liberal. Highlanders say costeños are "superficial, stupid, impulsive, violent, and conceited." Some even go so far as to call people from the coast *monos* (monkeys) and claim that their women are loose, the men violent, and both given to immoral behavior. For costeños, in turn, serranos are "two-faced, charlatans, hypocritical, stingy, crafty, gossip mongers and traitors." (1998, 33)

While both groups are aware that these images are stereotypes, they easily give in to them, thus coloring their perceptions of each other in such a way as to often hinder collaboration and communication.

These oversimplified and often denigrating views of each other are reinforced by important economic and political differences between the two regions. Guayaquil is the banking and commercial center of Ecuador as well as the country's principal port and export center; as such, it is more connected to the global economy and, thus, more cosmopolitan than Quito. Historically, costeños have favored liberal politics and policies, and they now favor neoliberal ones. Quito and the sierra region, in contrast, are more inward-looking and more conservative as well. Social pedigree and family reputation are important there, and social mobility less common. Agriculture and business in the highlands cater to the domestic market, and consequently people tend to be more preoccupied with internal affairs than they are with the global economy.

Given these fundamental differences between the two regions' economies and societies, it is not surprising that they sometimes seem to communicate at cross-purposes. Coastal residents typically regard the central government as a leech that primarily serves to tax and regulate them for the benefit of highland interests. The highlanders, in contrast, view the coastal region as an unruly appendage, important for its export income but otherwise bothersome and rebellious. Animosities between the two areas are so heated that there have been movements for regional and even provincial autonomy. Recently, the province of Guayas, which includes Guayaquil, voted overwhelmingly for autonomy from the central government. Furthermore, the southern provinces of Cañar, Azuay, and Loja see themselves as being constantly ignored and slighted by Quito, so they would likely vote for autonomy as well if given the opportunity.

The Sense of Being Ecuadorian

Despite the numerous differences among Ecuadorians, there are certain attributes that unite them and contribute to a shared sense of being Ecuadorian. At an ideological level, many national leaders have attempted to create a bond of affiliation among the diverse population based on the premise that Ecuador is a mestizo nation, whose inhabitants are the product of Spanish and Indian genetic and cultural blending. In fact, the majority of Ecuadorians really are mestizos, making up anywhere from 60 to 80 percent of the national populace. However, many criticize the "official" version of *mestizaje*, because it disavows Ecuador's ethnic diversity and instead posits mestizaje as a long process in the direction of "lightening" and Westernizing the Ecuadorian population. Supposedly, according to this blending formula, both the Native Americans and the Ecuadorians of African descent are destined to eventually disappear through absorption and acculturation into the white/mestizo majority.*

This controversial interpretation of Ecuador's supposed ethnic future does not, despite intentions, serve to unify the very diverse Ecuadorian people; however, other characteristics do. One is the Catholic religion. Ninety percent of all Ecuadorians are Catholic, and in the nineteenth century, President Gabriel García Moreno (1861–1865, 1869–1875) even made being Catholic a prerequisite for Ecuadorian citizenship. The Church is the one institution that cuts across all social, racial, ethnic, economic, political, gender, and age boundaries to offer Ecuadorians something they can nearly all agree on. Today, members of the clergy are powerful figures at all levels of society, and the Catholic Church operates many schools and universities and exerts enormous moral authority.

* This is understood as a cultural process and not necessarily a biological one. For more about this topic, see Erika Silva, *Los mitos de la Ecuatorianidad*, 2d ed. Abya Yala (Quito, 1995); Norman E. Whitten Jr., "Etnocidio ecuatoriano y etnogénesis indígena. Resurgencia Amazoníca ante la colonización andina," in *Temas Sobre la Continuidad y Adaptación Cultural Ecuatoriana*, 2d ed., edited by Marcelo Naranjo et al. EDUC. (Quito, 1984); and Ronald Stutzman, "El Mestizaje: An All-Inclusive Ideology of Exclusion," in *Cultural Transformations and Ethnicity in Modern Ecuador*, edited by Norman E. Whitten Jr. University of Illinois Press (Urbana, 1981).

Probably the most notable trait that Ecuadorians share is a proclivity for group activities and fun. Ecuadorians of all classes and ethnicities take pleasure in being *alegre*, or "happy" in the broad sense of joie de vivre; and they seek to create an alegre atmosphere wherever they are and whatever they are doing. Alegría implies talk and noise, music and conversation, motion as in walking or dancing, bright colors, food and drink. Ecuadorians prefer to share this happiness in groups and nearly always prefer company to solitude—as they say, "*Chulla vida*," meaning "There is just one life, so enjoy it."

Related to this is a love of jokes, stories, puns, and gossip. A good joke or story is almost never out of place. Even when referring to themselves or to their country or region, Ecuadorians love to joke, and they can be quite self-effacing. For example, a graffito seen on a Quito wall read, "Property for sale—excellent location, sea views, many resources. Inquiries: contact the government of Ecuador."

This national sense of humor is given full expression during the New Year's holiday, during which time most families, neighborhoods, or other kinds of associations construct a scene or diorama depicting or satirizing some event from the past year. These representations are typically life-size (or larger) with realistic dummies, masks, and props. Most families simply dress a mannequin in the clothes of a family member and paint a face mask to match the likeness. All these *años viejos* (last years) are exuberantly destroyed at midnight, symbolically vanquishing the old year as they welcome the new.

Another New Year's custom is The Will. A few family members or neighbors get together and write up a list of inheritances, mostly metaphorical, to be bequeathed to the other members. These "wills" are then read out on New Year's Eve before the assembled family or neighbors to great hilarity, for they often comment on taboo subjects, are suggestively humorous, or are uncharacteristically frank. For example, one person's alleged venality might be exposed in the bequest of a reputation for generosity.

The alegría continues on January 6, celebrated as the Day of the Innocents, which is something like April Fool's Day in the United States. People try to convince each other of contrived truths while maintaining a serious demeanor. In a recent example, a local newspaper announced the national president's wedding and honeymoon at the Mexican resort at Cancún, in full detail and with the total authority of the diligent press. The president, of course, knew nothing of the engagement.

More exuberant joy takes place during Carnival, the three days before the beginning of Lent. Rules of propriety are suspended, their violation becoming the norm. Water mixed with flour, pink foam, or any sticky substance at hand is liberally applied to strangers as well as to family and friends. Rich food and strong drink are consumed in quantity. Social roles are forgotten as the normally passive behave aggressively; affront must be borne with good grace.

Finally, there are certain symbols about which nearly all Ecuadorians feel proud, one of which is the artwork of internationally renowned painter Oswaldo Guayasamín (1919–1999). Of indigenous heritage himself, Guayasamín drew inspiration and motifs from pre-Columbian peoples and their descendants, and he championed their causes. He is best known for his representations of huge hands, downtrodden Indians, and exhausted mothers. A huge Guayasamín mural covers one wall of the congressional chambers; it depicts foreign oppressors and defiant Ecuadorians, a triumphant nation in the face of external threat.

An "Island of Peace" versus Lack of Cooperation

External threat seems to be a most effective unifier of the Ecuadorian people, as can be noted in the nation's long struggle with Peru over its Amazon region and southern border, which remains a sensitive issue between the neighboring countries and a heated topic in international diplomacy. This conflict extends back to the days of the rubber boom (1870–1910) in the Amazon basin area, when Peruvians began to tacitly occupy what was then a relatively large but quite neglected portion of Amazonian Ecuador.

This area, in fact, made up about one-third of Ecuador's territory at the time. After the rubber boom eventually ended, Peruvian leaders nonetheless maintained economic and strategic interest in Ecuador's Amazonian area. In 1941 the Peruvians finally decided to establish definite sovereignty over this region and launched a military invasion. Being significantly weaker militarily than the aggressors, Ecuador appealed to the international community for mediation and redress, but to no avail (in large part because of the onset of World War II). Consequently, Ecuadorian leaders were forced to accept a large territorial loss that significantly shrank the nation's borders and was a blow to national pride.

The formal agreement that brought an end to the hostilities, known as the Protocol of Rio de Janeiro, is still considered by many Ecuadorians to be a permanent insult to national pride and honor. Especially contentious has been the boundary of one small section along the Cordillera del Condor, which proved impossible to identify, thus providing continuing opportunities for Ecuador to contest Peruvian sovereignty. These challenges to Peru have escalated into open warfare twice—the last time being in 1998. This time a definite boundary was finally agreed to and, as a face-saving gesture, Ecuador was granted one square kilometer, designated a peace park, inside Peruvian territory to symbolize its sacrifice.

Despite such apparent bellicosity, Ecuador is often called an "island of peace" in the midst of its tumultuous and violent neighbors. Certainly compared with Peru and Colombia, it has been calm. In general, Ecuadorians prefer to avoid violence both as a nation and among themselves. At the individual level, an aversion to direct confrontation allows social relationships to continue despite serious disagreement. This national characteristic may be due, in part, to the fact that historically, Ecuadorians lived in small communities where withdrawal or removal was not feasible.

Although Ecuador may be called an island of peace and Ecuadorians considered rather pacific in character, they are nonetheless remarkably unable, or perhaps disinclined, to cooperate with each other. In 1865 Friedrich Hassaurek, the U.S. ambassador to Ecuador at the time, made the following observation, "An important trait of the (Ecuadorian) character is their great distrust of each other, which precludes all spirit of association. Partnerships are not customary, co-operation unheard of. Great enterprises, therefore, are an impossibility" (Hassaurek 1967, 62).

This comment still rings true today and can be observed in various aspects of contemporary Ecuadorian life, including its politics. Ecuadorians rarely agree on what sort of policies the government should follow or even what sort of government the nation should have. All eighteen political parties are adamantly opposed to the others, and, as mentioned earlier, movements for regional and even subregional autonomy are strong throughout the nation.

In the economic sphere, lack of national consensus has served, at least in part, to waste the potential benefits from petroleum exploitation, revenues from which make up approximately half of Ecuador's foreign income. While petroleum income has, in recent decades, indeed served to modernize some aspects of the nation, the degree to which these oil reserves have actually contributed to improving the living conditions of Ecuadorians is open to debate. These sentiments are understandable in light of certain deleterious facts:

> The fact is, relatively few Ecuadorians have profited from the oil boom. The sudden influx of oil incomes caused rampant inflation, which is devastating to people already living a marginal existence. The oil money that went to wealthy Ecuadorians immediately went out of the country...worse, Ecuador's foreign debt has exploded...foreign lenders demand austerity programs from Ecuador's government, resulting in civil service layoffs and cuts in food and fuel subsidies. Penniless Amerindians, displaced from their Amazon homes by oil companies, come to Ecuador's cities and swell the rank[s] of the poor. So Ecuador's poor are indeed getting poorer. (Morrison and Conway 1997, 167)

In part, international factors can be blamed for Ecuador's apparent inability to take full advantage of its petroleum revenues.

Fluctuations in the international price of oil have led to boom-bust cycles in the national budget, with disruptive consequences for the economy as a whole. In 1992 Ecuador renounced its membership in Organization of Petroleum Exporting Countries (OPEC), claiming that this international organization of oil producers did not adequately represent the interests of smaller producers. Ecuador needed to export more oil than its quota permitted in order to address budgetary deficits. Probably more significant, however, is the role of internal factors, including misguided and/or inappropriate government policies, spending on consumption rather than investing productively, and the concentration of revenues in the hands of a small group of elites.

Since the heyday of high oil prices a few decades ago, Ecuadorians have come to realize that oil will not be the magic elixir many had expected. Disenchantment with the results of the oil bonanza is widespread among Ecuadorians of all classes and is responsible for more than just the country leaving OPEC. Recently, most Ecuadorian cities had graffiti that proclaimed the following: "*más petroleo = más pobreza*" ("more petroleum = more poverty").

Repercussions from its petroleum dependency combined with a huge foreign debt and vulnerability to global trends have contributed to the serious economic difficulties currently facing the country, which is experiencing its worst economic crisis since the 1930s. In a controversial and desperate move, Ecuadorian leaders decided to convert the nation's currency to dollars in 2000, thus forgoing internal control over its economic affairs.

Another quite different response to the economic difficulties in Ecuador has been emigration. In recent years many Ecuadorians from the lower social strata, and increasingly from middle and upper sectors as well, have decided to seek greater opportunities and income abroad. The United States is the principal destination for most of these emigrants, with Spain an increasingly popular second choice. Presently, there are over one million Ecuadorians in the New York City area alone, many of them undocumented.

This emigration has had widespread repercussions in Ecuador, both positive and negative. On the one hand, remittances to the migrants' families have fueled markets for land, construction, motor vehicles, and household furnishings while increasing demand for financial services, couriers, migrant smugglers, and even traditional sorcerers and healers who treat all the fallout from the migrants' small bonanzas. On the other hand, migration often results in family dissolution, troubled children, and community disintegration. It also deprives Ecuador of its entrepreneurial labor force. These newly wealthy families of migrants now constitute a novel and ambiguous social sector in the stratification system, namely economically secure, cosmopolitan ex-peasants or workers. It remains to be seen how this structural anomaly will be resolved.

Communication Patterns

Ecuadorian alegría is reflected in communication patterns; one of the key components of an alegre character is a willingness to engage in conversation. A witty conversationalist is greatly appreciated, and verbal acuity and a sense of humor are indispensable in business and politics. In contrast with some other SSSAs, who are sometimes reticent about talking with strangers, Ecuadorians are, as a general rule, quite gregarious. Thus, talking with strangers is not considered forward or intrusive behavior in Ecuador; instead, it is simply one more manifestation of Ecuadorian alegría.

Ecuadorians can be very creative in their use of language, and metaphoric speech is a highly developed art. There are famous political examples such as "*la mano negra*" ("the black hand"), referring to illicit, behind-the-scenes maneuvering; and "*las vacas flacas*" (the thin cows), referring to a time of belt-tightening or limited resources. This inclination for linguistic elaboration and invention can, and often does, extend to outright lying. In fact, lying, distortion, and inaccuracy are frequent ingredients in conversation and may be preferred in many cases to indelicate directness or unpleasant frankness.

There are many different reasons for lying and different kinds of lies. There is lying to be friendly and polite, to please one's audience. There are lies to create impressions, to have one's listener believe in nonexistent events, personal qualities, deeds, relationships, or intentions. There are lies crafted to get one's listener to take a certain action or assume a certain attitude. And there are simply gratuitous lies with no apparent goal beyond creative play.

Friendly lies support cordial relationships: "I've been *dying* to see you! Why haven't you called?" Manipulative lies aim at producing a certain result: "My grandmother just passed away, and we must have $150 for her burial and we don't have a cent, but next week I'll get my paycheck, so couldn't you help us out?" Lies can be used to obligate one person to another: "While you were gone, some thieves nearly broke into your house, but I scared them off even though they tried to attack me. Then I checked all the doors and windows and posted my handyman here the rest of the night." There are even behavioral equivalents of lying: talking into a deactivated cell phone in public carries the subtext, "I'm rich enough to afford one of these phones and have important contacts to maintain at *all* times."

This combination of highly sociable, amenable, and ingratiating self-presentation with manipulative lying is not contradictory, by local reckoning. Ecuadorians are practiced at recognizing cues and circumstances conducive to lying, and especially creative and outrageous lies are quite admired. Because they are considered normal behavior and are frequently employed, Ecuadorians know when to expect them, how to detect them, and how to compensate or correct for them. For the unskilled, however, this practice can be highly disconcerting if not infuriating. Indignation and anger are not appropriate responses to the realization one has been misled; the preferred strategy is to dissemble and play along, hiding any offended feelings you may have.

The strong regional differences in Ecuador are reflected in variations of accent, vocabulary, rate of speech, and intonation. In fact, these verbal differences are so great that speakers from one region sometimes have difficulty understanding those from another. Not surprisingly, the most significant variation is between people from the coast and those from the highlands. In the sierra region, a strong Quichua influence can be noted in speech patterns and vocabulary. The use of diminutives is also more common in the highlands, presumably due to the Quichua influence. In contrast, people from the coast are said to swallow their words, leave off endings, omit consonants, and speak very fast. However, even within the sierra and the costa, there are significant local variations in dialect. For example, people of Cuenca are said to "sing," while those of Loja are considered to speak clearly.

There are also regional differences in matters of social etiquette. While handshakes and mutual arm pats are the universal greeting throughout most of Ecuador, in the urban highlands women kiss friends and some acquaintances on the cheek and men kiss women but only shake hands with men. In contrast, in the rural areas and on the coast, cheek kissing is not practiced at all.

Living and Working in Ecuador

Living and working in Ecuador can encompass both great frustrations and great pleasures. Learning to maneuver your way through daily life in Ecuador in order to fully appreciate all this nation has to offer can be challenging. Time allocation can be one area of particular frustration for many English-speaking North Americans (ESNAs). Ecuadorians demonstrate little regard for punctuality and compliance with scheduled events. People regularly make appointments they don't keep—and possibly never intended to keep—and they do this without qualms. In fact, timely arrival is not expected. A telling example of how punctuality is perceived is the concept of *hora judicial*, or judicial time, which is encoded in Ecuadorian law as follows: a given judicial proceeding may begin any time between the designated time and one hour later and still be considered "on time"; only after an entire hour has elapsed can tardiness be proclaimed and the corresponding blame be assigned. Foreigners, however, must exercise caution in following local customs regarding promptness (or lack of it). Because they are thought to be more punctual than Ecuadorians, it is good policy to uphold this stereotype, even if it means waiting for your Ecuadorian counterpart.

As in many other places in SSSA, Ecuadorian bureaucracy is usually tortuous and inefficient. Ecuadorians know how to deal with this pernicious reality of daily life through a combination of subterfuge and the strategic employment of kinship and friendship ties, bribes and gifts, personal connections, and/or a well-connected lawyer. One frequently used option for foreigners is to hire the services of special facilitators, called *tramitadores*, who, for a fee, will see that bureaucratic hurdles are successfully negotiated.

One misguided expectation held by many foreigners is that public services will work. In fact, water, electricity, garbage collection, police, firemen, or telephones should not be assumed to function reliably, if at all. Those who can afford to do so have water storage tanks and pumps in their homes. Police usually require payment if their services are required, and people usually resort to them only when all else has failed. Businesses, hospitals, and other public institutions have their own power generators to fill in for the inevitable public power failures.

Driving can be yet another area of frustration for foreigners in Ecuador. The key to safe driving is defensive driving. One must always expect a sudden obstacle in the road—whether it be a pothole, a landslide, a pedestrian, or another vehicle. Most Ecuadorian drivers are accustomed to these obstructions, and adapt to present circumstances by spotting the easiest route around the obstacle. In urban areas, the situation is exacerbated by the commonly accepted practice of public bus drivers frequently stopping their vehicles whenever and wherever they want; since there are no bus stops outside the stream of traffic, other drivers must be prepared to stop whenever the bus ahead does so.

In case of an accident, Ecuadorian drivers avoid involving

the police to the extent possible. Since few drivers have insurance, dealing with an insurance company is usually not possible. Instead, the parties involved often reach an agreement or intimidate each other into one, arranging payments and repairs among themselves. In the case of serious accidents, when such ad hoc agreements are not usually possible, the police are still thought to further complicate the problem; oftentimes drivers responsible for a serious accident will flee the scene rather than face the police, because they believe that they will be found guilty, even if they were not at fault. Experience has shown that this is not an unreasonable conclusion.

One of the most challenging aspects of life in Ecuador is finding the ethical path. There are many opportunities and even strong pressures to participate in unethical or corrupt practices, and in certain circumstances, to act ethically may actually be self-defeating, from a business perspective. According to the 2001 Transparency International Corruption Index, Ecuador "boasts" about the same level of corruption as Russia and Pakistan do, all three countries tying for a seventy-ninth ranking, out of a total of ninety-one countries polled, on a scale from least to most corrupt. The economic and political problems that now threaten the country's stability and the welfare of its people are due in no small way to this corruption, which is deeply embedded in Ecuadorian national life.

The frustrations of living in Ecuador are more than offset, in the opinion of many foreigners, by the many pleasures of residing in this aesthetically delightful, geographically diverse, and culturally unique nation. Ecuadorians nearly unanimously claim to love the countryside, and members of the middle and upper classes often own country homes, or *quintas*, where they spend weekends and vacations. Even those urban residents who do not have rural retreats still flock to the countryside whenever possible to enjoy a picnic or country outing. There are many good locations for hiking and climbing in the highlands, and the beaches on the coast are lovely.

Though soccer is the most popular spectator sport, and many

young men play it on the weekends, volleyball is the all-around most popular participant sport—for both men and women. Motorcycling, bicycling, and running are also popular sports. Ecuador's only Olympic gold medal was won by Jefferson Perez, of Cuenca, in the speed-walking competition.

For many visitors to Ecuador, wandering thorugh Indian markets and enjoying village festivities for patron saints' days or other local celebrations are among the highlights of their Ecuadorian experience. In addition, in the larger cities there are myriad churches, museums, galleries, and cultural centers of interest, many reflecting Ecuador's pre-Columbian or colonial past. Finally, there is no lack of worthy projects and urgent necessities to address in Ecuador, and some foreigners take advantage of the relatively weak national control to carry out their own personal or collective projects designed to make a positive impact on the nation and its residents.

Despite the serious economic and political situation currently facing Ecuador, there is a sense of continuity, of sameness to it all. The word *crisis* has been used to describe Ecuador's economic and political institutions for the last thirty years, if not before; this suggests that whatever "crisis" means, it is normal for Ecuador. In keeping with this assessment, Ecuadorians seem to have adjusted to present conditions and are attempting to get on with their lives. They maintain their sense of alegría and joking, oftentimes utilizing the current situation as a source of inspiration for their puns and verbal exchanges. Although they are as divided among themselves as ever, Ecuadorians are united in lamenting their nation's current situation, which might prove to be the strongest bond of all.

References and Selected Bibliography

Benner, Susan E., Kathy S. Leonard, and Marjorie Agosin. 1998. *Fire from the Andes: Short Fiction by Women from Bolivia, Ecuador and Peru*. Albuquerque: University of New Mexico Press.

Colloredo-Mansfeld, Rudi. 1999. *The Native Leisure Class: Consumption and Cultural Creativity in the Andes*. Chicago: University of Chicago Press.

Conaghan, Catharine, and James Malloy. 1995. *Unsettling Statecraft: Democracy and Neoliberalism in the Central Andes*. Pittsburgh: University of Pittsburgh Press.

Crowder, Nicholas B. 2002. *Culture Shock! Ecuador*. Portland, OR: Graphic Arts Center Publications.

Franklin, Albert B. 1943. *Ecuador, Portrait of a People*. Garden City, NY: Doubleday Doran & Company.

Handelsman, Michael. 2000. *Culture and Customs of Ecuador*. Westport, CT: Greenwood Press.

Hassaurek, Friedrich. [1867] 1967. *Four Years among the Ecuadorians*. Carbondale and Edwardsville: Southern Illinois University Press.

Kane, Joe. 1995. *Savages*. New York: Alfred A. Knopf.

Miller, Tom. 1986. *The Panama Hat Trail*. New York: Vintage.

Morrison, Terri, and Wayne A. Conway. 1997. *The Internatinal Traveler's Guide to Doing Business in Latin America*. New York: Macmillan Spectrum.

Newson, Linda A. 1995. *Life and Death in Early Colonial Ecuador*. Norman: University of Oklahoma Press.

Pareja, Miguel Donoso. 1998. "Ecuador: Identidad o Esquizofrenia." *Eskeleta*.

Reyes, Marco A. Encalada. 1983. *Medio Ambiente y Desarrollo en el Ecuador*. Quito: Salvat Editores Ecuatoriana, S. A.

Thomsen, Moritz. 1978. *The Farm on the River of Emeralds*. New York: Vintage.

———. 1969. *Living Poor, A Peace Corps Chronicle*. Seattle and London: University of Washington Press.

Yépez, Martha Traverso. 1998. *La identidad nacional en Ecuador: un acercamiento psicosocial a la construcción nacional*. Quito: Abya Yala. 194.

15

Paraguay: The Bilingual Nation

Danna Lee* and Skye Stephenson

> *El territorio de la paraguayología nos ofrece, mientrastanto, el desconcestante atractivo de los arcanos, el misterio de lo remoto, la paradoja de ser más desconocido cuanto más cerca esté de nuestros ojos.*
>
> —Helio Vera

> *The terrain of Paraguayology has the disconcerting attraction of the arcane, the mystery of the remote, the paradox of being more unknown the closer it is to our eyes.*

Paraguay is perhaps the least known of the Spanish-speaking South American (SSSA) countries, and there are few tourists who include this relatively remote country on their travel or work itineraries. Those who do make it to this landlocked nation of five and a half million inhabitants discover it to be one of the best spots to learn about many aspects of the traditional culture of SSSA, because Paraguay has probably changed less in recent decades than any of the other SSSA nations. While all

* Danna Lee served as a U.S. Peace Corps volunteer and technical trainer in Paraguay from 1992–1995 and has returned to Paraguay periodically since then. She was also the coordinator of the CIEE study abroad program in Santiago, Chile, from 1997 to 2000. Danna is currently the associate director of Off-Campus Study at Colby College.

the others have witnessed dramatic and significant population outflows from their rural to their urban sectors, with the ensuing economic and cultural changes that typically accompany this process, Paraguay stands as the only SSSA country where over half of its populace still resides in the rural sector and derives a livelihood from agriculture. This one fact explains much about Paraguay.

Paraguayan history also sheds light on many of its contemporary cultural patterns. Extensive *mestizaje* took place between the Spanish conquistadors and the local Native American peoples, principally the Guaraní, during the colonial period; consequently, its populace has the highest percentage of mestizos in all the Americas—over 90. Today, Paraguay is the only country in the hemisphere where nearly everyone speaks a European language, Spanish, and a Native American language, Guaraní. In fact, Guaraní is an obligatory subject in all Paraguayan schools and the bane of many students because of its extremely complicated grammatical structure, which is very different from Spanish.

Consider these additional facts about the Paraguayan nation and its people:

- Even with a strong Native American imprint, Paraguay's popular culture is primarily of European origins, such as its world-renowned harp music and its national dance, which is a variety of the polka.
- Although the colonial period in Paraguay was more peaceful than it was for many of its neighbors, its postindependence history has been marked by periods of great belligerence, such as the War of the Triple Alliance, which occurred in the nineteenth century and is considered to have been the bloodiest conflict to ever take place in the Americas.
- Paraguayans are known for their hospitality and are usually very welcoming to outsiders. At the same time, corruption and distrust are no strangers to Paraguayans and can have serious implications for forming relationships and conducting business.

- Paraguay is probably the most isolated SSSA country, yet a great variety of immigrants have made this nation their home, including Mennonites and Japanese as well as some people who could not find refuge elsewhere, such as former Nazis and lawbreakers of various types.

In order to have a more complete understanding of Paraguayan culture, we will examine the following: geographic and regional influences, key cultural characteristics, communication styles, and living and working in Paraguay. Among the key cultural characteristics of the Paraguayans to be explored are the Guaraní influence and the "gentle" conquest; isolation, defeat, and fatalism; traditional ways; and Paraguay as a safe haven for criminals.

Geographic and Regional Influences

Paraguay's most defining geographical characteristic is its isolation. Spanning 406,752 square kilometers (254,220 square miles), the nation is tucked away in the continental landmass, far from either ocean. This central location, rather than placing the nation in the middle of regional events and interactions, actually functions as a deterrent to communication with its neighbors because much of Paraguay's border is shaped by formidable geographic impediments, including rivers, waterfalls, swamps, and arid areas. For instance, even though Paraguay shares an ample border with the other landlocked South American nation—Bolivia—to the northwest, this region is inhospitable, and communication and travel between the two countries are difficult.

Paraguay's eventual isolation could not have been foreseen when the Spanish first began to settle the area. In fact, Asunción, the Paraguayan capital, was the first urban site the Spanish founded in the Río de la Plata area, and it served as the beachhead for exploration and settlement of the rest of the region—including Buenos Aires and Montevideo. However, this upriver city was soon overtaken in size and power by the newer settlements located at the mouth of the Río de la Plata and closer to the Atlantic Ocean. Eventually, Asuncion became a backwater and Paraguay, relatively ignored. This reality is critical to comprehending Paraguayan culture. As a Paraguayan social commentator elaborates,

> The first of these facts (clues to understanding Paraguayan culture) is geographic isolation. Far from the routes of international commerce, without control of any strategic vantage point, without precious metals, and without any product coveted in the rest of the world, very soon Paraguay began to be forgotten. An Argentine writer produced a work—*Zama*—in which he narrates the misadventures of a colonial Spanish functionary that was sent to Asunción and forgotten. It was [as] if they had sent him to Siberia. (Vera 1988, 94)

Another clue to understanding Paraguayan culture is its climatic realities, which serve to shape both the rhythm and texture of life. Paraguay is one of the hottest and most humid places in the continent. Located far from the ocean breezes and the lofty Andes Mountains further to the west that bring in cool air, Paraguay can be likened to a continental oven. This is especially true during the long summer months, when the heat can be unrelenting.

In spite of having no direct access to the ocean, waterways play a crucial role in Paraguayan national life, leading some to dub the nation an "island surrounded by land." Principally, the country is divided in two by the Paraguay River. To the northwest of the river lies the Chaco region, which is largely arid and desolate, supporting only 3 percent of the population: mostly indigenous groups, Mennonite colonists, and cattle ranchers. This sparsely populated region produces large amounts of beef products and accounts for most of the nation's dairy production. To the southeast is the fertile central region, where the remaining 97 percent of the population lives and where the two main Paraguayan cities, Asuncíon and Concepcíon, are located. In this region agriculture predominates; the principal crops are soybeans, cotton, and sugarcane.

Paraguay is most famous among tourists as an important route to the majestic Iguazú Falls, which are located very close to the Paraguayan border and shared with Argentina and Brazil. These falls are much wider than Niagara Falls and far more dramatic. They stretch for nearly 4 kilometers (2.5 miles) and are made up of approximately 275 individual cascades, some of which drop 82 meters (269 feet).

Located near the Iguazú Falls and within Paraguayan territory is Itaipú, one of the largest dams in the world. In 1983 construction began on another dam on the Rio Paraná, Yacyretá, which will be about half the size of Itaipú. Since Paraguay's relatively small population cannot use all of its share of the electricity generated at these sites, the national leaders have benefited by selling the excess to the country's much larger and more industrialized neighbors and partners in the construction projects, Argentina and Brazil. This interregional exchange has served to lessen Paraguay's isolation in recent years to some degree.

Keys to Understanding the Paraguayans

The Guaraní Influence and the "Gentle" Conquest

While there were, and still are, other Native American groups that reside in Paraguay, the Guaraní take center stage in Paraguayan life and culture. In fact, the imprint of this Native American group on Paraguayan culture is so strong that it is difficult to separate what is Guaraní from what is Paraguayan. The Guaraní influence can be noted not only in the linguistic patterns of the Paraguayans but also in the ethnic makeup of the population and in popular culture.

At the time of the Spaniards' arrival, the Guaraní were a very large linguistic group of seminomads who occupied nearly all of the Atlantic coast of South America as well as vast interior regions of the continent. While the Guaraní resided in a region that was much more extensive than contemporary Paraguay, it is in this country that the deepest and most lasting echoes of the Guaraní resonate.

The early interaction between the Caucasian invaders and the Native American locals was relatively "gentle," at least in comparison with what occurred in other parts of the continent. The Guaraní repulsed the first Spanish contingent that arrived in Paraguay, but the second one received a very different reception. Led by Juan de Salazar Espinoza and consisting of more than 2,500 soldiers, the Spaniards were welcomed by Guaraní chieftains in a very special way—they were offered some of the "surplus" Guaraní women.

What had begun as a gesture of hospitality on the part of the Guaraní soon became a conscious policy of the Spaniards. In a process that came to be known as *mestizando*, the Spaniards made a deliberate attempt to mix the blood of the local indigenous groups with their own. Domingo Martínez de Irala, the governor of Paraguay from 1539 to 1556, exemplified this policy, having as many as seventy Guaraní mistresses himself. He then married off his many daughters to high-ranking local officials, thus expanding his connections throughout the colony. While Governor Irala had more women than the lower-ranking Spaniards in the territory, it is estimated that the majority of European males each kept between thirty and fifty Guaraní women during the early colonial period.

This "amicable" introduction portended the direction of the demographic future of the nation. It was primarily through these intimate relations between the Spanish men and the Guaraní women—and the incorporation of each into the culture and lifestyle of the other—that the conquest of Paraguay was achieved. This approach contrasted sharply with the traditional methods of conquest and appropriation that occurred in most of the other Spanish colonies in the New World. In fact, there was probably nowhere else in all the Americas where the Europeans and the Native Americans procreated as openly and prolifically as in Paraguay during the early colonial period. The consequence of this approach to European-indigenous relations can be noted in the ethnic composition of contemporary Paraguayans; according to estimates, more than 90 percent of the population can claim a mestizo ancestry.

Paraguay was also the site of a very different yet equally fascinating attempt to deal with the "indigenous question." The Jesuits, who arrived in 1609, wanted to find a new way to convert and educate the Native Americans—a way that would be considered more humane and more complete than what had occurred in the colonies previously. With this goal in mind, the Jesuits developed what came to be known as *reducciones*. These were closed communities within which a relatively harmonious and egalitarian lifestyle was promoted between the Spanish priests and the Native Americans who had been enticed to live there.

In their heyday, more than thirty reducciones held as many as 200,000 people within their walled confines. The Native Americans were instructed in Christian doctrine, literacy, and the arts. In general, the education was very Eurocentric in pedagogy and content. However, the priests soon discovered that many of the indigenous peoples possessed exceptional artistic talent and began to encourage this natural proclivity among them. As a consequence, many different types of arts and crafts flourished, particularly music and masonry, and were produced in the reducciones. Beautiful churches were also constructed, largely by Native American craftsmen.

Despite the paternalistic approach of the Jesuits, their experiment is laudable, particularly if one considers the realities that most Native Americans on the continent were facing at the time. Even so, Voltaire, in his famous work *Candide*, satirizes the Jesuit missions in Paraguay as follows:

> "So you have already been to Paraguay?" said Candide. "Indeed I have," replied Cacambo. "I was once a servant in the College of the Assumption, so I know how the reverend fathers govern...the reverend fathers own the whole lot, and the people own nothing; that is what I would call a masterpiece of reason and justice." (Morrison and Conway 1997, 307)

The Jesuits were expelled from Paraguay in 1767 due to political pressures from Europe as well as to more immediate opposition from local landowners desiring to use the indigenous Americans for cheap labor. After the Jesuits left Paraguay, most of the Native Americans in the reducciones dispersed. Many ended up working as slaves or laborers on agricultural plantations. Today, visitors can still see some of the ruins of Jesuit reducciones, although the condition of many is quite deteriorated.

Even though the physical presence of the Jesuits in Paraguay ended centuries ago, they left important legacies that continue on in the nation's contemporary cultural patterns. One of the most noteworthy is music. Because of the excellent Jesuit instruction, the Guaraní were indoctrinated into European music. As a result, despite the strong indigenous influence in Paraguayan culture, the nation's popular music is almost entirely European in origin.

The Paraguayans are most known for their beautiful harp music. This genre gained world attention at the end of World War II, when several Paraguayan harpists, for example, Luis Alberto del Paraná and Los Paraguayos, achieved international renown for their melodies. The guitar is the only other instrument widely played in Paraguay. Most Paraguayan songs are slow and sentimental, and quite a few are about important events in the country's history.

Paraguayan dances are also primarily European in origin, although they have been modified over the years. Most are a variety of polka (see German influence, page 283); there is the lively *polca paraguaya* and the *galopa*. The former is a dance for couples, while the latter is usually danced by groups of women, the *galoperas*, who swing around barefoot, balancing a bottle or jar on their heads. There is even a special polca for the two principal Paraguayan political parties, the Colorados and the Liberales.

The Franciscans both preceded and outlasted the period of the Jesuit missions in Paraguay. Although some of the early Franciscans were quite vocal in support of the rights of the Guaraní and other Native American groups, as the political power of the Spaniards increased and formal local governments were established, the Franciscans provided little support for the welfare of the indigenous peoples.

Today, the general attitude of Paraguayans regarding their indigenous history and identity is quite complex. Because of the extensive mestizaje that occurred there, almost all Paraguayans feel a personal sense of affiliation with their indigenous ancestry, and they take great pride in the Guaraní language. This contrasts strikingly with the situation in some of the other SSSA countries (such as Ecuador and Peru) with large Native American populations, where there is often a clear division between the worlds of those of indigenous ancestry and those who are of primarily European lineage.

Nonetheless, Paraguayans often attribute many of their national and individual shortcomings to the same mestizaje and Guaraní influences in their culture. For instance, Paraguayans often blame laziness or a lack of motivation on their indigenous heritage and see productivity or innovation as tied to European influence. Rather than focusing on the tremendous assets of this bicultural nation, some instead claim that it is this merging of the Guaraní with the Spanish that explains the country's supposed lack of development.

Isolation, Defeat, and Fatalism

In contrast to certain periods in Paraguayan colonial history that were notable for a relatively harmonious coexistence among the local population and a receptivity to outside influences, the country's postcolonial history developed along almost opposite lines. No other SSSA nation has endured such a tragic saga as Paraguay. Its people have had to cope with tremendous losses, bloodshed, isolation, and heavy-handed rulers. In fact, Paraguay's reputation as an "island surrounded by land" is due not just to geographic features but also to its psychological isolation from its neighbors. This insular attitude is attributable in large part to the political and military history of postindependence Paraguay, which has been marked by the rule of several dictators whose personal attitudes and policies have strongly shaped the direction and destiny of the nation.

This pattern began right after Paraguayan independence from Spain, with the ascension to power of José Gaspar Rodríguez de Francia, known as *El Supremo* (the Supreme),[†] who governed from 1814 to 1840 and ruled the fledgling nation with an iron hand. During his nearly three decades of leadership, he enforced a strict policy of isolation and self-sufficiency that virtually sealed the nation's borders and minimized interaction with the outside world.

The man who succeeded Francia, Carlos Antonio López, spent much of his twenty-two-year term reversing his predecessor's policies. He reopened the nation's borders and recruited foreign specialists, particularly in the areas of technology and military formation. Unfortunately, his son, Mariscal Francisco Solano López, who took over upon his father's death, did not continue this political strategy. Instead, he pursued a more aggressive approach to foreign policy, launching Paraguay in 1864 into the infamous six-year War of the Triple Alliance against the allies Argentina, Brazil, and Uruguay.

This war proved to be disastrous for Paraguay and was probably the bloodiest conflict ever to take place on American soil. By the time it ended, what had been one of the most prosperous SSSA countries was literally decimated. The large Paraguayan army had been reduced to 480 soldiers. Even the president himself, who had commanded the troops, was killed. Of nearly a million and a half Paraguayans prior to the conflict, only 6,000 men and 220,000 women and children survived. The nation also lost a large portion of its territory, including an area along its border with Uruguay. Paraguay's current borders are a consequence of this decisive defeat. Some say that Paraguay has never totally recovered from this conflict, either psychologically or economically, and even today, the War of the Triple Alliance is a subject of much discussion and debate among Paraguayans.

[†] The most well known Paraguayan author, Augusto Roa Bastos, wrote a novel nearly a century later titled *Yo, el Supremo* about a fictitious dictator who was strikingly similar to Francia.

However, the country did begin to recover demographically by the mid-twentieth century, due in part to immigration. One of the more important immigrant groups to Paraguay was the Mennonites, who first arrived around 1927 from Russia, Canada, and Mexico, in search of educational independence and escape from the military draft. Most of them settled in rural communities in the Chaco region, where many still remain. Currently, about 28,000 Mennonites reside in Paraguay; most still retain their own particular identity and lifestyle. They have proven to be very successful farmers and currently control about 70 percent of the country's dairy production.

Another important immigrant group to Paraguay has been the Germans, who also began arriving in the early twentieth century. Today, Germans make up the largest Caucasian group in Paraguay, about 1.7 percent of the total population. More recently, there has been an influx of Asians, particularly Japanese and Koreans, and they have fared quite well economically.

Paraguay's military travails did not end with the infamous War of the Triple Alliance. In the twentieth century, from 1932 to 1935, Paraguay entered into yet another armed confrontation known as the War of the Chaco, with its western neighbor, Bolivia. The cause of the conflict was the issue of which nation would control a portion of their border area where petroleum had been found. The war ended in a stalemate, and Paraguay did not lose any territory, as it had in the previous conflict, but the impact on the nation was still profound. This time, Paraguay lost about 36,000 citizens in the fighting.

In more recent years, Paraguay held the hemispheric record for the longest reigning dictator in the twentieth century. Until his overthrow by his son-in-law in 1989, General Alfredo Stroessner ruled the country as president for thirty-five years. Originally gaining power through military means, he was then reelected seven times—in elections of questionable transparency. His administration was tainted by human rights abuses and corruption; nevertheless, it also enjoyed strong popular support, mainly among the lower classes and government officials. Even today,

Stroessner is both criticized and lauded, and he still remains a subject of dispute.

All of these historical national realities of postindependence Paraguay have contributed to shaping and reinforcing a very Paraguayan trait, a marked sense of fatalism. While such a sense of *destino* is a key cultural characteristic of SSSA cultural patterns in general, it is particularly strong in Paraguayan culture. This is not surprising, considering the many heavy losses and long dictatorships that the Paraguayan people have had to weather over the centuries.

For many natives, this sense of fatalism is inextricably linked with religious beliefs. Even by SSSA standards, the populace is extremely Catholic, except, of course, for such minority groups as the Mennonites and the Asian and German communities, among others. This religiosity can be noted in numerous ways; it is even reflected in the spoken language. Many Paraguayans liberally dose their speech with hopeful pleas for kindly assistance of all sorts from the heavens; the theme of the petition may range from the profoundly significant to the mundane. It is not uncommon for some Paraguayans, especially the older generations, to solicit God's intervention (*si dios quiere*) automatically and in an offhand manner for anything ranging from a trip to the capital to the preparation of a birthday cake.

This belief that fate, rather than individual initiative, controls much of what transpires contributes to another very Paraguayan trait, which is a strong conformist bent with a tendency to not want to "make waves." This attitude leads many Paraguayans to have rather limited expectations and aspirations for themselves as well as for the nation. In fact, few truly innovative policies or actions have sprung from Paraguayan soil. Even the literary arts, so strong in much of the region and such an important means of expression, have never taken much hold in Paraguay. This nation boasts few well-known authors or poets, and the citizens are notorious for being rather uninterested readers for the most part.

Traditional Ways

The Paraguay of today, at the beginning of the twenty-first century, is similar in many ways to other countries in the region half a century or more ago. For instance, class differences are very apparent among Paraguayans. The social gap between the few rich and the multitudinous poor is so marked that some have even called it a caste system. There are few middle-class Paraguayans, and it is extremely difficult for someone from the lower echelons of society to raise his or her position. The family and class one is born into strongly shapes present and future opportunities and limitations.

Contrasts in the standard of living between the rich and the poor are striking. In 1990, only 50 percent of the urban population and 17 percent of the rural population had piped water (Valdez and Gomariz 1995, 118). In contrast, wealthy Paraguayans live quite lavish lifestyles, entertaining in their social clubs and large homes. Many of the urban elite derive at least some of their income from landholdings in the rural sector, which have often been passed down from generation to generation. While such patterns of land distribution were prevalent in many other SSSA countries in the past, government leaders in quite a few of them (such as Bolivia, Peru, and Chile) undertook land reform measures that redistributed at least some of the larger landholdings to needy rural residents. Such initiatives were never undertaken in Paraguay.

Neither has Paraguay experienced the massive rural-urban migration so typical of the other SSSA countries in the last half century. As a consequence, Paraguay is the only nation in the continent where, as mentioned earlier, more than 50 percent of its population still resides in the rural sector, and agriculture and livestock production are still by far the most important sources of revenue and employment for most Paraguayans.

The rhythms and configuration of life in Paraguay are very much shaped by this reality, and even in the urban areas most people interpret events from an agricultural mindset. In fact, the predominance of the rural sector is one of the most important and defining characteristics of the Paraguayan nation and its peoples, shaping in powerful ways perceptions of space, time, work, leisure, and life in general.

> The rural life has an inevitable and powerful influence on the cosmovision of the [Paraguayan] people, with its routine of slow days, of scanty shadows and malevolent sunlight, with its ambivalent dependence on water, cursed when it pours and yearned for when it makes itself scarce; with its religious fear of authority, before whose arbitrariness and depredations there is no recourse. (Vera, 98)

Another defining and traditional Paraguayan characteristic is the centrality of family in personal as well as national life, a trait typical of many relatively isolated and primarily agrarian societies. Even more than in many of the other SSSA nations, family is the key for much of what transpires in Paraguay. This can even be noted in the political realm. Membership in one of the two traditional political parties—the Colorados and the Liberales—is usually decided by family affiliation. So too are many of the twists and turns of the political events in the country. Probably the most famous of these situations was the 1988 rumor that the marriage between former dictator Alfredo Stroessner's daughter and the son of then General Andrés Rodríguez was suffering. Many have speculated that this personal strain between the two was somehow significant in the events leading up to Stroessner's fall at the hands of General Rodríguez one year later, in 1989.

For most Paraguayans, family is the single most important point of reference in their lives. Not only does family affiliation serve to both shape and define one's place in Paraguayan society, it is also the realm in which the greatest amount of time and energy is invested. Here, even more than in other places in the continent, the extended family is revered, and relations among cousins, aunts and uncles, in-laws, grandparents, and the like is the main focus of many Paraguayans' social life. For instance, many families, especially those who have the financial means, lavishly celebrate such events as baptisms, fifteen-year-old parties for females, and marriages. Having a large party when a child reaches one year of age is a local tradition. Because many children used to die during the first year of life, this one-year celebration became an important milestone, symbolizing the likelihood that the child would survive to adulthood. Some of these parties among the elite can cost enormous sums of money and often include hundreds of guests—both adults and children.

The importance of family in Paraguayan national life does not usually impinge on their way of interacting with nonfamily members. In fact, as a general rule, Paraguayans are extremely warm and friendly, even by SSSA standards; they are notably hospitable and generous. Many, in fact, pride themselves on their hospitality and consider it to be the most positive Paraguayan attribute. This trait runs through the social spectrum; even those Paraguayans who are the most economically stressed will graciously invite visitors to partake of a meal, dividing the portions in such a way that each and every participant receives his or her allotment. Extending the table, adding another chair, and squeezing one more person into the gathering are sources of pleasure for the Paraguayan host.

This sense of hospitality and sharing can be noted in one of the most typical Paraguayan customs, the drinking of cold maté, known locally as *tereré*. While maté is popular throughout the Southern Cone region and the south of Brazil, only in Paraguay is it consumed cold, due largely to the hot climate. Often, other herbs are added to *yerba maté*, many of which possess supposed medicinal properties, such as serving as a diuretic, promoting weight loss, reducing blood pressure, and others. Tereré is typically served in a cow horn, referred to as a *guampa*, which is filled to the brim with the herbs and topped off with water. The resulting tea is sucked through a metal straw with a sieve at the bottom, known as a *bombilla*. The drinking of this popular beverage is always a communal activity, the container being passed, in turn, to all those present, who share the same bombilla.

Safe Haven for Criminals

Paraguayan hospitality extends not only to family and friends but also to welcoming some rather unsavory characters. Paraguay is infamous as a haven for criminals and political characters who cannot find a home elsewhere. As Pico Iyer summarizes,

> Paraguay has the reputation of being the darkest country on the planet…this was the place where deposed dictators found a new home…. This was the place where fugitive Nazis received a hearty welcome—Eduard Roschmann, "The Butcher of Riga," allegedly died here; Josef Mengele, "the angel of death," was a Paraguayan citizen for much of the time he was the world's most wanted war criminal; and Martin Bormann lived just across the border. This was also the place where Italian neo-Fascists gave lectures, Croatian thugs trained security details, Chinese tong kings picked up tips, and the new president himself—the "clean one"—was associated with drug kingpins who'd made $145 million in shipping heroin. (Morrison and Conway, 307)

Hand in hand with the welcoming of criminal elements and/or perpetrators of actions condemned by most of the world community is the attitude of many Paraguayans themselves. Paraguay is a place where smuggling, corruption, and dishonesty run rife. Many of the nation's top leaders have turned a blind eye to illegal activities as long as funds flowed into personal and government coffers. Such an attitude is not exclusive to the elite; it permeates all levels of Paraguayan society in one way or another. For instance, large numbers of Paraguayans knowingly drive stolen cars, most of which have entered the country from Brazil. These vehicles do not have legal papers, so they cannot be taken out of the country. Nonetheless, within Paraguay they can and do circulate freely. Such cars cost about half that of a legally acquired automobile.

One of Paraguay's most booming cities is Ciudad del Este, a free-trade zone located near Iguazú Falls. According to one U.S. university student, this city seems very much like "a more chaotic Tijuana." In this border town, both authentic and, more often, counterfeit goods are sold at less expensive prices than in the neighboring countries. Busloads of Brazilians arrive for the weekend from destinations as far away as Saõ Paulo to go shopping. It is estimated that from Ciudad del Este alone, anywhere from five to ten billion dollars of counterfeit goods per year enter the continent.

Recently, Paraguay has become an important smuggling center for another type of product—illegal drugs. Due to antinarcotic policies in some of the other countries in the region, some drug lords are moving their operations and distribution facilities to Paraguay. Many are rumored to be located in the more remote parts of the country, such as in the Chaco region.

Communication Patterns

One of the most defining characteristics of Paraguayans is that the vast majority are bilingual. While other SSSA countries, such as Peru, have more than one official language, and while Native American languages are spoken by many of indigenous descent, only in Paraguay do so many people, whatever their ethnicity, speak both Spanish and Guaraní. This bilingualism has received strong governmental support in recent years; since 1990, efforts have been made to implement educational reform whereby both languages are taught in all the public schools throughout the country. In addition, Guaraní is used frequently in the media, especially radio.

However, Paraguay cannot be classified as a totally bilingual nation. Even though nearly all Paraguayans speak at least some Guaraní, only 75 percent speak Spanish.[‡] Those who are monolingual in Guaraní usually hail from the poorest and often the most remote sectors of the nation. Most of those Paraguayans who do speak both languages do not usually do so interchangeably; rather, the decision of whether to use Spanish or Guaraní

‡ There are about 90,000 Paraguayans who speak a Native American language other than Guaraní.

is dependent upon geographical, functional, and social factors. For instance, Spanish tends to predominate in the urban areas, while Guaraní is more common in the rural zones. Also, Guaraní has developed as the language of daily routines and colloquial interactions, whereas Spanish is used as the language of law, politics, official functions, and higher education. The division is so marked that the vocabulary itself is unique to each purpose.

Many Paraguayans say that Guaraní is the language of the heart. Even those for whom it is a second language feel they express some things better in Guaraní, which utilizes actual sounds to describe many things. For instance, the word for "stream" sounds like running water, *ysyry*.

As commonly occurs in multilingual settings, many Paraguayans, when they speak colloquially, combine Spanish and Guaraní into a creative and ad hoc lingua franca known as *Jopará*. Often, Spanish roots with Guaraní suffixes and prefixes or, alternatively, Guaraní roots with Spanish conjugations are employed. Often, Paraguayans traveling outside of the country choose to speak in Guaraní or Jopará among themselves so that outsiders cannot understand them.

In contrast to Guaraní and jopará, Paraguayan Spanish is similar to that of the other Río Plate countries—Argentina and Uruguay. For example, like Argentineans and Uruguayans, Paraguayans use the word *vos* instead of the more common *tú* for the informal second-person singular pronoun. However, unlike Argentineans and Uruguayans, Paraguayans do not enunciate *ll* and *y* like "sh." Rather, like the rest of the continental Spanish speakers, they give these letters a "y" sound.

Although Paraguayans have the greatest cultural affinity with their Argentine neighbors, they are also influenced by Brazilians. Along the border region near Brazil, many of the locals also speak Portuguese. Also, in contrast with the greeting patterns of nationals from all of the other SSSA countries, Paraguayans prefer to give two salutatory kisses, one on each cheek, as the Brazilians do. In fact, Paraguayans are quite fond of their Brazilian neighbors, considering them to be *alegre* and friendly; and when given a choice as to preferred vacation destinations, the majority would probably select the Brazilian coast.

Living and Working in Paraguay

For visitors to Paraguay, the heat more than any other factor will probably serve as a backdrop to much of their experience, due not only to its physical effects but also because many aspects of daily life in Paraguay are a response to the nation's climatic patterns. The Paraguayan concept of time is consistent with that of many other countries with hot, humid climates: there simply is no hurry. Paraguayans frequently use the expression *tranquilopa*, which means "Relax, take it easy." There is generally no rush, and people prefer *tranquilidad,* or a "laid-back" attitude, to urgency. Another frequently used expression is *en seguida*, a phrase that literally means "right away" but should more accurately be interpreted as "eventually." The use of the terms *mañana* (tomorrow), *esta tarde* (this afternoon), and *a la tardecita* (a little later) to specify hours can also be less precise than many English-speaking North Americans (ESNAs) are accustomed to.

Paraguayan working hours also function according to the nation's heat. Nearly every business, office, and school commences very early in the day, usually around 7:00 in the morning, in order to get some time in before it gets too hot. Some places, such as banks, then close for the day around 2:00 P.M. Other institutions with a more extended workday typically have a long period in the afternoon when they are closed, commencing business once again around 4:00 P.M., when some of the heat has abated.

Paraguayan hospitality is a second important aspect for foreigners. In some of the other SSSA countries, especially in the more urbanized areas, invitations to locals' homes may not be readily forthcoming; in Paraguay, however, foreigners often receive such invitations, and great efforts are usually made to effusively welcome the visitor. Due to the country's relative isolation and to the fact that so few outsiders make it to Paraguay, many Paraguayans are fascinated with foreigners, and outsiders are often treated as revered guests, in part because the foreigner has knowledge and expertise that most Paraguayans do not. There is even a well-known Paraguayan expression that sums up this attitude, *después de Dios, el gringo* (after God, the gringo). As one professional woman working in Paraguay stated, "In most (employment) situations, the Paraguayan employer will give preference to the foreigner over the Paraguayan."

For foreigners planning to live and work in Paraguay, learning some Guaraní phrases can go far in helping to establish bonds of warmth and trust with Paraguayans. So, too, can taking the time for relationships and interactions; even more than in the rest of SSSA, relationships are pivotal for all that transpires in the country.

Just as in the rest of SSSA, fashion is important, especially for those with the economic means. Preference in clothing style is often taken from neighboring Argentina or Brazil, and, just like in those two nations, plastic surgery is a quite common procedure among the wealthy in Paraguay. Perhaps the most distinguishing characteristic of Paraguayan clothing is a marked flair for the baroque that is most evident at social events. Many women use ample make-up and wear an abundance of jewelry to accent their fashionable clothing. In daily affairs, more casual attire is the norm.

Nepotism and tips given to obtain a desired result are not only legal, they are standard practice in Paraguay. Such paybacks can involve more than small tips in some instances. Many people in government and business will facilitate almost any transaction, given sufficient economic incentives. Foreigners living and working in Paraguay need to pay special attention to this cultural characteristic in order to avoid financial difficulties. Someone who lived and worked for five years in Paraguay explains the situation in a personal interview with the author: "Foreigners need to be careful doing business in Paraguay; you can be taken advantage of. While Paraguayans are usually very warm and friendly, at the same time they might be thinking not about the conversation at hand but rather about ways to take your money."

Of course, not all, or even the majority, of Paraguayans are involved in such questionable activities or engage in corrupt practices. Many worry about the impact of this corruption on the country's political and economic institutions and on its future well-being, and they are concerned that the prevalence of corruption is impeding the growth and stability of the country. Nonetheless, Paraguayans in general recognize how entrenched these patterns are and how difficult they are to change. As one Paraguayan in an interview with the coauthor stated, "We are missing a civic maturity. We need to pass into another generation, or maybe two, so that a new Paraguayan can be formed...this is true because the corruption is so deep inside the Paraguayan—it occurs at all levels of society, from the highest classes down to the lowest ones."

* * * * * * *

As Paraguay confronts the twenty-first century, this most isolated of the SSSA nations is undergoing important transformations that most likely portend a different future, which serves to underscore the importance of not dwelling excessively on the traditional configurations of Paraguayan culture to explain all that occurs within national boundaries. In fact, in recent years much of the populace has undertaken a sustained effort to transform key aspects of life in Paraguay. This can be noted in the move toward democratic governance, which has, for the first time in the country's history, managed to sustain itself to date despite several attempts by powerful leaders to seize power through extralegal means. Paraguay's increasing economic integration with its neighbors is another indicator of the desire to modernize. The full implications of these events are hard to predict, but it is clear that important changes are percolating in Paraguay these days.

Despite these very important recent trends, however, much still remains the same. The predominance of the rural sector, the stratified social structure, and the conformist bent of many locals as well as their ebullient hospitality are still very notable aspects of Paraguayan life and culture. So, too, is the mestizo nature of the Paraguayan people who, as a collectivity, have managed over the centuries to integrate within themselves and their predominant national culture both the European and the Native American to an extent unmatched anywhere else in the continent.

References and Selected Bibliography

Bailey, Gauvin A. 1999. *Art on the Jesuit Missions in Asia and Latin America, 1542–1773.* Toronto: University of Toronto Press.

Bastos, Augusto Roa. 1974. *I the Supreme.* Translated by Helen Lane. New York: Alfred A. Knopf.

Cultural Survival, Inc. 1980. *The Indian Peoples of Paraguay: Their Plight and Their Prospects.* Special report, no. 2. Cambridge, MA: David Maybury-Lewis.

Estragó, Margarita Durán. 1990. *Le Iglesia en el Paraguay. Una Historia Minima.* Asunción: RP Ediciones.

Lambert, Peter, and Andrew Nickson, eds. 1997. *The Transition to Democracy in Paraguay.* New York: Macmillan.

Lewis, Paul H. 1982. *Socialism, Liberalism, and Dictatorship in Paraguay.* New York: Praeger.

Melià, Bartomeu. 1993. *Una Nación Dos Culturas.* Asunción: RP Ediciones—CEPAG.

Morrison, Terri, and Wayne A. Conway. 1997. *The International Traveler's Guide to Doing Business in Latin America.* New York: Macmillan.

Reed, Richard K. 1995. *Prophets of Agroforestry: Guaraní Communities and Commercial Gathering.* Austin: University of Texas Press.

Roett, Riordan. 1991. *Paraguay: The Personalist Legacy.* Boulder: Westview Press.

Valdés, Teresa, and Enrique Gomariz, coords. 1995. *Latin American Women: Comparative Figures.* Santiago: FLACSO.

Vera, Helio. 1988. *En Busca del Hueso Perdido.* Tratado de Paraguayología. Asunción, Paraguay: RP Ediciones.

16

Peru: Heir of Empires

Linda Greenow* and Skye Stephenson

Nosotros, los Peruanos, siempre estamos recreandonos
—Manuel de Cossio Kluver

We Peruvians are constantly re-creating ourselves.

Peru is the second largest of the Spanish-speaking South American (SSSA) countries, covering a territory about the size of Alaska. However, Peru's significance is far greater than even its size suggests, for it is as if within this one nation were crystallized nearly all the historical, political, economic, and cultural variants that have ever been manifested in the region as a whole. In Peru, more than in any other country in the continent, can be found both the diversity and complexity of SSSA cultural patterns, and attempting to comprehend this multilayered na-

* Linda Greenow is associate professor and chair of the Department of Geography at the State University of New York at New Paltz, where she teaches courses in geography and Latin American Studies. She has published articles and book reviews in such journals as *Journal of Historical Geography*, *The Professional Geographer*, and *Hispanic American Historical Review* as well as textbooks and textbook units for K-12 social studies. She received a Ph.D. in geography from Syracuse University and is currently codirector of a U.S. Department of Education Title VI grant for Latin American Studies at SUNY New Paltz.

tion with its multitoned citizens can be both challenging and deeply rewarding.

The most enduring image many people have of Peru is that of the stunning and seemingly ethereal mountaintop remains of the sacred Incan city of Machu Picchu. Peru was indeed the center of not only the Inca empire but several other important pre-Columbian civilizations as well. This nation was also the seat of Spanish power in colonial South America and the most important part of the Iberians' extensive holdings on the continent.

Contemporary Peruvians reflect their nation's long history of harboring diverse human settlements of various types. There are more Native Americans in Peru than in any other place in the western hemisphere, and the Hispanic presence is very strong as well. Peruvians of African heritage first arrived in this Andean nation as slave labor, while those of Asian ancestry arrived later as a source of cheap labor. Today, large numbers of Peruvians are mestizos, with ancestry of varying ethnic combinations.

Much of contemporary Peruvian life is driven by the dynamics of this multiracial and multicultural populace. On the positive side, Peru's amazing cultural richness is reflected in its folk culture, arts, music, crafts, and cuisine. On the downside, despite decades of effort to distribute resources and opportunities more equitably among the different groups, entrenched racism and classism still exist to some degree and color the nature of many interactions among Peruvians.

Some key features of Peruvian contemporary reality include the following:

- More Peruvians speak Native American languages than in any other country in the Americas. At the same time, Peruvian Spanish is among the easiest to understand of all the Spanish-speaking nationalities.
- Sharp differences exist between the coastal cities and highland towns and villages—in their economies, cultures, and ways of life. Many longtime residents of coastal cities such as Lima and Trujillo are well educated, self-assured, and knowledgeable about other countries and cultures. Residents

of highland towns and villages are, for the most part, quieter and more traditional in their lifestyles.

- What is now Peru was the center of both the Incan and the Spanish empires and the site of the most important and opulent human settlement during these periods; however, these days, Peru ranks toward the bottom of the region in economic and social development, at least according to most standard scales.
- Peruvians are noted for their relaxed friendliness and openness, both among themselves and with outsiders. Nonetheless, despite recent social transformations, Peruvians are, as just mentioned, still deeply entrenched along class and racial lines.

This chapter provides information that will help the reader better understand and appreciate Peru and its people. The following themes will be covered: geographic and regional influences, keys to understanding the Peruvians, communication patterns, and living and working in Peru. The defining characteristics of Peruvian culture that will be discussed are Peru, land of empires; hierarchy; flexibility and openness to change; and creativity and aesthetics.

Geographic and Regional Influences

Peru is not only diverse ethnically but also geographically. Few countries can portray their differences with such certainty on a map, with clear and convincing boundaries that separate regions of markedly distinct physical environments, cultures, and historical experiences. In fact, Peru is very nearly three countries in one: its coastal desert plain serves as the urban, industrial, and commercial/agricultural base of Peru's modern economy; the Andean highlands are the home of the indigenous population, descendants of the great Inca empire, and the site of colonial cities, rural estates, and mines; and the eastern two-thirds of the country includes the edge of the Amazon basin and is isolated from the rest of Peru both physically and psychologically. Considering Peru's geographic realities, it is not surprising that a lack of national integration is often cited as one of the country's most challenging problems.

La Costa. Peru's all-important coast (*la costa*) is a narrow plain over 2,240 kilometers (1,400 miles) long that makes up only about 10 percent of the national territory but is home to over 40 percent of Peru's population. An unlikely place for such a concentration of the national populace, la costa is in general an arid zone; however, the presence of numerous rivers crossing this region on their way to the Pacific Ocean creates river valleys that, when irrigated, are extremely fertile. There are about forty such oases located throughout the costa, supporting a wide variety of produce that includes sugarcane, rice, grapes, fruits, and olives. Extensive industrial production is also synonymous with the coastal region.

Life along the entire coastal strip is strongly influenced by its maritime location. Especially significant is the existence of a cold ocean current that flows northward along this portion of the Pacific coast. Peruvians call it the Peruvian Current, but it is more commonly known as the Humboldt Current. This cold current brings with it high levels of oxygen and an abundance of plankton and algae, which act as a magnet attracting a plenitude of fish, especially anchovies. Peru is one of the major fishing countries in the world today, although recently overexploitation has had a serious effect on production. Fish meal, fertilizer, and other fish products are processed in factories located in many of the coastal cities, lending an odoriferous air to such sites.

This cold ocean current also affects weather patterns along the coast, especially levels of moisture. During part of the year, prevailing inshore winds bring a blanket of sea mist and clouds, known as *garzua*, to the coastal lands, enveloping them with a grayness that can last for days at a time and providing much-needed moisture.

The increasingly well-known phenomenon of El Niño is related to this current as well. About every five to six years, warmer equatorial waters flow southward to converge with the

Peruvian (or Humboldt) Current, raising maritime temperatures and changing coastal life in profound ways.

Due in part to the rich ocean resources as well as to la costa's fertile valleys, important indigenous groups thrived in this area prior to the arrival of the Europeans. Probably the most well known is the Nazca people, who are famed for the mysterious lines—long extensions of geometric shapes that are observable at high altitudes—they ostensibly configured in the desert sands. Another important indigenous group were the Chimú, who practiced irrigated agriculture in coastal valleys and built the city of Chanchan, considered to have been one of the largest cities in the Americas during its time.

Despite this indigenous legacy, the imprint of Spanish culture and tradition is more uniform here than in the other regions of Peru, and it is here where most of Peru's largest cities, including its capital Lima, are located. In true Hispanic style, Lima's importance outshines by far its closest national rival in population and power. In fact, more than half of all the country's city dwellers reside in the nation's capital, which currently has a population of about seven million. Political and economic decision making is highly concentrated here as well.

Rural-urban migration to Lima has been extensive in recent decades, swelling the ranks of the poor and contributing to the many shantytowns and squatter settlements, known as *pueblos jovenes*, that ring the outskirts of the city. Several of these settlements have grown to such a degree that if their populations were counted separately from the Lima metropolitan area, each would be on the list of the ten most populated cities of the country. Despite the many difficulties of living in the capital, many of the migrants believe that living conditions and future possibilities are nonetheless better in the capital than in their rural birthplaces.

Because of the cities, industrial plants, businesses, and port facilities that characterize la costa, many of the residents from this part of Peru, who are known as *costeños*, are quite cosmopolitan, and the typical urban lifestyle, complete with noise, traffic jams, rapid speech, and street-smart youths, is found here. Costeños tend to have a broad worldview and a general receptivity to foreigners. In fact, many have either traveled abroad themselves or have relatives who have.

La Sierra. Peru's second region, the highlands, or *la sierra*, is another world entirely. Most highland towns are quieter than coastal cities, with a slower rhythm and more formal public behavior. Costeños are reputed by highlanders to be aggressive, fast-talking, and ready to take advantage of others. In contrast, people of the highlands, or *serranos*, are often regarded by costeños as naïve, reserved, and behind the times. Serranos also tend to be mistrustful of outsiders, a phenomenon that some attribute to the Spanish conquest period and its aftermath.

The highlands were, of course, the stronghold of the Inca and other precolonial indigenous civilizations. As a result, it was the most densely settled part of South America before the Europeans arrived, and it is still home to about half of Peru's population, even though it encompasses only about one-quarter of the country's territory. The sierra is the place where one is most likely to find Peruvians of Native American affiliation who still live a rather traditional lifestyle and speak Quechua, Peru's second official language. Naturally, this zone has attracted tourists, especially to places of great historic interest such as Cuzco and Machu Picchu, "the lost city of the Incas."

It is a continuing source of amazement to tourists and scholars alike that so many preconquest peoples were able to thrive in this extremely rugged and seemingly inhospitable environment. Many of South America's highest peaks are located in the Peruvian Andes. But high peaks (ten over 6,000 meters, 19,685 ft.) are just one component of this challenging terrain. Slopes are extremely steep in most places, with deep, narrow canyons and ravines separating rugged, steep mountainsides. Colca Canyon, located in the department of Arequipa, is the deepest in the world.

Volcanic eruptions are not as common in Peru as in Ecuador and Colombia, but earthquakes and tremors of all intensities are frequent, as are landslides, mudslides, rockslides, and flash floods. To overcome these obstacles, the indigenous peoples constructed highly sophisticated bridges, roads, irrigation systems, and terraces that enabled them to take advantage of a wide diversity of climatic conditions available at different elevations, at different angles to the sun, and at different precipitation levels to practice intensive agriculture.

The Native American presence is very strong in the highlands, and the Spanish influence is also notable. The highlands were transformed during the colonial period with the introduction of haciendas—large estates held by Spaniards and worked with subservient indigenous labor—and of extensive mining in the central and southern highlands. As a result, the sierra today contains an interesting mixture of traditional Indian communities that hold most of their land in common, large and lucrative farms and ranches, tiny private farm plots, and the newest landholding unit on the scene, agrarian reform units carved from large estates and run in any of a variety of ways today.

La Oriente. Peru's third region, the east, or *la oriente*, is literally a region removed from the rest of the nation. Located inland beyond the Andes and skirting the Amazon basin area, this area makes up over 60 percent of Peruvian territory but is home to only about five percent of the nation's populace. One of the reasons that the Oriente is isolated from the rest of the country is the paucity of transportation links into or out of the zone to the west, making the principal means of transportation the Amazonian river basin, thus tying many of the locals more closely to communities downstream in Brazil than to Peru itself.

Until just recently, most of the residents of this zone were indigenous peoples of varied ethnic and/or linguistic groups who led primarily a subsistence lifestyle based upon fishing, trading, and simple agriculture. This has changed quite significantly in recent years, as the presence of valuable resources in the region, such as oil, gas, and timber, has attracted outside commercial interests. Just as in many other places in South America (and elsewhere where such a phenomenon has taken place), the arrival of technicians, prospectors, and so forth in parts of the Oriente has been a cultural onslaught for many of the region's original inhabitants, and the cultural integrity of many of the tribal groups as well as their actual survival is precarious at present.

Keys to Understanding the Peruvians

Peru, Land of Empires

History is an important backdrop to much of the situation in Peru today, and the contemporary nation cannot be understood without first looking at its past. Parts of what is now Peru had been heavily populated for millennia prior to the arrival of the Spanish. The oldest human remains found in Peru have been dated back to 7,500 B.C., and the first permanent human settlements appear to have been established sometime around 2,500 B.C. From that period onward, diverse cultures developed and took root in what is now modern-day Peru, several of the best known being the Chavin-Sechin, the Paracas-Nazca, the Moche, and the Huari-Tiwanaku.

Of course, the most important Native American group to settle in what is now Peru was the Incas, whose civilization incorporated much of what had been developed by earlier cultural groups as well as by adjoining tribes. Although the actual origin of the Incas is shrouded in mystery and myth, this Amerindian group seems to have emerged from the Cuzco Valley in what is now central Peru in the early fifteenth century. Fewer than one hundred years later, the Incas were ruling over a far-flung empire that encompassed nearly a million square kilometers (625,000 square miles), stretching all the way from what is now northern Ecuador to central Chile, and served as home to between five and seven million people, the vast majority of whom were not Incas but rather other ethnic groups that had been subsumed into the Inca empire either through conquest or capitulation.

No one knows how the Incas were able to consolidate such a successful empire so rapidly. They had no writing system, as the Mayas did, which makes it even more difficult to obtain historical information about them. What they did excel in was administrative and organizational skills, and their kingdom at its height was one of the most extensive and dynamic to be found anywhere in the world. The Incan overlords were relatively benign in the running of their empire. "One secret of the strength of the empire was the concern of the Inca for the well-being—if not the happiness—of his subjects. The physical needs of the people were taken care of by the state: hunger and acute hardship were unknown" (Herring 1968, 56–58).

The Inca empire was very hierarchical in organization. At the base of the pyramid were the commoners, who made up the vast majority of the empire's populace. They worked their lands jointly and were prohibited from leaving their community. In addition, they had to spend a certain number of days every year performing services for the nobility. If one member of the community disobeyed the Incan overlords, the entire community would be punished.

The merchants, traders, and skilled craftsmen and artisans, many of whom were town and city dwellers, occupied the middle of the pyramid. Their skills helped to create the famed buildings and temples, gold jewelry, ceramics, textiles, and other objects of art for which the Incas were renowned.

At the top of the pyramid was the nobility, who lived a very different lifestyle from the commoners. Many of the empire's elite resided in the capital city of Cuzco, which at its largest had a population of about a hundred thousand people, making it one of the most important urban settlements of the era anywhere. Even though the top members of the aristocracy were predominantly Incan, elites from the subject tribes also participated in the governance of the empire, providing a very effective means by which to meld the diverse tribal groups together under Incan auspices.

The great Inca emperor himself, known as the Sapa Inca, stood at the apex of the entire structure, and exerted near total control over his many subjects. He was thought to be partially divine and traced his lineage to the sun itself. To maintain the purity of the royal bloodline, the Inca's main wife was his full sister, and the next heir was to be born from the consummated union of these two siblings.

The rigid hierarchy of the Inca empire at first proved to be its greatest strength and then, eventually, the main reason for its demise in 1532 at the hands of the Spaniards. Led by the infamous Francisco Pizarro, who had an entourage of only 300 men, the conquistadores set foot on Incan domains just when the empire had been plunged into a civil war over succession between two half-brothers. Exploiting this divisive struggle and aided by the Incas' belief that the Spaniards might be the returned legendary Viracocha, a light-skinned and bearded Incan semideity, the conquerors were able through both subterfuge and direct confrontation to wrest control from the much more numerous Incan elites and to establish themselves as overlords of the entire empire.

This change in command, often with heavy-handed tactics, was nearly cataclysmic for the Incan and other Native American groups, shattering not only the empire itself but, even more fundamentally, instigating far-reaching changes in the belief systems, ways of life, and cultural practices of the region's indigenous inhabitants. One of the most significant changes for the Native Americans was their relegation to the bottom rungs of the colonial hierarchy, where they were expected to serve as a ready pool of exploitable labor for the Spaniards. There was indeed great demand in colonial Peru for workers of various types—including agricultural field hands, household servants, and miners—as this region soon became the most important part of the Spanish empire in South America and the hub of colonial affairs. The demand for labor was such that eventually African slaves were brought to colonial Peru to augment the pool of indigenous workers.

Lima, founded by the Spanish in 1535 and nicknamed "City of Kings," became the capital of the Viceroyalty of Peru. In Lima resided the viceroy himself—the Spanish monarch's direct representative in the colonies—as well as a large ensemble of colonial leaders. Until colonial reorganization in later centuries, Lima was the site from which all of Spanish South America was ruled.

In addition, Lima's port of Callao was the only port in the entire region where the Spanish fleet was legally permitted to dock until the late eighteenth century. This effectively meant that any wealth sent to Spain, including the vast amounts of gold and silver obtained through both mining and pillage, had to pass through Lima. It also meant, parenthetically, that these riches also passed through the hands of the colonial bureaucrats, which led to the amassing of great fortunes.

In keeping with its importance and wealth during the long era of Spanish rule, colonial Lima developed into an opulent city whose elite lived very lavishly. This period in Lima's history has been described as follows:

> Lima is the court and emporium as well as a kind of perpetual fair for the entire realm and the other provinces that trade with the city. Everyone—nobles and those who are not—dress stylishly and richly in silk garments and all kinds of fancy clothing…." (Joseph and Szuchman 1996, 66–67)

As the colonial era progressed, Lima, and Peru in general, slowly lost some of its power as other viceroyalties such as Nueva Granada and Río de la Plata were designated and began to be administered from their own viceregional capitals of Bogotá and Buenos Aires, respectively. Nonetheless, throughout the more than three centuries of colonial rule, the Viceroyalty of Peru with Lima as its capital was by far the most important site of Spanish control in South America.

Even in the early nineteenth century, support for the Spanish monarchy was so strong among the Peruvian colonial elites that independence from Spain had to be imposed by outsiders—individuals hailing from less important parts of the Spanish colonial empire, such as José de San Martin from Argentina and Simón Bolívar from Venezuela. In fact, freedom from Spain was not warmly embraced by many of the local elites.

Lima and other urban areas still have numerous colonial structures, many in varying degrees of deterioration, which attest to their former days of glory, while in the highlands many residents coexist daily with concrete reminders of a different historical era of glory—the pre-Columbian one. Quite a few farmers, in fact, still use the terraced fields and irrigation systems constructed many centuries before the first white man ever set foot in Peru.

Most modern-day Peruvians are very proud of their nation's history as a center of empires; nevertheless, many also wonder why postindependence Peru has never been able to reestablish the colonial and pre-Columbian prominence it once had within the continent, and this may be a sore point best not asked about by foreign visitors. Some Peruvians, especially those of Native American lineage, may be particularly sensitive to the fact that their ancestors' lives were better in past eras than theirs are today, a realistic conclusion in view of the fact that Peru currently ranks toward the bottom of the SSSA nations, according to most standard measurements of development.

Hierarchy

Among the legacies of Peruvian history is a penchant for structuring society along lines of hierarchy and status differences, a pattern inherited, as discussed in the previous section, from both the Caucasian and Native American lineages. Even though hierarchical structure is the predominant one throughout most of the continent, what makes the Peruvian case unique is both the intensity of social hierarchy and its close interrelationship with issues of race and ethnicity, due in large part to the great racial diversity of the populace. A Peruvian resident in Chile explained the connection between racism and classism in his home country as follows:

> The most negative thing about Peru is the class divisions...Chile is classist for economic reasons, but in Peru you must add to this the racial part. The *cholos* (people with Native American

> ancestry) who have access to education, and even if they have a very good educational level, better than some whites, are still rejected by society. It is terrible. Even as recently as three years ago the blacks and cholos could not enter discos in the fancy Lima neighborhood of Miraflores.

In Peru, much of the colonial social structure still shapes current configurations in very powerful ways, and the lower rungs of the social hierarchical ladder are primarily occupied by the ten million Native American Peruvians who make up about half the population. The vast majority of these indigenous Peruvians are descendants of the Incas, and in fact more than 40 percent of all Peruvians speak Quechua as their first or, in some instances, sole language. Another 5 or 6 percent of the Native American population is Aymara, a Native American group originally from the altiplano region near the Bolivian and Chilean borders and never totally assimilated by the Incas. Other indigenous groups also reside in Peru, especially in the Oriente region, many of whom have their own unique cultural patterns and languages. In fact, a recent survey found that ninety-one different languages are currently spoken in Peru, all of which, except Spanish, are of Native American origin.

The cultural patterns and lifestyles of these many Peruvian Native Americans vary widely; some are quite "Westernized" while others, especially those in more remote areas, lead a primarily subsistence lifestyle. Many of the latter, especially those who do not know Spanish well or at all, may have little sense of being Peruvian, defining themselves instead primarily by local and/or ethnic affiliation.

Many outsiders may visualize the lifestyle and cultural mores of these indigenous people romantically, yet in truth survival is difficult for many. Aggregate statistics corroborate this. For instance, the indigenous population of the Peruvian Andes has the lowest literacy rate of any comparable group in South America, and the nutritional value of their diet is 50 percent below acceptable levels (Box 1966, 1105). Julia Meyerson described daily life in the highland village where she lived as follows: "Life in a Quechua village is simple and hard, based on subsistence agriculture, so that the activities of every member of each family are determined throughout the year and, indeed, for most throughout their lives by the needs of the crops" (1990, xiii and 3).

For many Peruvian Indians, living in the cities—which may offer more physical amenities and possibilities for mobility—can nonetheless be very harsh as well. Economic hardships are often compounded by racism and prejudice, a reality that is a recurrent theme in much of Peruvian literature. For instance, Peruvian authors Ciro Alegria (*The Golden Serpent*) and José María Arguedas (*Deep Rivers*) have examined the life and treatment of Peruvian Indians in their writings, often taking their side; other writers, such as Mario Vargas Llosa, have examined the ethnic and class differences that are played out in urban settings.

The second largest segment of the Peruvian population is the mestizos, who make up about one-third of the total. Many of these people, some of whom might in actuality be little better off than the Indians, nonetheless feel quite different from and superior to the indigenous people, or campesinos, as the Native Americans are often called in Peru, and would most likely be insulted if confused with an indigenous person.

Adding to Peru's racial smorgasbord are relatively small, yet visible, populations of blacks and East Asians. Most of the ancestors of these two groups arrived in their new American home with the status of either slave or indentured servant, typically working under very onerous labor conditions for little if any pay and enduring all sorts of prejudice and difficulties. Many of their offsprings' situations, however, have changed dramatically, especially in recent decades. Today, many of these people, especially those of East Asian lineage, have been able to "make good," and some have become quite prominent in their professions. Probably the best example of this phenomenon is the former three-term Peruvian president Alberto Fujimori, of Japanese descent, who was one of the most important Peruvian politicians in recent history.

Rounding out the diverse populace at the top of the hierarchical ladder is the approximately 15 percent of Peruvians classified as Caucasians. Among the smallest of the different ethnicities in terms of absolute numbers, these "European" Peruvians have nonetheless dominated the nation politically, economically, and culturally since the colonial era, and though there has been some loosening of their hegemonic control in recent decades, white Peruvians continue to hold much of the power in the nation today.

Flexibility and Openness to Change

Providing a crucial counterpoint to the Peruvian peoples' inclination for hierarchical social organization based on racial and ethnic divisions is their renowned *flexibility and openness to change*—traits that have enabled them to weather dramatic and often traumatic national events and to bring about far-reaching societal transformations. For instance, Peruvians have experienced both bold victories and humiliating defeats. At the end of the nineteenth century, Peru lost a large part of its southern territory to Chile in the War of the Pacific; several decades later, Peruvians were able to wrest from Ecuador much of that nation's Amazonian territories, permitting Peru to expand in size once again. Both border areas, but especially the Amazonian zone, are still bitterly disputed; however, it seems that recently this contentious issue might finally have been resolved to the satisfaction of both parties.

Peru's changes extend beyond border redrawing, reaching much deeper into the heart and soul of the nation and its peoples. In recent decades Peruvian society has undergone significant structural transformations that have brought about greatly increased possibilities for social mobility for many of the nation's citizens. These changes were spearheaded in large part by a reformist military junta that led the nation from 1968 to 1980. Quite different in ideology and performance from most of the military rulers who have held the reins of power in the continent, this very unique group of Peruvian military men was quite leftist in political inclination and relatively benign in its use of power and force. The leaders' main agenda was to enact reforms designed to benefit the lower sectors of the Peruvian population—most particularly workers and rural Indians.

Many far-reaching changes took place in Peru during this era of military rule. A significant number of industries were nationalized, and workers were actively encouraged to participate in the management of the enterprises where they were employed. An extensive agricultural reform was carried out, designed to redress, at least in part, the centuries of very skewed land distribution in the country. Agricultural cooperatives and farms were created from expropriated estates, ranches, and haciendas, with mixed results. In certain places, violence accompanied the process of agrarian reform, as landowners refused to comply with laws and/or as campesinos took matters into their own hands. Even today, this agrarian reform is still a significant topic of discussion and dispute among many Peruvians.

As a consequence of these policies, contemporary Peruvian society is less hierarchical now than it was a generation or two ago—and less blatantly racist as well, a reality that is a source of great pride for most Peruvians. Even the racial and ethnic composition of the Peruvian business sector, often among the least resistant to change in many societies, has been significantly modified as a result. A Peruvian diplomat describes the current situation as follows:

> The business sector in Peru has changed quite a bit over the last three decades, and it is not possible now to apply a stereotype that the businesspeople will all be white, as is the case in many other countries in Latin America. In fact, there has been a lot of mobility and it is not so much of an oligarchy as some people might think. This means that Peruvian businesspeople, even in high positions, can be a very heterogeneous group—you could have at a meeting a black, a Quechua speaker, and a Chinese person, to give just some examples.

Some disenchanted Peruvians, however, believed that these

reforms did not go far enough and wanted even more profound transformations of Peruvian society. A segment of these rebels were even willing to pursue their goals through extralegal means. Several revolutionary groups arose during the latter decades of the twentieth century, the most well known being *Sendero Luminoso*, or the Shining Path. The brainchild of philosophy professor Abimael Guzman, who taught at the Universidad de Ayacucho located in the Peruvian highlands, the group's platform was based on redressing the social inequities in Peru, particularly the dramatic differences between the sierra and the costa regions. While this goal may indeed be laudable, the methods employed by these far-leftist groups brought havoc and destruction to many parts of Peru and claimed the lives of thousands. Ironically, those most hurt were the highland indigenous peoples, many of whom were either pressed into forced service with the guerrillas and/or had to flee their homes in order to escape from them.

Government attempts to curb the revolutionaries proved ineffectual for several years, and from its original center deep in the Andes, the movement spread in waves of guerrilla activities and violence throughout the nation, eventually reaching Lima and even further north. Finally, in 1992, the Shining Path guerrillas were defeated, and most of their top leadership, including Guzman, were captured and locked in prison—where they continue to be held today.

One reason that the Shining Path proved so difficult to defeat was not so much due to its numeric strength or ideological appeal, but was rather a result of the financial and logistical support the group received from an unlikely accomplice, the cocaine dealers who have become an increasingly important presence in Peru in recent years. These drug lords benefited greatly from the atmosphere of fear that Shining Path guerrillas unleashed in their wake and took advantage of the situation to further expand the production of coca leaves in Peru.

In fact Peru, along with its eastern neighbor Bolivia, is one of the most important sources of coca leaf production in the world today, although most of the actual refining is done in Colombia and elsewhere. Although the cultivation and consumption of coca leaves extend back for millennia in Peru (coca leaves are used by many indigenous Peruvians as a mild narcotic that is either chewed or taken as a tea), the scale and purposes of coca leaf production have changed dramatically in recent decades due to the increased demands for this product. Many Peruvian farmers now grow coca leaf exclusively for economic reasons, thus becoming often unwitting accomplices of the global cocaine trade. The drug dealers' involvement in Peru has brought about a marked escalation in violence, crime, arms smuggling, and other types of illicit activities in certain sectors of the nation and has placed it in the spotlight of the fight against drugs.

Creativity and Aesthetics

Peru has other important legacies stemming from its colonial and precolonial periods, one of the most noteworthy being a great respect for and pride in artistic creativity in many forms. This aesthetic inclination is apparent in many aspects of Peruvian culture. Some claim that even Peruvian workmen, such as mechanics, demonstrate great manual creativity in their work style. As one young Peruvian commented, "The best thing about Peru is the aesthetics. Art is appreciated in so many things, and it seems that the art transcends time. This Peruvian penchant for aesthetics is reflected in how the horses dance in the north, in the interminable carnivals in the mountains, in the colors used in the streets, and in the food that is full of flavors. People in Peru try to make whatever they come into contact with a beautiful artistic creation."

In fact, a significant number of Peruvians make their living based on their artistic skills, and so great is the proliferation of Peruvian objects of art (e.g., gilded paintings, religious figurines, woolen goods of various types, and silver jewelry) in stores and markets around the world that many outsiders consider, incorrectly, Peruvian crafts to be synonymous with SSSA arts and crafts in general.

Peruvian cuisine exemplifies the artistic inclination of the populace, and many consider it to be the most tasteful and imaginative in all South America. Peruvian dishes typically include diverse and seemingly incongruous ingredients that somehow blend together deliciously and look beautiful when served. *Ceviche*, a dish made from fresh fish marinated in lemon juice, is a source of pride among Peruvians, and visitors are often invited to eat this dish, with or without the addition of hot peppers, as an introduction to Peruvian coastal cuisine. Other Peruvian specialties are *papas a la huancaina* (boiled potatoes served with a zesty sauce of cheese, chili, and cream), *causa a la limeña* (a combination of mashed potatoes, shrimp, ripe olives, cheese, yucca, corn, and hard-boiled eggs), and *aji de gallina* (chicken in a spicy sauce made of bread crumbs, chili paste, and nuts topped with olives and hard-boiled eggs).

The many and diverse festivals held in Peru also reflect the Peruvian penchant for creative expression. This practice is particularly strong in the sierra region, where nearly every village has its own festival day, often to honor a local saint or virgin. While the actual happenings at these festivals vary widely, depending on the place and the purpose of the event, music is a dominant component in all of them. It is said that almost every village has its own dance and, to date, more than two hundred different dances have been recorded in the Peruvian highlands, and there are most likely many others.

While the music of the sierra region often has a melancholy tone, the rhythms and sounds of coastal music are more lively, and an African influence even comes through in some of the tunes and dances, such as the famous Marinara dance in both versions—*limeña* and *norteña*. The most recent and popular musical genre to emerge from Peru is what is known as *musica criolla*, which usually has a lively beat and a guitar accompaniment.

Communication Patterns

Perhaps because of their artistic bent and despite the hardships and economic difficulties of many, Peruvians pride themselves on being *alegre*, or happy. In contrast with many of the people from the Southern Cone nations, who tend to be less spontaneous and approachable at first, Peruvians are noted for their relaxed sociability, which they call being *llano*. A Peruvian describes what this means: "The Peruvian, in general, is pretty llano. [We are] informal, direct. There is not much distance with people. We will enter rapidly into familiarity and try to transcend roles to really get to know the person." Some attribute this trait to Peru's very diverse and multicultural society, which makes many of the nation's citizens comfortable with people who may speak, act, and look different from themselves. Whatever the reason, Peruvian sociability is renowned throughout the region, and many Peruvians consider their llano temperament to be one of their positive national attributes. The following anecdote told by a Peruvian university student studying in Santiago, Chile, illustrates this:

> I was in a park the other day in Santiago taking some photographs, and I started talking to a person who seemed to be a foreigner. We were having a good conversation, when this person turned to me and asked me if I was Chilean. I said, "No, I am Peruvian." To which she replied, "I should have known because a Chilean never would have been so friendly in approaching me."

Peruvian Spanish seems to reflect the outgoing personality of the speakers, for it is reputed to be among the clearest and easiest to understand of all the national variants in the region. Part of the reason for this is Peru's importance during the colonial era, when the Spanish spoken in Lima set the standard of correct Spanish throughout the region. This linguistic purity carries over into the modern era, and in general Peruvians use less slang and dialectical variation when speaking Spanish than do, for example, their southern neighbors, the Chileans.

Despite the relative standardization of the Peruvian dialect, there are a few words and/or pronunciations that are unique to Peruvians. One is the use of *pe* or *pues* at the end of a sentence or phrase to indicate agreement; another is the employment of *oah* to get attention, instead of the more common word *oye* ("do you hear?") employed by most other SSSAs.

When discussing Peruvian language, it is important to remember that Peru is officially bilingual—Spanish and Quechua—the latter being the mother tongue of many Peruvians, especially in the highlands area. Many of these native Quechua speakers don't know Spanish very well, and when they speak it, they do so in a monotone, with a soft, high voice, a speech pattern that is sometimes interpreted as a form of resistance to the dominant culture.

Living and Working In Peru

Peruvian sociability is manifested in many aspects of daily life, including the importance of entertaining and enjoying human relationships. This is even true in the business sector, when getting to know the people involved in a prospective business deal is considered more crucial than the actual business itself. As a Peruvian businessman explains, "A Peruvian is open. In business or personal relationships, he or she likes to create a friendly atmosphere. A Peruvian will probably be very hospitable and invite a businessperson to the house, a restaurant, or whatever. We always try to transcend the formal part of the relationship and get to know the other person as a person, that is how it goes. While we could most likely do a deal with someone we did not get along with if we had to, it would be much harder for us."

Such sociability, however, does not preclude attention to status and position, and throughout Peru professional titles are common in the work setting, often serving to indicate a person's place in the group hierarchy in terms of position and authority. Among the most common of such titles are *arquitecto* (architect), *ingeniero* (engineer) and *tecnico* (technician). In some cases, the title does not even reflect the person's actual degree, training, or specialty; rather, it is used as a sign of respect.

If sociability is one of the positive aspects of life in Peru, then one of the most frustrating must be the complexity of carrying out many even apparently simple tasks. Peruvian bureaucracy is onerous, and endless numbers of signatures, stamps, seals, permits, and licenses can be required for routine business. Case studies revealed that fourteen years were needed to start up a market legally, and over two years were required to open a minibus route or a city bus route concession that complied with all regulations. For foreigners or visitors, the best hope in achieving necessities in the Peruvian bureaucratic mayhem is to adopt the approach of *personalismo*—develop contacts with local liaisons who can smooth the way and cut through much of the red tape.

Given such realities, it should come as no surprise that it was a Peruvian scholar, Hernando De Soto, who wrote one of the most important books to date about the "informal sector," using Peru as an example. Current estimates place the informal sector as the source of employment for about half of Peruvian workers and the source of close to half of the recorded gross domestic product. The number of self-employed Peruvians who somehow eke out a living selling objects of various types along the street in most cities in Peru is just one among many visible manifestations of this reality of modern-day life in Peru.

Living in Peru will inevitably require the presence of a maid or housekeeper, no matter how simple one tries to keep one's lifestyle. The reasons are practical and also help explain why it is difficult for many women to work outside the home. For instance, one daily chore in households with small children is to personally accompany them to and from school each day because public streets are considered unsafe for children and school-bus systems are virtually nonexistent. Other daily chores may include accepting deliveries of mail, milk, gas for the stove, packages, and assorted other things that cannot safely be left sitting out in public view. Peruvians generally use fresh ingredients in their cooking, and someone needs to go to the market, butcher, and bakery each day. In addition, many tasks may need to be done in person, such as paying bills, mailing letters, banking, and so forth.

The presence of service people to help both in the home and

workplace can sometimes feel a bit suffocating to an English-speaking North American (ESNA). For instance, every building has a doorman or security guard, and messengers, gofers, and errand boys are everywhere. It is not unusual for government employees and business managers to have "official vehicles," each with its own driver. These are all manifestations of personalismo as well as of low average wages and the high percentage of the labor force engaged in the service sector.

* * * * * * *

Peruvians face the early years of the twenty-first century in much the same way as their ancestors confronted their own particular time periods—flexibly trying to adjust to current realities while still remaining true to their significant historical and cultural legacies. With one foot in the future and the other foot in the past, the present for Peru becomes a sort of balancing act. This sometimes awkward but highly creative position is especially true these days as Peruvians face political issues of transition, questions of economic relevance, and perhaps even more importantly, the long-standing question that has yet to be truly addressed in all its magnitude—how to deal with the large Native American population and what role these descendants of the Incas and other pre-Columbian groups should play in modern-day Peru.

References and Suggested Bibliography

Babb, Florence. 1989. *Between Field and Cooking Pot: The Political Economy of Market Women in Peru.* Austin: University of Texas Press.

Bourque, Susan C., and Kay Barbara Warren. 1981. *Women of the Andes: Patriarchy and Social Change in Two Peruvian Towns.* Ann Arbor: University of Michigan Press.

Box, Ben, ed. *South American Handbook.* 72d ed. Suffolk, England: Clays.

Cameron, Maxwell A., Philip Mauceri, Abraham F. Lowenthal, and Cynthia McClintock. 1997. *The Peruvian Labyrinth: Polity, Society, Economy.* College Park, PA: Pennsylvania State University Press.

Cobo, Bernabé. 1882. "Historia de la fundación de Lima." In *Colección de historiadores del Perú.* Translated by Sharon Kellum. Lima: Imprenta Liberal.

Crabtree, John, and Jim Thomas. 1998. *Fujimori's Peru: The Political Economy.* Washington, DC: Brookings Institute.

Davies, Nigel. 1998. *The Ancient Kingdoms of Peru.* New York: Penguin.

De Soto, Hernando. 1989. *The Other Path: The Invisible Revolution in the Third World.* New York: Harper & Row.

Herring, Hubert. 1968. *A History of Latin America.* 3d ed. New York: Alfred A. Knopf.

Joseph, Gilbert M., and Mark D. Szuchman, eds. 1996. *I Saw a City Invincible: Urban Portraits of Latin America.* Wilmington, DE: Scholarly Resources.

Kirk, Robin. 1997. *The Monkey's Paw: New Chronicles from Peru.* Amherst: University of Massachusetts Press.

Llosa, Mario Vargas. 2001. *The Storyteller.* Translated by Helen R. Lane. New York: Picador.

Meyerson, Julia. 1990. *Tambo: Life in an Andean Village.* Austin: University of Texas Press.

Starn, Orin, Robin Kirk, and Carlos Degregori. 1995. *The Peru Reader: History, Culture, Politics.* Durham, NC: Duke University Press.

Stern, Steve. 1998. *Shining and Other Paths: War and Society, 1980–1995.* Durham, NC: Duke University Press.

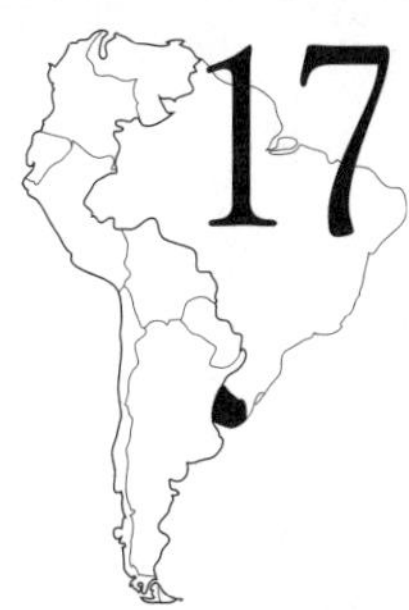

17

Uruguay: The Buffer State

Skye Stephenson

Una cosa que los uruguayos saben, pero no dicen, es que realmente somos más europeas que latinoamericanos.

—Gabriel Rey

One thing that most Uruguayans know deep down, but will rarely admit, is that we are really more European than Latin American.

Uruguay has the smallest population and size of all the Spanish-speaking South American (SSSA) nations; about three million Uruguayans in total reside in a country approximately the size of the state of Oklahoma. The entire nation can be traversed in just a few hours! Uruguay's scale is so strikingly different from that of its colossal neighbors, Brazil and Argentina, that Juan Carlos Onetti, considered one of the finest Uruguayan authors, once described his homeland as "a little joke of a country" (Onetti 2002).

In a way, Onetti is correct because misunderstandings about Uruguay abound, some of which reach almost comic proportions. For instance, many people wrongly place Uruguay somewhere in Central America, while others readily confuse it with nearby Paraguay, an unfortunate mistake, as the two nations are markedly different. The commonly used nickname "*orientales*" for Uruguayans, derived from the country's full name (which is the

Republica Oriental de Uruguay*) also contributes to misperceptions; upon hearing it, some foreigners leap to the conclusion that Uruguay must have a significant Asian population and/or influence when, in actuality, there is none.

In fact, Uruguayans are the most Caucasian of any nationality in the continental Americas, North or South. There is literally no indigenous presence to speak of in the modern-day nation, and except for a relatively small number of black Uruguayans, the populace is of European descent—a demographic phenomenon that has an enormously strong impact on the nation's cultural patterns and mores. Many visitors to Uruguay have felt the need to readjust their preconceived ideas about supposedly "exotic" SSSA during their sojourn in the country when they observe how the Uruguayan people seem in many ways to be more European than South American.

Although there are not many Uruguayans, they have historical patterns and cultural characteristics that also set them apart from their larger neighbors.

- Uruguay was created as a buffer state between Spanish-speaking Argentina and Portuguese-speaking Brazil, and the country shares important commonalities with both, sometimes making it a challenge for Uruguayans to figure out exactly what it is that makes them unique as a people.
- Uruguayans have the strongest democratic tradition of all the SSSA nations. However, during its only period of military rule in the last century, which extended from 1973 to 1984, the nation had the sad distinction of harboring more political prisoners per capita than any other place in the world.
- Uruguay boasts the highest literacy rate and the greatest degree of social and gender equality in the entire region, yet despite these impressive social accomplishments, the country has not prospered in recent decades, and many Uruguayans have felt the need to leave their homeland in pursuit of better opportunities elsewhere.

---

* This name is derived from the country's location to the *oriente* (east) of the Uruguay River.

A closer look at the Uruguayan nation and people shows why this country's significance is greater than its size may suggest. The following topics will be covered in this chapter: geographic and regional influences, keys to understanding the Uruguayans—including Uruguay's role as a buffer state, the gaucho and the European, maté and egalitarianism, and pessimism and grayness—communication patterns, and living and working in Uruguay.

Geographic and Regional Influences

W. H. Hudson's nineteenth-century book based on his travels in Uruguay was titled *The Purple Land*, but probably a better name would have been *The Flat Land*, because Uruguay is the only SSSA country with no mountains at all. The highest point in the whole country reaches only 600 meters (2,000 feet) above sea level! Most Uruguayan terrain is flat grassland, part of the pampas that extend further south into Argentina, and is very well suited for livestock production. Among the most fertile lands in the world, the pampas are rather dull from an aesthetic standpoint, with few majestic natural features or dramatic vistas to break the visual monotony of the endless grassland. Charles Darwin himself described the area's scenery as "cheerless" and "uninteresting" (Morrison and Conway 1997, 341).

What does add texture and dimensionality to the landscape are waterways of various types. Not only does the nation face the Atlantic Ocean, but in addition its entire southern border is the monumental Río de la Plata, which, when it passes by Uruguay, is the widest river in the world. In fact, many locals call it a sea rather than a river; from the Uruguayan coastline, it does indeed seem so. Added to this are no fewer than five different rivers that cross the country's heartland, all of which eventually empty into the Río de la Plata.

Nearly all Uruguayan cities and towns have access to at least some form of waterway—whether it be river, estuary, or the Atlantic Ocean—and the capital itself, Montevideo, literally abuts the Río de la Plata. Since most of the populated areas are within a walk or a bus ride from a beach of some sort, Uruguayans are avid beachgoers; people, summer and winter, "hang out" along the waterfront. One Uruguayan woman, in her English-language memoirs about coming of age in Uruguay during the 1960s, describes her own feelings about the Río de la Plata as follows:

> (It) was moody, rough, gentle and wild, and to me, always beautiful. The river rejected unwanted offerings, harbored life, and took it.... I had walked its shores, loved its changing colors, and been buffeted by its waves all my growing-up years. (Bridal 1997, 10–11)

One of Uruguay's principal sources of revenue is derived from those who frequent its extensive beaches. During the summer months, the nation's shorefront is crowded with sun worshippers from many places, especially Argentina. The most well known resort of all is Punta del Este, which is ideally situated on a peninsula where the vast Río de la Plata empties out into the Atlantic Ocean, thus providing in a relatively compact area a wide variety of different surf conditions. Famed as a getaway for the rich and famous, in truth tourists of all types flock here. Sharing some of the prized coastal areas with the human beachgoers are numerous sea lions, whose hulking bodies and odoriferous presence make them easy to spot.

While they may congregate at the beach, Uruguayans are, for the most part, urban folk. Over three-quarters of the population reside in cities, and half the nation lives in just one, Montevideo. Even in a region like SSSA, where capital cities typically overshadow all else, the Uruguayan case is extreme. In many ways Montevideo *is* Uruguay; there is little of import that takes place in the country that is not Montevideo based. That said, the capital is still relatively small by regional standards, with a more provincial feel than the other Southern Cone capitals of Santiago and Buenos Aires. The placid mood of this port city can be misleading, however, for it teems with artistic, political, and diplomatic energy.

Keys to Understanding the Uruguayans

The Buffer State

The nation's small size and the concentration of its population in the capital make regional differences insignificant among Uruguayans, although some subtle distinctions exist, especially among residents in the outlying rural areas. More significantly, differences between the Uruguayans and their neighbors, especially the Argentines, are not very pronounced either. In fact the two nationalities are frequently confused because they share many cultural and linguistic patterns due, in large part, to their common history. In fact, present-day Uruguay had no real separate identity during the long colonial era; it was just one part of the Viceroyalty of the Río de la Plata, although its strategic location between the Spanish and the Portuguese South American empires made it a hotly contested area.

One small but concrete indication of the intensity of the rivalry between Spain and Portugal over control of present-day Uruguay is the still-heated debate over the derivation of the rather unusual name of Montevideo. One group traces its origins to a Portuguese sailor's exclamation in the first-ever European expedition to this zone. He said, upon seeing a small hill arising from the future site of the capital, "*Monte, vide eu*" (Portuguese for "I see a mountain"). Proponents of a second school of thought claim the name comes from an entry in a Spanish navigator's logbook during a somewhat later visit, where the site was described as "Monte VI D.E.O.," meaning that it was the sixth mountain as one moved up the river from the Atlantic Ocean and that it was located in an east/west direction. Some Uruguayans even today affectionately call their capital "Monte VI" (Sixth Mountain).

Dispute over control of modern-day Uruguay did not end with the Spanish demise. If anything, it became stronger. The area was successfully invaded by Brazil, which at the time was still under Portuguese rule, and it seemed as though the territory would end up being incorporated into the Portuguese rather than the Spanish realm. Great Britain's intervention decisively changed Uruguay's fate. Desirous of pacifying the strategically important southern Atlantic flank of the continent, British diplomats strongly urged the two rivals to make Uruguay a separate nation that would serve as a buffer between them. Thus, Uruguay came to be a separate entity due to the efforts of external actors rather than to any strongly marked geographic, historical, and/or cultural differences with either Brazil or Argentina.

Because of how their nation was born, Uruguayans actually recognize two different dates for their independence. The first is August 25, 1811, when Uruguay declared independence from Spain in conjunction with two other provinces of the Río de la Plata. The second, July 18, 1828, represents when Uruguay truly became a nation in its own right, with the expulsion of the Brazilian invaders and the signing of a constitution. Uruguay's most important hero, José Artigas, led the country during this critical period. His venerated remains are located in a mausoleum in Montevideo's main plaza.

Indeed, Uruguay has fulfilled its intended purpose as a buffer zone and, since its founding, has peacefully coexisted with both its neighbors. Not just geographically but also culturally, Uruguay bridges Hispanic and Luso-South America. As one cultural guide puts it, "The Uruguayans are in the middle. Although they are linguistically and ethnically closer to the Argentines, Uruguayans are more relaxed and informal. But Uruguayans are not quite as uninhibited as Brazilians are" (Morrison and Conway, 354).

Not only do Uruguayans have strong commonalities with both of their colossal neighbors, Argentina and Brazil, but frequently people move back and forth among them as well, both as temporary visitors and permanent residents. Over 400,000 Uruguayans (almost 15 percent of the total population) reside in Argentina, and there is also a significant Uruguayan presence in Brazil. In fact, along the nation's northern border, a Portuguese-Spanish dialect known as *brazilero*, *fronterizo*, or *portuñol* is spoken colloquially.

Interestingly, the European nation that Uruguay is most frequently compared with is Switzerland. Despite the obvious differences between the two, they are both indeed buffer states strategically located between continental powers. One indicator of Uruguay's status in this sense can be noted in the way that it (just like Switzerland) has served as a site for numerous important international meetings, such as the well-known Uruguayan round of General Agreement on Trade and Tariffs (GATT) negotiations. Montevideo has also been designated the administrative center of MERCOSUR, the regional free trade organization founded to promote increased trade and business flow among the southernmost South American countries.

In their view of themselves and others, Uruguayans are very much like other small nations located between larger and more powerful neighbors. As a general rule, they are not very nationalistic; patriotic symbols such as the flag and the national anthem are not as fervently revered here as in some of the more insular nations in the continent. Even so, they are justifiably proud of their country and on good terms with their neighbors. For example, Uruguayans have a friendly rivalry with the Argentines, especially in sports rather than a sense of mutual suspicion such as that which characterizes relations between the Argentines and their Pacific neighbor, the Chileans.

The Gaucho and the European

Uruguayans also have a strong connection with the Argentines due to similar settlement patterns, which have influenced both nationalities profoundly. Despite this commonality, some distinctions, more in degree than in kind, can be made between the experiences of the two. Even more than in central and southern Argentina, Uruguay had few *indigenas* at the time of the Europeans' arrival. The largest group was the Charrúa, who were renowned for their prowess and ferocity. Popular culture claims they were cannibals, although this has never been definitively corroborated. What is clear is that they were intransigent opponents of the Caucasian invaders, whom they managed to ward off in 1516, when an initial attempt was made to settle the area. They killed the entire group! Their success proved short-lived, however, and the tide turned against them. Their violent opposition incited the Spanish conquerors to carry out an indigenous eradication policy that was so successful it culminated in the complete elimination of the Native American populace from the República Oriental de Uruguay by the nineteenth century. These days, Uruguay is the only nation in all continental America (North and South) with *no indigenous population* at all.

Although there are no surviving Charrúas, some claim that their presence still reverberates in the nation, a supposition most frequently put forward to explain the Uruguayans' resounding success in soccer. Uruguay is the only country with such a small population to have won two World Cups. The first victory was in 1930, when Uruguay hosted the World Cup and the second in 1950, when Uruguay upset the favored Brazilians in Río de Janeiro. In both of these famous soccer victories, the Uruguayans claimed that it was their garra charrúa (Charrúa claws) that enabled them to defeat their rivals.

To an even greater degree than its larger neighbor, the gauchos—those independent cowboys of the southern Atlantic region of South America—were the predominant inhabitants in the lands that were to become Uruguay. In many ways, these lands were an ideal site for them: the zone was sparsely populated, far from the centers of colonial control, and replete with free-roaming cattle and horses they could use for food, transport, clothing, and in some cases, even shelter (some lived in leather houses). Shunning the settled life and deprecating anything that smacked of culture or sophistication, each gaucho was truly a law unto himself—living as autonomously as possible, unhindered by material possessions or emotional ties of any sort.

Contemporary Uruguayans, for the most part, revere their gaucho past and celebrate these cowboys in popular folk culture. Some even wear gaucho-style ponchos crafted from raw wool during the chilly winter months, and during certain festivities men will don wide gaucho pants known as *bombachas*.

More significantly, Uruguayans' dietary patterns reflect the gaucho imprint; they, along with the Argentines, are the greatest meat consumers in the world, eating an average of 200 pounds of beef each year. Most Uruguayans' favorite meal is a type of barbecue known as *asado*, which includes many types of entrails such as tripe, tongue, kidney, and blood sausage as well as different cuts of beef. Sometimes these asados even have *asado con cuero*, meat cooked with the skin still on, which serves to tenderize the beef. (The leather skin, of course, is not consumed!) Even when Uruguayans are not eating barbecued beef, they still like their meat; another popular dish is *milanesa*, a breaded meat cutlet.

Another gaucho attribute that has survived to the present day is a strong sense of individualism. Some contend that the Uruguayans are the most individualistic of all the SSSAs, a supposition corroborated in several cross-cultural studies. One such study described the Uruguayans as follows: "Individuals are responsible for their decisions and individualism is respected....because each person is deemed unique" (Bosrock 1997, 342).

This individualism is manifested in numerous ways, two of the most obvious being their typically direct communication style and their fondness for debate. In contrast with many other SSSAs, Uruguayans have no problem espousing personal opinions, even if they differ from others in the group; they will usually gleefully contradict and/or argue with anyone who says something they do not agree with.

Despite the frequent accolades to the gaucho, it is actually the European immigrant who has had the strongest impact on contemporary Uruguayan culture. At the time of independence, Uruguay was sparsely populated; the capital had only about 20,000 inhabitants and the nation's interior, even fewer. Uruguay's demography changed with a large influx of Europeans, about 650,000 in total, who flocked to the fledgling nation between 1836 and 1926 in search of better opportunities and fewer restrictions than were offered in their lands of origin. The vast majority hailed from Spain, Italy, France, and Germany, and though most were Catholic, a significant number of Jews also migrated, giving Uruguay one of the highest percentages of Jews in the Americas today.

The impact of these immigrants was profound. Because there was so little indigenous culture, much of the European settlers' cultural patterns were absorbed almost directly into the still-forming Uruguayan traits, giving a decidedly European flavor to the nation. This influence can be noted in many ways today, including architecture, cuisine (Uruguayans' favorite dishes along with the ubiquitous beef include many Italian foods such as pizza, pastas, and gelato ice creams), and most importantly, its people. Today, over 90 percent of all Uruguayans are totally of European ancestry, making them the most homogeneous populace in the region, and many still feel very connected to the old continent, especially to their forebears' homeland.

Although the Spanish, Italian, and, to a lesser extent, German influences are prevalent in Uruguayan patterns, probably the most influential country of all, from a cultural standpoint, is France. French influence is especially marked in the country's educational system; French was, until recently, the predominant second language in the public schools and is still taught, along with English, in most of them today. Consequently, most educated Uruguayans know French quite well, oftentimes better than English, and many Uruguayans can sound resoundingly like their French friends in their views of the United States, which they often say they feel only *más o menos* (more or less) about. The Uruguayan connection with France extends so far that two well-known French poets are actually Uruguayan in origin—Jules Supervielle and Conde de Lautréamont. The French also reciprocated, at least in part, the strong cultural connection with Uruguay: French author Alexandre Dumas wrote one of his novels, titled *The New Troy*, about Uruguay, and in Voltaire's famed *Candide*, the port of Montevideo figures prominently.

The only other important ethnic group of note in Uruguay is a relatively small black populace, whose presence can be most strongly felt in the nation's music. While most of Uruguay's music is similar to that of Argentina—the rural gaucho-type strains and the urban tango tunes—once a year staid Uruguay pulsates with the rhythms of Carnival. During this festive week, as well as in the period leading up to it, *candombe* groups of up to fifty people playing drums of four different sizes (*chico*, *repique*, *piano*, and *bajo*) circulate through the main streets and plazas of Uruguayan cities and towns, and almost everyone gathers around them to revel in the pulsating beat.[†]

Maté and Egalitarianism

Although the Uruguayans have incorporated many aspects of European culture into their own, one practice is definitely non-European: the drinking of an herb tea known as maté. Although maté is drunk throughout the Southern Cone region, its use is most widespread in Uruguay, where it is usually taken *amargo* (bitter), without the addition of sugar or any other ingredients (see chapter 15, "Paraguay: The Bilingual Nation," for more details concerning how maté is prepared and consumed). In contrast to tea and coffee, which are similar to it in caffeine content, maté is communally imbibed; the group passes the herb-filled gourd from hand to hand and shares the metal straw, known as a *bombilla*. One visitor to Uruguay described his experiences with the drinking of maté as follows:

> Maté is the Uruguayan symbol of hospitality. Custom requires that all in the same circle of friendship drink from the same pot and the same silver pipe.... There is a belief that germs cannot live on the hot silver pipe, that it is self-sterilizing. I hope that the belief is true, for the rite is as unavoidable as kissing the bride.... Uruguayans set much store by it and believe that it is food, drink, and vitamins all wrapped in the same package. (Morrison and Conway, 343)

Perhaps the many hours spent drinking maté together have contributed to Uruguayans' uncomplicated manner of relating.

---

† These are musical groups similar to the Carnival groups in Brazil, whose origins can be traced back to the era of slavery.

Even though they are not usually as extroverted as many of the tropical SSSAs, they can be quite open and easy to get to know, with an unpretentious attitude. This characteristic is due, at least in part, to their marked egalitarian inclinations, which contrast sharply with the perspective of most other SSSAs. A popular Uruguayan saying, "*Nadie es más que nadie*" ("No one is better than anyone else is"), succinctly reflects this point of view, and for the most part, Uruguayans try to minimize rather than emphasize hierarchy in their interactions. Take their linguistic preferences, for example; they usually opt for the informal *you*, even in conversations between people of different social status. It is extremely rare for deferential terms such as *don/doña* and *patrón* to be used. Uruguayan attire, which is typically informal and unpretentious, also mirrors this lack of concern for social status markers.

There are several reasons for Uruguayans' decidedly non-Hispanic way of conceptualizing human interactions. Both the aforementioned gaucho mentality and the influence of some of the more politicized of the European immigrants who arrived in Uruguay full of ideas then popular among many sectors in the Old World (anarchism, socialism, and communism) contributed to the "Uruguayan way." An even more important influence is the legacy of one of the most revered of all Uruguayans, José Batlle y Ordóñez. This farsighted and very democratic leader served as president of the nation twice, from 1903 to 1907 and again from 1911 to 1915, during which time he transformed Uruguay into the continent's first welfare state. Among his policies were free medical care, old age and service pensions, and unemployment compensation for all qualified citizens. He also made significant progress in separating church from state, legalizing divorce, and giving full legal status, including the right to inherit property, to illegitimate children.

Batlle y Ordóñez's significance extends even beyond the very important policies he helped to establish, for he enunciated for the Uruguayan people a vision of what they should strive for as a society that came to be embraced by nearly the entire populace, becoming a pivotal component of the national leitmotif. It was a vision that was decidedly secular, statist, and pragmatic, with a marked social welfare concern. As one Uruguayan explains,

> *Batllismo* (Batlle's ideas) could be (and were, without a doubt) an alternative or program for the modernization of the country, but it was also a cosmovision, an ideological synthesis with very concrete declarations about the world, about God (or god), about human relations, and about life. (Conteris 1978, 53)

Batllismo continues to be extremely influential in twenty-first century Uruguay, and nearly all Uruguayans are fervent supporters of a government heavily involved in promoting the national welfare. Decades of such an approach have had concrete results. Today, Uruguay leads the region in many indicators of social well-being, including having the highest degree of social equality, the highest literacy rates, and the highest percentage of retired people living on their own. Although most Uruguayans are nominally Catholic, the Church seems less omnipresent here than in the rest of the region, and there is little public evidence of religious commitment; statues of Jesus, virgins, or saints are rare, shrines for devotees are mostly unheard of, and even religious holidays are few.

Intergender relations have also been shaped by the Uruguayans' liberal orientation. According to international statistics, Uruguayans have the greatest degree of gender equality and intergender wage equity in the region, and most women work outside the home. Not surprisingly, Uruguayans are usually quite modern in their view of male-female relationships. Many couples live together before they marry, a practice that is routinely accepted by family and friends, and homosexuals are more readily accepted here than in some of the other SSSA countries.

Especially in the literary field, Uruguay boasts a disproportionately high number of internationally renowned authors, including Eduardo Galeano, Mario Benedetti, and Juan Carlos Onetti, to name but three. These writers display in their works a marked concern with social welfare as well as a decidedly secular orientation and, oftentimes, a quite open view about sexual relations.

Pessimism and Grayness

Despite (or maybe due to) the egalitarian social conditions in Uruguay, Uruguayans are not a very happy lot. Many (including some of the aforementioned writers) exhibit a kind of existential angst that is frequently manifested externally as an erudite and usually pessimistic criticism of both self and others. Critics par excellence, Uruguayans are as harsh, if not harsher, on themselves as they are on others. All the Uruguayans I interviewed described themselves as a sad people, uptight and depressed. In true Uruguayan style, Carlos Zeballo, a diplomat who has lived throughout the continent, classified his compatriots as follows: "We Uruguayans are repressed and unsure of ourselves. We don't know how to have a good time because we fear appearing ridiculous in all types of human relationships. I can assure you, if it looks like Uruguayans are having a good time, it is because they drank some alcohol."

This attitude lends a kind of heaviness to life in Uruguay, a gray pallor that hangs over not only the scenery but also many of the people. Life in Uruguay frequently seems more like an Ingmar Bergman movie than a Federico Fellini or Pedro Aldomavar clip. A Colombian, during his first-ever visit to the country, made the following observation: "I don't understand Uruguay at all, people seem to do pretty well, but nonetheless the whole country seems so gray. In Colombia, in contrast, we have so many problems, but we are always smiling and enjoying ourselves. Here, nobody seems to have a good time."

Various explanations have been put forth to explain this characteristic Uruguayan "grayness." Some claim this phenomenon, which seems to be most pronounced during the dismal winter months, is simply a result of Uruguay's rather dull natural environment. Others attribute it to issues of identity, arguing that Uruguayans can have a hard time expressing themselves because they really don't know how to. Hiber Conteris, a Uruguayan author, told the author in a personal interview that

> Uruguayan "grayness" has historical roots: Uruguay is really an artificial country and should truly be part of Argentina. As a consequence, Uruguay is a country without folklore or history. The Uruguayan is not like Brazilians or Colombians who manifest their happiness in dance and music. Uruguayans, in contrast, are timid—not by character but because it is hard for them to express themselves because they don't have the culture to do so. Even though Uruguayans are very cultured, there is nothing that is authentically Uruguayan. We are a pueblo of critics who look at what happens in the world, reflect on it but do not generate anything new, nothing from the *pueblo* itself. This is a sad characteristic of the Uruguayans.

Economic problems and political upheavals in the last half century or so have also contributed to reinforcing the somber mood of contemporary Uruguayans, leading many to believe that their nation's past, particularly the Batlle era, was better than its present reality and future prospects. Actually, Uruguay has been a nation out of balance since at least the 1950s, exhibiting a decided lack of fit between the Uruguayan people, with their twenty-first century perspectives and expectations, and the country's very traditional economic base, which continues to rely quite heavily on cattle and sheep exports for national revenues, products which have not fared well in international markets recently. As a consequence, the country's economy has not performed well, making it increasingly challenging for many to maintain the kind of lifestyle they feel is their due.

Uruguayans have had different responses to their country's economic woes. Some have chosen to leave, in search of better opportunities elsewhere, and out-migration is quite high. Others, especially during the highly politicized era of the 1960s, chose a very different path, becoming staunch advocates for radical change in Uruguayan society. Quite a few of these social critics became part of the Tupamaro[‡] movement, which was a leftist

‡ This name came from an Inca leader, Tupac Amaru, who bravely fought, and was eventually killed by, the Spanish conquistadores.

group originally formed to support rural workers' rights in the early 1960s but rapidly came to encompass much broader goals, including radical social and political changes. The Tupamaros were considered one of the best-organized social change groups on the continent, and their methods of confrontation were largely nonviolent. They prided themselves on their Robin Hood-like escapades. As the decade progressed, however, they became increasingly bold and carried out a few kidnappings of carefully targeted individuals. The most infamous of these kidnappings was the 1970 abduction of U.S. adviser Daniel Mitrone,[§] who was eventually killed when the kidnappers' demands were not met.

This event marked a watershed in the struggle between the government and the guerrilla forces. The same day that Mitrone's body was discovered, the Uruguayan president was granted a state of emergency that included a temporary suspension of many civil liberties. Constitutional rights continued to gradually erode as the fight against the Tupamaros became increasingly violent and repressive until, in 1976, the formerly apolitical armed forces assumed total control of the nation, deposing the Uruguayan president and permanently closing down the legislature.

The armed forces proved resoundingly successful in destroying the Tupamaro movement, but at a tremendous human cost. During this period of military rule, formerly peaceful and democratic Uruguay became one of the most repressive nations anywhere. While actual casualties were not that high, the number of arrests and imprisonments was exponential: "One in every fifty (Uruguayans) was detained at one time or another for interrogation; and one in every five hundred received a long prison sentence for political offenses" (Wescheler 1990, 89).

True to their democratic tendencies, the vast majority of Uruguayans never supported the armed forces' intervention,

---

§ Mitrone was ostensibly an adviser to the Uruguayan police, but many allege he was actually instructing Uruguayan military in counterinsurgency techniques, including methods of torture. A Costa-Gavras' movie called "State of Siege" is based upon this story.

and when finally given a chance in 1980 to vote on a constitution designed by the military, 90 percent of them rejected the proposal. It took another four years, until 1984, for the military to willingly relinquish power. At that time democratic rule was restored with the free election of a new president.

Although Uruguay's democracy has remained intact since this atypical interlude in the nation's history, the military era forever changed the nation and its people. Today, nearly two decades later, most Uruguayans know someone who was directly affected by the repression in one way or another. These often heart-wrenching sagas seem to cast a dark shadow upon the collective soul of the nation.

Communication Patterns

One of the most salient aspects of Uruguayans' communication patterns is—not surprisingly—how similar they are to the Argentines. For most outsiders, it is nearly impossible to distinguish the two. Just like the Argentineans, Uruguayans have incorporated much of the Italian lilt into their language. Also, like their southern neighbors, Uruguayans tend to be direct, as mentioned earlier. Many other SSSAs try to avoid giving a negative response; however, Uruguayans, for the most part, have no problem at all offering a resounding no if that is what they think.

While others may confuse the two nationalities, Uruguayans and Argentineans rarely do; they can usually tell each other apart almost immediately by certain clues. Even more than their southern neighbors, the Uruguayans pronounce the *ll* or *y* with a very clear "sh" sound: *playa* (beach) sounds like "plasha" and *uruguayo* (Uruguayan), like "uruguasho." Also, while most Argentineans consistently use *vos* for the second-person informal pronoun instead of the more common *tú*, Uruguayans typically alternate the use of the two: commonly opting for *tú* when speaking among themselves, but switching to *vos* when talking with Argentineans.

There are a few words that are unique to Uruguayans, as well.

The most characteristic is the colloquial term *ta*, which is an abbreviated way to say the Spanish verb *está*, which means "it is." However, the Uruguayan *ta* signifies so much more; its broader meaning is quite similar to the English *okay*. In telephone conversations and friendly discussions, for instance, Uruguayans will frequently interject *ta* when the other party is talking, to demonstrate that they are following the line of argument. Another very Uruguayan term is the use of the word *championes* for sneakers. Originally the name for a particular brand of athletic shoes, *championes* somehow evolved into a generic term for all athletic shoes, whatever the brand. In Argentina, in contrast, sneakers are called *zapatillas*, as they are in the rest of the region.

Differences in communication style and attitude also serve to distinguish Uruguayans from the Argentines, especially people of Buenos Aires. While the latter often give the impression of being garrulous, confident, and extroverted, Uruguayans tend to be less flashy, somewhat hesitant in manner, and more introverted. In fact, Uruguayans claim that they can often tell an Argentinean just by a particular confident lilt in a person's voice. Uruguayan author Mario Benedetti humorously explores this difference as follows: "They say that a Uruguayan is an Argentinean without a complex of superiority...perhaps, perhaps. It also could be that an Argentinean is a Uruguayan without a complex of inferiority" (1997, 52).

Living and Working in Uruguay

One of the most surprising aspects of living and working in Uruguay is the seemingly incongruous juxtaposition of a very modern people with an often antiquated infrastructure, largely due to the economic situation of recent decades. In many ways, the country seems to be literally "frozen in time." Montevideo, for instance, has probably changed less in recent decades than most of the other SSSA capitals, and until just a few years ago, Uruguay was a godsend for antique-car collectors from around the world because there were countless classic automobiles actually in circulation, lovingly kept in working order by their owners, who could not afford a newer car. There is even an antique-car museum in Montevideo, established in tribute to these vintage vehicles.

What was true until recently concerning cars is still oftentimes true regarding the nation's industrial infrastructure. Many Uruguayan businesspeople will willingly use reliable goods that are not always state-of-the-art if the price is right.

> Many of Uruguay's industries have not had the resources to upgrade their technologies. This has made Uruguay a good market for used and/or obsolete machinery. This also minimizes difficulties with incompatible technologies. If something works, Uruguayans are happy to use it, even if a newer version is available. (Morrison and Conway, 349)

Conducting business in Uruguay has certain unique characteristics that extend beyond material aspects. For one thing, Uruguayans typically like to "get down to business" right away, without much of the preliminary conversational niceties that are so important in the rest of the region. Uruguayans are also quite punctual, and meetings usually begin at the designated time. The nation is also among the most transparent in the region; corruption and/or bribery is nearly unheard of, both because of the strong democratic inclination of the citizenry and because of the fact that the small market size lessens the possible benefits to be derived from payoffs.

The pace of work in Uruguay tends to be more relaxed than in the other Southern Cone nations. Due both to the difficulties of finding appropriate employment opportunities for the very competent populace and to the nearly century-long welfare state, many employees are not avid workers, commonly having the attitude that it is best to "just ride the tide" at work, putting in the required years and awaiting a future pension upon retirement. A remarkably high number of Uruguayans, even by regional standards, take over their parents' business and/or profession, a rational response to marketplace realities.

That said, Uruguay is very much plugged into the globalization process, and the nation has undergone important changes in recent years. These days, it is rare to see antique cars along Uruguayan streets; the nation ranks among the most computerized in the region; and Montevideo has experienced a building boom of sorts. All of these events attest to the typically slow but steady way in which Uruguayans have characteristically assimilated new currents into their national life and culture.

* * * * * * *

It is symbolic of Uruguay's character that the twentieth century both began and ended with a Batlle as president (a Batlle was elected president in 1989, a relative of the famed former president). This one fact reflects a lot about the Uruguayan personality: although Uruguayans number among the most modern of the SSSAs in many ways, they also have great reverence for their past and a preference for stability and continuity. Created originally to be a buffer between the continental giants of Argentina and Brazil, the nation gradually developed its own unique role in the hemisphere, many of its citizens contributing in various ways to promote regional cooperation and to propel dialogue about the issues of social equity, justice, and peace.

References and Selected Bibliography

Benedetti, Mario. 1997. *Andamios*. Buenos Aires: Ediciones Alfaguara-Grupo Santillana.

Bosrock, Mary Murray. 1997. *Put Your Best Foot Forward: South America*. St. Paul, MN: International Educational Systems.

Bridal, Tessa. 1997. *The Tree of Red Stars*. Minneapolis, MN: Milkweed Editions.

Conteris, Hiber. 1978. *Virginia en Flashback*. Montevideo, Uruguay: Arca.

Gillespie, Charles G. 1991. *Negotiating Democracy: Politicians and Generals in Uruguay*. New York: Cambridge University Press.

Gonzalez, Luis E. 1992. *Political Structures and Democracy in Uruguay*. Notre Dame, IN: University of Notre Dame Press.

Kaufman, Edward, ed. 1979. *Uruguay in Transition*. New Brunswick, NJ: Transaction.

Langguth, A. J. 1978. *Hidden Terrors*. New York: Pantheon Books.

Morrison, Terri, and Wayne A. Conway. 1997. *The International Traveler's Guide to Doing Business in Latin America*. New York: Macmillan.

Onetti, Juan Carlos. 2002. *Junta cadáveres (The Body Snatcher)*. Madrid: Alianza Editorial.

Servicio Paz y Justicia Uruguay. 1993. *Uruguay Nunca Más: Human Rights Violations, 1972–1985*. Translated by Elizabeth Hampsten. Philadelphia: Temple University Press.

Sosnowski, Saul, and Louise B. Popkin, eds. 1992. *Repression, Exile and Democracy: Uruguayan Culture*. Durham, NC: Duke University Press.

Weschler, Lawrence. 1998. *A Miracle, A Universe: Settling Accounts with Torturers* (section about Uruguay). Chicago: University of Chicago Press.

Venezuela: The Tropical Beat

Richard S. Hillman*

Encontré tu retrato en un manual de geografía,
Me mirabas con lagos azules, me reis con costas ardientes,
Me abrazabas en el regazo neblinoso de las cordilleras,
Y eras una llamura tendida en mi espera.

—Arturo Uslar Pietri

I found your portrait in a geography atlas,
You looked at me with blue lakes, you laughed with burning coasts,
You hugged me in the foggy lap of the mountains,
And you are an extended plain awaiting me.

Venezuela is a midsized nation of twenty-five million people that lies along the northeastern corner of the South American continent. Due to its location, it is the closest Spanish-speaking South American (SSSA) nation to English-speaking North

---

* Richard S. Hillman is director of the Institute for the Study of Democracy and Human Rights at St. John Fisher College and the Central University of Venezuela. He has a diploma in Hispanic Studies from the University of Madrid and a Ph.D. from New York University. Hillman's other major accomplishments in Latin America include three terms as a Fulbright scholar in Venezuela; an edited book, *Understanding Contemporary Latin America;* two authored books; and numerous articles about Venezuela as well as a book and several articles on the Caribbean.

America (ESNA). This closeness extends beyond geographic proximity. Linkages between Venezuela and the United States include both strategically significant economic exchanges and marked cultural commonalities. For instance, Venezuela is the largest Latin American supplier of petroleum to the U.S. It is also the only SSSA country where baseball is widely played.

Even with such important connections, Venezuela is not as well known among ESNAs as one might expect. There is actually less written about Venezuela in English than about other smaller and more distant nations in the region, such as Chile. This paucity of information may be partly because Venezuela does not fit neatly into many of the categories typically used for the SSSA countries. It does not belong either to the Andean countries with their ethnic variety, the Southern Cone region with its distinctive political and economic histories, or Colombia, which has drug and guerrilla problems to deal with. Rather, this most Caribbean of the SSSA countries exhibits certain cultural patterns that set it apart from all of the other nations in the region and makes trying to grasp and explain the Venezuelan identity a real challenge.

Consider also the following opposing facts about Venezuela and the Venezuelan people.

- Venezuelans have stronger ties and greater cultural affinity with the United States than do any other of the SSSAs. At the same time, Venezuelan leaders have played a key role in policy initiatives that apparently run counter to U.S. government policy. For instance, Venezuela was a founding member of the Organization of Petroleum Exporting Countries (OPEC).
- Venezuela achieved the highest per capita income in SSSA, largely because of its revenues from petroleum exports. Shortsighted use of such revenues, however, means that many Venezuelans currently live below the poverty level and suffer from unemployment and underemployment.
- More Venezuelan women have won international beauty pageants than any other nationality, and physical appearance

is accorded great importance by many Venezuelan women. At the same time, Venezuelan women are considered among the most independent in the SSSA region, and the country has the highest divorce rate in the continent.

- Venezuela's most revered national figure is Simón Bolívar, who liberated the northern part of South America from Spanish colonial rule and tried to create a unified Spanish-speaking South America along the lines of the United States. However, until recent decades, Venezuela's post-independence history was marked by dictatorship, regime changes, and political repression. Venezuela is, at the same time, the most Caribbean and among the most fervently South American of any of the countries in the region.

This chapter illustrates certain key aspects of Venezuelan culture, including its geographic and regional influences, defining cultural characteristics, communication style, and living and working in Venezuela. The defining cultural characteristics include Caribbean and SSSA traits, a consideration of the positive and negative aspects of petroleum, and appearance and identity.

Geographic and Regional Influences

Venezuela straddles two distinct geographical areas. This single fact explains much of the country's history as well as its contemporary cultural patterns. On one hand, Venezuela is a Caribbean nation with approximately 2,800 kilometers (1,750 miles) of coastline along the Caribbean Sea and includes within its territories seventy-two cays, coral atolls, and islands. At the same time, Venezuela is a gateway to continental South America and has as its neighbors Brazil, Colombia, and Guyana.

Due to its proximity to the Caribbean, Venezuela was the first place on the South American mainland that the conquistadores explored. Columbus landed there in 1498 on his third voyage to the Americas and originally called the area *Tierra de Gracia*. One year later this area's name was changed to Venezuela, which means "little Venice." The Spanish explorers were reminded of the famed Italian city during their explorations because some of the native inhabitants built their houses on stilts along certain waterways.

Because of its strategically important location, Venezuelan settlement patterns developed in large part as a response to security concerns and international realities. Most of the colonial outposts were placed along coastal areas to protect the shipping routes into and out of the Caribbean Sea, which were frequently attacked by pirates (some of whom actually resided in the more remote of the Venezuelan islands). This pattern continues even today, and international and domestic development is quite weak. Although Venezuela is not very large (it encompasses 912,068 square kilometers [352,150 square miles] of territory), it is divided into five regions that are clearly distinguishable due to geographic, demographic, and cultural features.

Litoral. The most important region in terms of population and power is the *litoral*, a strip of land that skirts the eastern and central coast. Here live many of the most urbanized and cosmopolitan of the Venezuelans as well as many poor shanty dwellers. In this heavily populated area lies the capital city of Caracas, with about four and a half million inhabitants. This largest Venezuelan city is renowned for its near-perfect climate. Its average temperature is between 75 and 80 degrees, with low humidity due to its two-thousand-foot elevation and a short rainy season. In recent decades, Caracas has also come to be known for less appealing aspects: urban congestion, infamous traffic jams, and a stressful daily existence for inhabitants because of the city's rapid population growth. Beyond the urban areas of the litoral lie fertile farmlands and plantations. Many of the traditional Venezuelan elites who have dominated the nation's economic and political life over the centuries hail from these realms.

Maracaibo Lowlands. The portion of coastal Venezuela that borders Colombia is known as the Maracaibo lowlands. This area lies along a narrow strip that extends for over 2,816 kilometers (1,750 miles) and is named for freshwater Maracaibo Lake. It is in this area where the largest deposits of petroleum have been discovered. In addition, agricultural lands, cattle ranches, swamps, and beautiful beaches can all be found here. Inhabitants of Maracaibo, known as *maracaibeños* (*maracuchos* in the vernacular), are renowned for having a strong sense of regional pride. This has sometimes created a rivalry with the natives of Caracas, known as *caraqueños*, with whom they compete for control of the revenues from the vast oil reserves.

Andes. Inland and along the Colombian border is the mountainous Andean area, which stands apart from the rest of Venezuela both geographically and culturally. Semi-isolated until recent decades due to its difficult terrain, people from this area are more traditional and conservative by reputation than many other Venezuelans are. This area boasts the only cold place in Venezuela as well as the highest peak, Pico Bolívar, which stands at 4,998 meters (16,400 feet).

Llanos. The llanos region is made up of flatlands that stretch from the coastal mountains inland to the Guyana Highlands around the Orinoco River basin. Here, tall grasses predominate, much like the pampa located farther south in Argentina and Uruguay. The inhabitants of this rugged terrain, known as *llaneros*, share similar traits with the gauchos, including a rough and tough manner and a fiercely independent spirit. Many of the caudillos (military leaders) who have played such a key role in the nation's politics come from this region.

Guyana Highlands. The last region is the Guyana Highlands, which lie to the south of the Orinoco basin. While this area is the largest in size, making up 45 percent of Venezuelan territory, it is sparsely populated largely because of its dramatic natural features. Here can be found inland tropical forests interspersed with tablelike plateaus, called *tepuis*. Angel Falls, the world's highest waterfall, is located here as well. Along the southern border with Brazil live the Yanomamis, a Native American group made famous by anthropologists' descriptions of them as "the fierce people" because of their cultural practices of having ceremonial fights and using of hallucinogenic plants.

Keys to Understanding the Venezuelans

Both Caribbean and SSSA Traits

Venezuelans' cultural patterns mirror their country's geographical realities, incorporating and combining the characteristics of both the Caribbean and SSSA regions in a very open and flexible way. Their Caribbean affiliation can be noted in numerous aspects of Venezuelan identity and lifestyle. As is true of most of the Caribbean nations, Venezuela has a strong African presence due to the relatively large number of African slaves who were brought to the area to work the many coffee and cocoa plantations that dominated the colonial economy. Today, the percentage of blacks in Venezuela is larger than in any other SSSA nation, making up 5 to 12 percent of the total populace, depending on the region.

Venezuela's approach to race relations is more Caribbean than SSSA; and prejudice and discrimination appear to be less of an issue in Venezuela than in other countries in the region with multiracial societies. From the beginning of the importation of African slaves, the practice of *mestizaje* was widespread. Consequently, today's Venezuela is one of the most ethnically blended of the SSSA countries. Some have even dubbed Venezuela a "*café con leche*" ("coffee mixed with milk") society, reflecting a pattern that is common in Caribbean countries (Hillman and D'Agostino 1992, 15–16). Anywhere from 65 to 90 percent of Venezuelans are *pardo*, a term used in Venezuela to refer to any combination of Indian, black, and European. Exact figures are, unfortunately, impossible to obtain because there has been no national census since 1926 and also because of the very subjective nature of racial classification in Venezuela.

This marked African presence is apparent in many aspects of Venezuelan society. As in other countries with significant black populations, hybrid or syncretic religions and practices (combining African, Indian, and Christian beliefs) have been incorporated into Venezuelan culture. For example, the María Lionza cult, one of the more popular examples of the religious syntheses, worships a goddess of nature who is similar to (1) the Arawak Indian water deity, (2) West African mythical figures, and (3) the Virgin Mary. A monument to María Lionza, a statuesque nude woman of Amazonian proportions astride a tapirlike animal, stands in the center island of the main highway in Caracas. Despite its inaccessibility due to omnipresent traffic, the statue is virtually always adorned with fresh flowers and wreaths. Also, many Venezuelans of all ethnic and social groups consult native *curanderos* ("witch doctors" or herbal healers) and use spiritualist practices such as mediums and artifacts to obtain desired ends.

The ethnic mixture in Venezuela can also be noted in the nation's music and dance, which combine European, Native American, and African elements. Its distinctive sound comes from the combination of harp, *cuatro* (a small, four-stringed guitar), and maracas. Many of the rhythms have a very fast beat that makes one just want to dance. The Venezuelan national dance is the *joropo*, derived from the Arab word *xarop* for "syrup." Other uniquely Venezuelan dances and songs are popular in various regions of the country, and Venezeulans also enjoy salsa, cumbia, and merengue as much as other Caribbean peoples do.

In keeping with their Caribbean temperament, Venezuelans are noted for their love of parties. The vernacular expression "*Al venezolano le gusta bonchar*!" ("Venezuelans love to party!") reflects this attitude. Throughout the country, music is often blasting, and people take any opportunity to feel the beat and dance. Perhaps the country's climate contributes to the party-like mood.

Of all the SSSAs, Venezuelans—especially those in the large urban areas—are probably the most avid beachgoers. Most of Venezuela is tropical, and the coast is lined with beautiful beaches. Caracas, notorious for its horrible congestion and traffic jams, becomes a driver's nightmare during the weekends, when the locals flock to the beaches. On the beach most Venezuelans of both sexes wear an extremely scanty bikini known euphemistically as *hilo dental* (dental floss).

Venezuela must be considered as more than a Caribbean

state, however. Its cultural patterns and historical realities are also profoundly SSSA. In fact, Venezuela was the birthplace of one of the most revered figures in SSSA, Simón Bolívar, who spearheaded the independence struggle against the colonial overlords. Venezuela was among the first areas to revolt against Spain. Bolívar's successful military campaigns liberated the northern and central portions of the South American Spanish colonies and played a key role in the exit of the Spanish from the continent.

Bolívar's struggle extended beyond achieving independence. He also dreamed of creating a "United States of South America" that would bring together all the Spanish colonies in a loose federation similar to the United States of North America. He fulfilled part of his dream in the creation of the Confederation of Gran Colombia, which included what are today Colombia, Ecuador, Panama, Peru, and Venezuela. But this was as far as he got. The Confederation lasted but briefly, soon breaking apart into several distinct nation-states. Bolívar was eventually banned from Venezuela and forced into exile. He died a poor man, far away from his beloved homeland, his health broken, and his dream shattered.

Contemporary Venezuelans proudly carry Bolívar's banner and feel deeply South American. Every city and village in Venezuela has a statue to Bolívar, and stiff penalties await anyone who speaks poorly of this hero in public. Recently, Venezuela was renamed the "República Bolivariana de Venezuela."

As if following Bolívar's example, various Venezuelan political figures in recent decades have played key roles in regional and international negotiations and agreements. For instance, Venezuela was a founder of and major player in OPEC. Venezuelan diplomats were also heavily involved in the Central American peace processes during the conflict in that region in the 1970s and 1980s.

Venezuela's postindependence political history in many ways echoes its most revered hero's own tendency toward domination.

Venezuela has been extremely challenging to rule despite its relatively homogeneous population and moderate size. One reason for Bolívar's ultimate failure was his authoritarian approach to ruling the Confederation of Gran Colombia, a style that soon resulted in opposition from many quarters. Venezuelan politics has been characterized until recent decades by a long succession of military dictators who often functioned with heavy-handed tactics against opponents. In fact, the country did not have a democratically elected president who completed a full term in office until 1958.

One reason for the dominance of the "strongman" in Venezuelan national life can be attributed to the lack of national cohesion. Although Venezuelans are passionately proud of their nation, as the bumper stickers adorning many residents' cars stating "*Soy Venezolanísimo*" ("I'm extremely Venezuelan") affirm, strong regional differences also divide them and contribute to making national integration a challenge. Both historical and economic factors help to explain this phenomenon. During the colonial period, Venezuela did not have much of a separate identity, and it was a relatively unimportant part of the Spanish empire. In fact, it was subsumed within the administration of the Viceroyalty of Nueva Granada, with its capital in Bogotá. In addition, throughout the colonial and postcolonial era, until the middle of the twentieth century, Venezuela was almost exclusively an agricultural economy. The vast majority of Venezuelans resided in rural areas, deriving their sense of identity more from their local affiliation than from a distant national allegiance. Although things have changed dramatically in recent decades, certain aspects of contemporary Venezuelan culture still reflect its strong rural and regional focus.

Petroleum—Blessing or Curse?

Venezuela became primarily an agricultural outpost after the Spanish conquistadores' hopes that the region was the site of El Dorado (the legendary lost city of gold) were dashed when no gold was discovered. These Spanish colonists never discovered the vast natural treasures that do lie beneath the ground in Venezuela. It was not until the twentieth century that the country's vast mineral bounty was recognized. Today, Venezuela's natural resources have proved to be its greatest source of revenue.

Coal, iron ore, and diamonds can all be found in Venezuela as well as gold itself. However, the most important mineral resource is not gold but rather petroleum, or "oro negro" (black gold). Three sedimentary basins—the Maracaibo, the eastern, and the Apure-Barinas—produce an estimated 64.5 billion barrels of oil. This makes Venezuela OPEC's third largest oil producer and the most important one in the western hemisphere.

The presence of this fossilized fuel was actually discovered before the Spaniards' arrival. The Native Americans called the sticky stuff "devil's excrement." However, it was not until the early twentieth century that the importance of oil was known. Petroleum exploitation was financed largely by U.S.-based multinationals, with British and Dutch companies playing a secondary role.

In the 1970s, under the leadership of Carlos Andrés Pérez, Venezuela rapidly began to gain more control over its petroleum production. The petroleum companies were nationalized in 1976, with control passing to the Venezuelan state-owned oil company, Petróleos de Venezuela. At the same time, Venezuela became a founding member and active participant in OPEC, as mentioned earlier.

Although the percentage of the country's revenues obtained from petroleum sales has fluctuated over time, nonetheless this single mineral product is by far the nation's most important export. The possession of petroleum has proven to be a mixed blessing for Venezuelan development. One Venezuelan intellectual warned as early as 1949 that petroleum wealth could "constitute one of the most grave obstacles for the implementation of a truly democratic regime in Venezuela" and that "paradoxically, [oil] is at the same time the problem and the solution" (Pietri 1989, 59–62).

On the positive side, the presence of petroleum has permitted the Venezuelans to achieve the highest per capita gross national product in Latin America. These revenues have, in turn, contributed indirectly to the consolidation of a uniquely Venezuelan brand of democratic governance based on an agreement between the country's two major political parties, the AD (*Accíon Democratica)* and the COPEI (Christian Democrats). Seven consecutive presidential terms were completed under this system, leading many political analysts to the conclusion that Venezuela was a fully democratic nation.

Oil revenues almost single-handedly transformed what had been a sleepy, traditional society dominated by a small elite of wealthy citizens into a modernized nation. Such changes are most visible in Caracas, formerly a red-roofed colonial city. It was razed during the petroleum boom and rebuilt with concrete, growing so rapidly that streets and buildings are still identified by proper names (rather than numbers), a throwback to a recent past when Caracas was considered a "town in which everyone knew each other."

Oil production has also propelled Venezuelans to interact with many new ideas and peoples. Waves of foreign in-migration accompanied the expansion of the petroleum industry, beginning in the 1930s. Most of these immigrants sought employment opportunities and upward mobility. These newcomers came to be commonly referred to as *musius* (from the French *monsieur,* in reference to their light skin). Except for the undocumented Colombians who flooded across the border to seek their fortunes, and who were often marginalized, the open and friendly Venezuelans warmly welcomed the foreigners. These new immigrants, in turn, proved to be quite influential in contemporary Venezuelan life. For example, large numbers of Italians migrated to Venezuela after the Second World War; as a result, it is the second largest pasta consumer in the world, after Italy.

Other foreigners came to Venezuela for political rather than economic motives. Because of Venezuela's strong democratic governance during the 1970 and 1980s as well as its prosperity, many SSSAs from countries experiencing political repression (most notably Argentina, Chile, and Uruguay) found Venezuela a safe haven. Many eventually returned to their native lands when democratic governments were established, but others have stayed and now consider Venezuela their second home, and many of their children are fully integrated into society.

Since much of the oil industry, especially in the early years of exploitation, was dominated by U.S. companies, many ESNA technicians, such as geologists and engineers, came to Venezuela to live and work. However, even prior to the development of Venezuelan oil, the U.S. presence in this country was stronger than in most of the other countries in the continent. This is attributable to Venezuela's strategic location along the Caribbean shipping lanes and its close proximity to the United States. Since at least the time of the Monroe Doctrine, Venezuela has in many ways fallen under the influence of the U.S. more than any of the SSSA countries located further south on the continental landmass.

The marked U.S. influence is apparent in certain aspects of Venezuelan popular culture. American fast-food chains, the echo of English language rock music coming from boom boxes, and the ubiquity of blue jeans and cell phones give Venezuelans the superficial appearance of New York City Puerto Ricans, Southwestern Chicanos, or Miami Latinos. Venezuela and the United States share a passion for the national pastime of baseball, and some Venezuelan players have become stars in the American major leagues. In addition, many Venezuelans travel to the U.S. whenever possible to shop and sightsee. At the height of the oil boom of the 1970s, there were so many wealthy Venezuelans who either frequently visited or set up second homes in Miami that the city earned the nickname, "Venezuela's 21st State."

Shortsighted and/or misguided use of petroleum funds during the boom years eventually paved the way for some of the difficulties that are currently plaguing the country. Even though several major Venezuelan leaders urged the policy makers to *sembrar el petróleo* (invest the oil), their sage advice was not heeded and petroleum revenues were used primarily for consumption rather than long-term investment.

The results of this lackadaisical approach became blatantly apparent during the so-called Black Friday of February 1983. On that day, the Venezuelan currency, the bolívar, was devalued in an attempt to ward off an impending debt crisis due to excess foreign loans. The initial devaluation was inadequate so the bolívar was devalued again, and again. The continent's most prosperous nation was rapidly plunged into an economic crisis, the ramifications of which were extensive, including the political and social instability of the country. The crisis clearly marked the end of Venezuela's boom period, and to some extent, the nation has yet to recover even now.

Recent political events seem to belie the once-popular belief held by some journalists and academics that Venezuela was unlike other Latin American countries because of its successful transition to a democratic government. By the 1990s the pacted party system (agreements between political and business elites to share government responsibility) began to break down, due in part to the end of the oil boom and the poor management of government revenues. Recently, the country has experienced two attempts to overthrow the government, several massive protests, and a strong student movement. In addition, two-time president Carlos Andrés Pérez was tried for corruption. The 1998 election of the very controversial former military *golpe* leader, Hugo Chávez, and his policy of "social revolution" can be largely explained by the political uncertainty in Venezuela these days.

Despite the large amounts of petroleum money and the nation's relatively high per capita income, resource distribution in Venezuela remains very skewed and social services are often quite poor. Today, poverty is still pervasive; well over 70 percent of the population are poor by any standard. Large numbers of illegal street vendors hawk merchandise laid out on blankets in the "informal economy" because they can find no other work (unemployment is officially estimated to be 16 percent but is really closer to 25 percent).

At the same time, many of the wealthier Venezuelans became used to the perquisites of a strong currency and developed a reputation for being *mimado*, or "spoiled," expecting their country, which almost literally "floats on oil," to provide for them. During the period of the oil boom, foreigners provided much of the labor in the economy, while a significant number of Venezuelans spent their energies in other pursuits. Many claim that the "easy petroleum money" has notably weakened the Venezuelan work ethic and acknowledge that most Venezuelans probably don't work as hard as they could. It is just not considered *chévere* (cool) to work too hard or exert oneself too much.

Appearance and Identity

Even more than in other SSSAs, Venezuelans have made a cult of the ideal of female beauty. This is apparent in the incredible importance given to beauty contests of all types. Venezuela boasts more Miss Worlds and Miss Universes than any other country, and in most international beauty pageants Miss Venezuela reaches at least the final round of competition. Producing beauty queens has become a true industry in Venezuela, one that has been copied by several other nations desiring similar success.

The cult around beauty pageants is but one example of Venezuelans' proclivity for placing great importance on physical appearance. Comments about physical appearance including weight, skin color, and other physical attributions are frequent in conversations, and most Venezuelans are very concerned with how they look. Nobody leaves home without sprucing up, and even those without much money spend a tremendous amount on clothes and cosmetics, often preferring the more expensive, imported brands. Plastic surgery is quite common as well.

Venezuelan women's preoccupation with glamour does not mean that they are unconcerned with professional success; they don't see the two as incompatible. Venezuelan women are leaders in every field, including politics and business. One former Miss Universe even recently ran for president. Another Venezuelan woman, Carolina Herrera, has been able to parlay her very Venezuelan fashion style in the world arena, having become one of the most important fashion designers today.

Significant movement toward greater gender equality has been propelled in part by necessity. The nation has the highest divorce rate in the continent, at over 70 percent, resulting in large numbers of single women. This high figure may be partly attributable to the relatively weak presence of the Catholic Church in Venezuela, at least compared with many of the other SSSA countries. It might also be explained by the marked Caribbean influence on Venezuelan culture; the divorce figures are quite similar to those of some of the island nations of the Caribbean. Whatever the reason, as a longtime resident in Venezuela put it, "You do not get a sense of the abnegated, resigned, stereotypical Catholic wife/mother here. Women, too, seek out sexual partners, pursue their own lives, and work for their own happiness even after having children, having been left by men." Paradoxically, life in the extended family is considered sacrosanct in Venezuela, despite the nontraditional family structure.

In keeping with many Venezuelans' relatively relaxed view of marriage vows is a similarly relaxed attitude toward marital fidelity. There is even political currency inherent in having a mistress, and extramarital affairs, politically problematic in the United States, are a sign of power in Venezuela. For example, Blanca Ibañez, *amiga* of former president Jaime Lusinchi, and Cecilia Matos, amiga of former two-time president Carlos Andrés Pérez, rather than the "first ladies," opened bridges and represented the presidents at foreign embassy gatherings.

Some claim that Venezuelans' preoccupation with physical appearance reveals a cultural penchant for superficiality. Little attention is devoted to introspection, deep conversation, and pondering the meaning of life. It should not be surprising, then, that among Venezuela's most well-known cultural exports in the Spanish-speaking world are its soap operas, which are regularly shown in many other countries on the continent. Actress María Conchita Alonso, often cast as the stereotypical Latin female, is Venezuelan and got her start on Venezuelan soap operas.

The emphasis given to appearances may also be partly the result of the need of many Venezuelans to have something concrete to cling to as a frame of reference. While appearances can often be deceiving, many other aspects of contemporary Venezuelan life have proved to be even more illusory. Tremendous social change has occurred in Venezuela within the last generation or two. With the migration to urban areas, the economic developments brought on in large part by oil revenues, and the influx of many foreign ideas and peoples into this relatively underpopulated nation, a profound transformation of culture and identity has taken place. Tradition and rural ways of living have been discarded in fond expectation of a brighter future. However, many of these expectations have been dashed or have yet to be realized. Consequently, many contemporary Venezuelans feel a great void; they know what they left behind, but they are not sure where they are right now or where they might be going in the future.

At the crux of many of the political and economic problems currently facing the country is the perhaps more profound one of identity. Consequently, many Venezuelans these days—underneath their typical friendliness, joy of life, and spontaneity—are pessimistic and distrustful. This pessimism has been exacerbated in recent decades due to the series of crises and economic difficulties the nation has experienced. The popular soap opera *In These Streets*, for example, depicted in the early 1990s a deteriorating quality of life, rife with personal insecurity and political uncertainty. The show's hit theme song contained the following repetitive refrain reflecting social alienation: "Be careful at the corners, don't be distracted when you walk… for in these streets there is no longer any compassion." The song sums up how many Venezuelans feel these days.

Communication Patterns

In keeping with their Caribbean temperament, Venezuelans, especially those living along the coastal regions, are usually more informal and relaxed in their communication style than are other SSSAs. For instance, the informal *tú* is much more commonly used than the formal *usted*. Even shop owners and taxi drivers commonly call their female customers *mi amor*, something that would never happen in Chile or Colombia.

Body language in Venezuela exhibits the Caribbean simpatico familiarity. Venezuelans enjoy conversation and remain physically close, with constant eye contact, frequent touching, and ample use of gestures to emphasize points. The variations in Venezuelan greetings can be distinguished from the typical South American *abrazo*. Venezuelans hug each other according to familiarity and gender, ranging from a full embrace to a mere pat on the shoulder for men. Women greet each other and men with hugs and/or kisses on both cheeks. The formal handshake is reserved for business or professional introductions.

The Venezuelan accent is quite distinct from that of the other SSSA countries. In speed and pronunciation, it sounds more like the Spanish spoken in Cuba or the Dominican Republic—more rapid, softer in intonation, and with many final consonants dropped when colloquially spoken. As one Peruvian diplomat put it, "When I speak Spanish…nobody can tell that I am from Peru…I could be from Ecuador or even Mexico…but when I hear a Venezuelan speaking Spanish, I can always tell that they are from Venezuela…sometimes I can barely understand what they are saying."

Venezuelan Spanish contains many *venezolanismos* (words and expressions that are used only by Venezuelans). A few examples follow:

- *cónchale, vale* (gosh or wow, man)
- *chévere* (cool)
- *la vaina* (a vulgar word for practically anything, although frequently used as a greeting, especially among young people)
- *¿Cómo está la vaina?* ("How's it hanging?" "What's up?")
- *arrecharse* (to be disgusted)
- *pana* (pal)
- *chamo/a* (boy/girl)

Despite its relatively homogeneous population, Venezuela's regional differences are reflected in different accents and communication styles. For instance, in the Andean region located near the Colombian border, people are more formal. They often use *usted* rather than *tú*, sometimes even among people they know very well. In some families, even husbands and wives address each other with *usted*.

Although Spanish is the only official language of Venezuela, in the major cities Portuguese is quite common, not surprising considering the nation's proximity to the continental giant, Brazil. Because of the large number of Italian immigrants, some Venezuelans also speak Italian. In the remote interior, Venezuela's approximately two hundred thousand Amerindians speak a variety of Native American languages.

Literacy in Venezuela remains at around 90 percent, and the press is quite open and often critical of government policies. In Venezuela, as in other SSSA countries, literature has often been a vehicle for the critical analysis of society. Rómulo Gallegos, the country's most famous novelist, wrote *Doña Bárbara* in 1929 and is known for his uncompromising description of the Venezuelan character. Ramón Díaz Sánchez's 1950 novel, *Cumboto*, addresses racial relations in Venezuela.

The movie industry has also produced several notable films, including *Oriona*, a magical realism romance; *Río Negro*, a graphic depiction of the horrors of colonial life; the internationally acclaimed documentary *Araya* by Margot Benacerraf; the dramas of Román Chalbaud; the experimental films by Diego Risquez; and the popular hits such as *Macú: the Policeman's Wife*. These two abbreviated lists reveal the Venezuelan penchant for articulating critical ideas, at times in an idiosyncratic way. A few final examples include Venezuelans' tendency to proffer directions even when they are uncertain. In so doing they are striving to be knowledgeable and helpful. Venezuelans like to debate, but rarely admit to error.

Living and Working in Venezuela

The Venezuelans' vivaciousness and openness have helped the many foreigners living and working in or visiting this country feel welcomed. Even the country's recent economic and political difficulties have not put a severe damper on this buoyant Venezuelan spirit that finds joy in the present, however uncertain the future may be. Nonetheless, at a more practical level, adjusting to life in Venezuela can be challenging for many ESNAs.

What first strikes many foreigners visiting Venezuela, or at least the larger urban areas, is the way people drive. Venezuelan drivers are bold and enjoy driving fast. At intersections, cars frequently run through red lights and drive in the wrong direction on one-way streets, a common practice called *comiendo la flecha* (eating the arrow). Similarly, "shortcuts" are frequent, especially at night. The many roadside monuments in memory of killed motorists attest to the dangers inherent in some of these practices.

Venezuelan working hours exacerbate the traffic problems in large cities. A typical workday, for example, begins early (around 8:30 A.M.) and incorporates a lunchtime siesta with a visit to one's home or a club (there are private clubs for every class but the lowest). Three-hour "business" lunches are the norm. Work resumes after the long lunch break, usually lasting until the early evening. This means that many workers have to fight the traffic not twice, but four times a day.

Rapid urbanization has had other dampening effects on Venezuelan spontaneity and relaxed lifestyles that were based on rural traditions. High crime rates have given new meaning to the Spanish architectural use of iron gratings (*rejas*) and walled courtyards. Reaching their reja-enclosed homes (windows and doors are secured with these), a lengthy process of entrance ensues. Different keys open the garage, the locked gate, the outer door, the inner door, and in the case of apartment buildings, the elevator, the reja, and the multiple locks on the apartment door! Ten-foot walls topped with cut glass or barbed wire surround homes and apartment buildings in the more affluent sections of the cities and can be seen in rural areas as well.

Venezuelans really want to please and enjoy being in charge. Consequently, many tend to promise everything with good intentions at the moment. However, constraints such as traffic, power outages, availability of materials, or other difficulties can intervene, hampering their ability to follow through on promises. This can often cause frustration and misunderstanding for ESNAs whose sense of rationally ordered efficiency may be offended. However, these misunderstandings can be at least partially avoided by applying a measure of cultural empathy. A sense of humor and patience are virtues that will go a long way in Venezuela.

So too does having a network of contacts. Even more than in some other SSSA countries, family position, nepotism, and "who you know" significantly affect business activities. The personal touch is imperative and is often more crucial to successful job realization than any contract or legal agreement. It may take time to establish credibility in Venezuela, but the time spent getting to know the right people will pay off. In some cases, it may be difficult to achieve goals and objectives without recourse to some form of leverage, known as *palanca* by Venezuelans.

Introductions are important, and one should respect the sense of dignity and status articulated in titles such as *doctor* for the university educated (even when no doctorate has been earned) or *don* and *doña* for the elderly. Until a personal relationship has been established, gifts are inappropriate in business meetings but are expected when one is invited to a Venezuelan's home (an event that symbolizes the consummation of a personal friendship). High-quality scotch whiskey will be much appreciated.

Fashion-conscious Venezuelans are, as discussed earlier, concerned with appearances. Business attire consists of conservative dark suits for men and women. Evening clothes are open shirts for men and glittery cocktail dresses for women. Jeans and halters are omnipresent on university campuses.

* * * * * * *

Venezuelans have experienced wide fluctuations and profound changes in recent decades. The nation has gone from being peripheral and quite poor prior to the discovery of petroleum to becoming the Latin American nation with the highest per capita income to experiencing severe economic hardships since the "lost decade" of the 1980s. Venezuelans have had to learn to tighten or loosen their belts accordingly.

Socially, rural-urban migration has transformed a rather bucolic society into one where the vast majority of Venezuelans fight urban sprawl, high levels of violence, and incessant traffic jams daily. Politically, periods of heavy-handed dictatorship have given way to decades of pacted democracy that have culminated in the controversial leadership of Hugo Chávez, the populist president who was democratically elected after participating in an aborted coup.

The recent polemic political situation during the Chávez presidency is a concrete manifestation of the frustrations of many Venezuelans and of the great challenges facing the nation in the early years of the twenty-first century. Despite it all, Venezuelans love their country, recognize its vast potential, and continue dancing to the irresistible tropical beat.

References and Selected Bibliography

Ewell, Judith. 1993. "Venezuela in Crisis." *Current History* (March): 120–25.

Hellinger, Daniel. 1991. *Venezuela: Tarnished Democracy*. Boulder, CO: Westview.

Hillman, Richard S. 2003. "Intellectuals: An Elite Divided." In *The Unraveling of Representative Democracy in Venezuela: Toward a Model of Participation*, edited by Jennifer McCoy and David Myers. Baltimore: Johns Hopkins University Press.

———. 1994. *Democracy for the Privileged: Crisis and Transition in Venezuela*. Boulder, CO: Lynne Rienner.

———, ed. 2001. *Understanding Contemporary Latin America*. 2d ed. Boulder, CO: Lynne Rienner.

Hillman, Richard S., and Thomas J. D'Agostino. 1992. *Distant Neighbors in the Caribbean: The Dominican Republic and Jamaica in Comparative Perspective*. New York: Praeger.

Hillman, Richard S., and Elsa Cardozo Da Silva, eds. 1997. *De una a otra gobernabilidad: el desbordamiento de la democracia venezolana*. Caracas: Editorial Tropykos/UCV.

McCoy, Jennifer, Andrés Serbin, William C. Smith, and Andrés Stambouli, eds. 1995. *Venezuelan Democracy Under Stress*. Boulder, CO: Lynne Rienner.

Myers, David J. 1996. "Venezuela: The Stressing of Distributive Justice." In *Latin American Politics and Development*, 4th ed., edited by Howard J. Wiarda and Harvey F. Kline. Boulder, CO: Westview.

———. 1986. "The Venezuelan Party System: Regime Maintenance Under Stress." In *Venezuela: The Democratic Experience*, rev. ed., edited by John D. Martz and David J. Myers. New York: Praeger.

Pietri, Arturo Uslar. 1992. "A Culture of Corruption." *Hemisphere* 4, no. 3 (Summer): 28–29.

———. 1989. *De Una a Otra Venezuela*. 6th ed. Caracas: Monte Avila Editores.

Rey, Juan Carlos. 1989. *El futuro de la democracia en Venezuela*. Caracas: Serie Estudios-Colección IDEA.

Romero, Anibal. 1997. "Rearranging the Deck Chairs on the Titanic: The Agony of Democracy in Venezuela." *Latin American Research Review* 32, no. 1: 7–36.

Tulchin, Joseph S., and Gary Bland, eds. 1993. *Venezuela in the Wake of Radical Reform*. Boulder, CO: Lynne Rienner.

Weyland, Kurt. 2001. "How Long Can Hugo Chávez Last? The Dilemmas Facing Venezuela's Neopopulist Leader." XXIII International Congress of the Latin American Studies Association, Washington, DC (September).

Index

A

B

C

D

E

F

G

H

I

J

K

L

M

N

O

P

Q

R

S

T

U

V

W

Y

Z